VIETNAM
PROTEST
THEATRE

DRAMA AND PERFORMANCE STUDIES

TIMOTHY WILES, GENERAL EDITOR

Johannes Birringer. *Theatre, Theory, Postmodernism.*

Katherine H. Burkman and John L. Kundert-Gibbs, editors. *Pinter at Sixty.*

Ejner J. Jensen. *Shakespeare and the Ends of Comedy.*

Jeffrey D. Mason. *Melodrama and the Myth of America.*

Eugène van Erven. *The Playful Revolution: Theatre and Liberation in Asia.*

VIETNAM PROTEST THEATRE

THE TELEVISION WAR ON STAGE

NORA M. ALTER

INDIANA
UNIVERSITY
PRESS

Bloomington & Indianapolis

The paper used in this publication meets the minimum requirements of American
National Standard for Information Sciences—Permanence of Paper for Printed
Library Materials, ANSI Z39.48-1984.

Manufactured in the United States of America

Library of Congress Cataloging-in-Publication Data

Alter, Nora M., date
    Vietnam protest theatre : the television war on stage / Nora M.
Alter.
        p.   cm. — (Drama and performance studies)
    Includes bibliographical references and index.
    ISBN 0-253-33032-7 (cl : alk. paper)
    1. Drama—20th century—History and criticism. 2. Vietnamese
Conflict, 1961–1975—Literature and the conflict. I. Title. II. Series.
PN1650.V53A48   1996
809.2'9358—dc20   95-32287

1   2   3   4   5   01   00   99   98   97   96

FOR MY PARENTS

What we see is neither real, because after all we are looking at actors acting, nor unreal, as everything that happens makes us aware of the reality of the war in Vietnam.

—Jean-Paul Sartre

C O N T E N T S

PREFACE

All the world's a stage. The coming extinction of art is prefigured in the increasing impossibility of representing historical events.   —Theodor W. Adorno

Adorno's bleak vision in *Minima Moralia* must not become a self-fulfilling prophecy.[1] Artists and critics around the world should never give up their responsibility to attempt to do something just because the task may be ultimately impossible, and their art may become extinct. There are always ways of re/presenting and re/staging even unusually complex and disturbing historical events. Such, in any case, is one lesson of Vietnam Protest Theatre, one thesis of this book.

1

I generally acknowledge that the theatrical response to the Vietnam War cannot be reduced to a single thesis. I also recognize, however, that among the several distinct but intertwined theses that can and should be proposed, a certain number have pragmatic priority. The most fundamental is the notion that the war generated, more or less "spontaneously," an international corpus of staged plays that forms an identifiable genre here to be called Vietnam Protest Theatre. This corpus is identified in the first place by the shared topic of all its plays—the Vietnam War—but it also displays a certain number of features that are present to different degrees in different works and yet are linked in a single network or problematic. Thus, all plays engage in a perennial problem of political theatre: the difficult relationship between "documentary fact" and "creative fiction." All seek to assign responsibility and guilt for the Vietnam War, if not also war *tout court*, focusing on individuals or nations, but rarely confronting deeper levels of causation. These plays written in America and Europe use the "foreign" war to speak, more or less obliquely, about other things, notably their own country's past or present. And almost all plays are extremely hesitant about presenting the point of view of the Vietnamese and Vietcong "other," with the horrific result that often this "other" appears on the stage only at the moment of torture or violent death. Above all, running through all the plays, there is the deeply ambivalent response (sometimes reactive, sometimes creative) to the filmic mediatization of the first "television war"—on TV primarily but in other media as well, including the fast-emerging computer technologies.

2

Every day we saw dead Americans, dead Vietnamese, bombings, all kinds of rather interesting things, but never one program on why; never one program on the history of it; never one program attempting to place it in context.   —Emile de Antonio

An excursus is in order about the specifically televisual aspect of "the television war." We may recall Raymond Williams's sensitivity to the problems faced by living theatre within what he called "dramatized society," which is to say a society that is always already significantly televisualized.[2] Williams notes the consequences for war reporting of what he also terms "the culture of distance":

> The representation of spectacular destruction may already, in many minds, have blurred the difference between exercise and action, rehearsal and act. For it is one of the corroding indulgences of the culture of distance that to the spectator the effect at least offers to be the same.[3]

To be sure, Williams was referring, in 1982, to media coverage of the then recent British military intervention in the Falkland/Malvinas Islands; but his analysis could just as easily be applied retroactively to Vietnam. His argument implicates both perception and ideology. Confirming Guy Debord's Situationist theory of the spectacle (which was developed, not by chance, at the time of the Vietnam War), Williams points out the domination of surface "effects" in society. One result is that the spectator no longer even looks for the reality of things but is satisfied to perceive their re/presented effect. As Debord noted in the 1960s, all public—and increasingly private—life is fast becoming "cinematographic" and "televisual."[4] So it was that the photographed and televised war in Vietnam was happening not only in Vietnam but also "back in the USA," through the transmission of all manner of ideological messages that were then incorporated—more or less consciously, visibly or audibly—into virtually all cultural productions and reproductions.

During the air and ground combat in Vietnam, the role of media as a source of information was particularly significant. However, it is the *cultural* production *during* the Vietnam War that is the major concern of this book. By the same token, with reference to the audiovisual transmission of images, I am concerned with the way theatre responded to television—

and not, say, to film, its main competition at the time for the title of *Gesamtkunstwerk*. The major motion pictures about the Vietnam War and its social and personal aftershocks were produced only after the hot war was over, and they have been the source of extensive scholarship to a degree that theatre has not.[5]

I should like to make particularly clear that the main focus of this study is tripartite: (1) on Vietnam Protest *Theatre*, as opposed to other media that are less live in terms of performance (e.g., film, photography, novels, printed poetry, documentary reports in various media, reprinted art works, recorded music, television itself); (2) on Vietnam *Protest* Theatre, as opposed to other types of narrative (e.g., those involving the returning Vietnam vet, or various apologia for the war); (3) on Vietnam Protest Theatre *written and performed while the war was still being waged* (during the theatre of war, as it were), as opposed to either anticipations or recollections of it in any media. It should go without saying that this focus is not intended to replace other approaches but rather to supplement them, and thus to make a contribution to understanding an exceedingly complex and contested cultural-historical moment and response to it. Theatre captured the full range of immediate audiovisual reaction to the actual waging of the television war.

The war as spectacle was consumed by the American public principally on television. For television had become the visual medium par excellence: the main supplier and conduit of films, shows, debates, and especially the nightly news reports that played a capital role in forming public opinion, having begun to supersede print journalism. There seems to be little doubt, as Murray Edelman points out, that news reports in general but televised ones particularly "stimulate the construction of political spectacles."[6] Any assessment of the public knowledge of the Vietnam War, therefore, needs to take into account the "image" of war as conveyed by television. It was over *that* image that public opinion about the war was waged in the United States, both for and against it. If indeed, as Marshall McLuhan contends, the United States had become "by far the most visually organized country in the history of the world,"[7] it was by the 1960s that the dominant visual media had become, in their turn, dominated by television so as to turn the *Vietnam* War into arguably the first (not the last) properly *television* war.[8]

To understand Vietnam Protest Theatre, particularly in America but also in Europe, one must have some grasp of the complex relationship between that theatre and the televised images of the war.[9] This relationship was deeply overdetermined and hence deeply ambivalent. The often revolting, almost always disturbing, nature of those images formed a major source of the global protest movement. By the same token, Vietnam Protest Theatre had to rely on television, even when it most hated doing so. As Jean-Marie Serreau, a French stage director, pointed out in 1965 (anticipating by nearly three decades our current concern with postmodern techno- and cyborg-culture), there had been for some time, especially in the so-called First World but elsewhere as well, a drastic conflation involving *all* images—no matter whether they appeared on stage or anywhere else. This in turn affects playwrights working for a living theatre that, as a medium, may no longer be "contemporary":

> Whether now these pictures are stage props or photographic pictures—we are the first humans who have a photographic or audiovisual memory—the theatre picture, the poetic picture, the film picture, the television picture, all have strongly influenced the intellect of all these writers.[10]

And Serreau went on to tease out some of the historical and hermeneutic consequences of this almost inevitable spectacular conflation:

> Since the invention of staging, besides acting, photographic and audiovisual signs or ideograms have been introduced to parallel the dramatic occurrences. That means the insertion of a picture of the modern world into the theatre. Of course, this picture has several interpretations; the photographic message is multilayered; it is a primitive but universal speech, yet it is the means of communication. The first medium of information for the masses. . . . We enter into a new oral culture that consists of the language of pictures . . . new myths are created through photos, radio, and television. (Serreau 1)

Vietnam Protest Theatre was also aware, however, that the global television image mainly supported the war and that the entire medium was suspected of manipulating reality to various ideological ends. While forced to rely on them, theatre also attempted to place a dialectical distance between itself and the televised images.

The power of televised images was acknowledged by both their producers and consumers. Just to *"be"*—i.e., to *"appear"*—on television came to be considered a confirmation of one's function in life. It is significant that U.S. soldiers on the field (just like war protesters at home who rushed back from rallies and sit-ins to see themselves on TV) were more concerned with their photographed and/or televised image than with written interviews. Discussing soldiers with whom he had gone into battle, Michael Herr noted in 1968: "The grunts were hip enough to the media to take photographers more seriously than reporters and I'd met officers who refused to believe that I was really a correspondent because I never carried cameras."[11] We will encounter this problematic often in Vietnam Protest Theatre in the mid-1960s—as in John Guare's *Muzeeka*, Jean-Claude van Itallie's *TV*, and several other plays.

Yet, while powerful and virtually omnipresent, television had its limitations. In terms of maintaining a vital, democratic public sphere, one limit was an ideological slant that can be recognized as such. Generically TV, like radio and film, does not normally allow for a direct interaction with its audience. Living theatre has the possibility of more or less *immediate* response to current events and can adjust itself to them in performance as film cannot.[12] Popular music (including a "rock musical" like *Hair*) can be more like theatre than film in this regard, and, when recorded, music is more like film than theatre in reaching the largest possible international audience.[13] Like the cinema and recorded music—the quintessential media of "mechanical reproducibility," at least before video—TV involves a one-way communication from producer to consumer. This dominant effect must be contrasted with a theatre that draws its "magic" from the possibility of a constant two-way exchange between stage and audience. To that extent, television suffers from the same alienation, the same "culture of distance," that Bertolt Brecht detected in 1932 in radio. For it

> would be the finest possible communication apparatus in public life.... [I]t would be, if it knew how to receive as well as to transmit, how to let the listener speak as well as hear, how to bring him into a relationship instead of isolating him.[14]

Developing Brecht's argument in 1970, Hans Magnus Enzensberger thus observes that

> In its present form, equipment like television or film does not serve communication but prevents it. It allows no reciprocal action between transmitter and receiver, technically speaking, it reduces feedback to the lowest point compatible with the system.[15]

The special alienation produced by television is also dictated by the conditions of its reception. Paradoxically, while serving to unite viewers, since they all see the "same thing," it also separates them into single entities or minimal groups: communally speaking, television viewing would be at most an activity for families and friends, even if everyone in the world could be seeing and hearing the same program simultaneously (which is theoretically possible). The images of Vietnam, brought into "the living room" (and bars and bedrooms, etc.), were not only removed from the reality of the viewer's social context; they also referred to a context that was unknown to the viewer and could neither be checked nor verified reliably with other people. Any information or disinformation tended to be equated in the viewer's mind. In that sense, television exemplifies the drawbacks that Debord finds in all spectacles:

> The spectacle originates in the loss of the unity of the world ... the spectacle is nothing more than the common language of this separation.... What binds the spectators together is no more than an irreversible relation at the very center which maintains their isolation. The spectacle reunites the separate but reunites it as separate. (Debord, Thesis 29)

Within this iron cage of alienation, and perhaps because of it, television succeeded in exerting ideological pressure much more effectively than written journalism. As Daniel C. Hallin has noted in *"The Uncensored War": The Media and Vietnam* (1986), the reasons are both formal and technological:

> Television as a medium is completely different from written journalism for a number of reasons. Television is considered to be more of a "thematic" medium "organized in time rather than space; the television audience must be 'carried along' from the beginning of the story to the end."[16]

In addition, as Hallin comments about a report by Peter Jennings that articulated several quite disparate narratives: "This kind of connection between different stories usually does not exist in newspaper coverage. It is one of the things that makes television a more ideological medium than the newspaper: television forces much more of the news into the unity of a story line" (Hallin 121).

To be sure, the jury remains out on the *precise* sociological effect of the televised coverage of the war. Did "bringing the war into the living room," i.e., the sight of Americans (not Vietnamese) dying on prime time, have *significant* bearing on getting the United States out of Vietnam? Accounts differ about the consequences of seeing the massive 1968 Tet offensive on TV. For advocacy groups such as "Accuracy in Media," this mediatized event was decisive in turning the tide of popular opinion against the war. Yet, in terms of news reporting and analysis of Tet, scholars like Hallin have found relatively little evidence of substantial antiwar bias on the part of the official media line. Some scholars have pointed to the deeply ambivalent nature of the coverage of events like the Tet offensive and the response to it.[17] And some historians writing about "the living room war" think that "the ghastliness of the war, as revealed on the nightly news, provided the crucial leverage for the antiwar movement that helped end it."[18]

Perhaps what is most significant is that the *U.S. government*, if no one else, felt that television was responsible for undermining the military's war efforts in Vietnam. This "paranoia" shaped future official government policy on press coverage—not the least of the legacies of the first television war. For instance, during the British/Falklands crisis, Britain's establishment took great pains to stifle a similar subversive possibility: television coverage was often three weeks late and news releases came out only after official reports by the ministry of war. The media was heavily censored throughout the crisis in order to prevent what was imagined to have occurred in the United States during the Vietnam War.[19] Later, in the same spirit, during the invasions of Granada, Panama, and the Gulf War, the United States has tried mightily—and effectively—to restrict the activities of all reporters, including of course live television coverage.[20] Alternatively, when U.S. troops landed in Somalia, they found American TV crews and floodlights waiting for them.

Nonetheless, it is also sobering to note that some scholars believe that "television's banalization or routinization of the war had the result of numbing the audience into a state of acquiescence before government policy" (Arlen xiv). Recent studies have confirmed that the media, despite their apparent protest, despite a widespread perception that they are "liberal," are actually tightly controlled by the government and military and that television has long served as a powerful tool for spreading U.S. and capitalist ideology, not only in the United States but through a global exportation of U.S. programs.[21] Thus, Fred J. MacDonald's *Television and the Red Menace* traces the strategy by which American ideals were programmed on television so as to counteract the "enemy," i.e., communism.[22] MacDonald argues that this constant anticommunist propaganda on all levels of televised entertainment prepared the U.S. audience to accept the war in Vietnam:

> Never in the history of American broadcasting had there been so many war programs. Even during World War II, radio discouraged excessive amounts of fictional drama re-creating battles and other forms of military violence. . . . During the Vietnam War, however, T.V. presented a procession of soldiers, heroes fighting for freedom in weekly dramatic series. (MacDonald 191)

The same overall bias dominated nightly or weekly reports of the Vietnam War: the so-called neutral or objective broadcasts. Images produced on television tended to reveal that "it was the American invaders who were regarded as the victims of the 'aggression' of the Vietnamese, and the war was reported from their point of view, just as subsequent commentary, including cinema, views the war from this perspective."[23] Even reputed liberal reporters, such as Chet Huntley or Walter Cronkite, were simultaneously producing government propaganda films and promoting their "objective reporting" on national television (see MacDonald 176). In fact, special broadcasts, purportedly critical of the war, rarely questioned the righteousness of the war or the ideology behind it (let alone socioeconomic structural pressures). They concentrated instead on empirical consequences: e.g., the financial cost to the United States or the devastating effects on the American and Vietnamese people as individuals.[24]

Between the two rival assessments—positive and negative—of media's influence on the war and the image of the war, there are of course meditiating positions. The somewhat contradictory stance maintained by television during the early years of the war may have been produced, as Hallin proposes, by the action of two conflicting factors: the ideology of the cold war and a professional striving toward the goal of objective journalism.[25] Increasingly, however, the "objective style" was turning into the so-called gonzo mode, involving participatory reporting at the expense of analysis and injecting often extreme subjectivity or "human interest" into the stories about Vietnam.[26] (There was no gonzo equivalent for TV; but this was before video technology made gonzo visual journalism possible.)[27] As Michael Herr notes, with at least some ambivalence, in his novel *Dispatches* (thought to be one of the first documents of a properly "postmodern sensibility"):

> conventional journalism could no more reveal this war than conventional firepower could win it, all it could do was take the most profound event of the American decade and turn it to a communications pudding, taking its most obvious undeniable history and making it into a secret history. (Herr 234)

Overall, mass media showed a basic adherence to the official representation of the war even though they also transmitted some subversive images. And certainly many images were received not as they were *intended* to be received. There was more mainstream American press than independent, left-wing, or alternative journals, such as *Ramparts*. Most of the media avoided "rocking the boat." They even abstained from using some "official" facts that could prove to be too disturbing. This silence was particularly notable during the Gulf of Tonkin incident, when significant information was not publicized in the media.[28] Michael Parenti is on the mark when he observes:

> What the business-owned media left unreported was far more spectacular than what it reported. From 1945-54 the United States spent several billion dollars supporting ruthless French colonialism in Vietnam, but the American public was never informed of this . . . and the dumping of 12 million tons of agent orange and other chemicals on the countryside. . . . The My Lai story was not broken until more than a year and a half after it happened and by a small news outfit, the Dispatch News Service.[29]

To a certain extent, however, "the American public" did somehow intuit—increasingly—that mass media did not accurately portray the war. Indeed, it seems that quite a few people relied on foreign newspapers and newscasts to learn what was "really happening."[30] There were some reports in the United States, on television and elsewhere, about war atrocities or casualties, but these stories were usually tainted by the dominant pro-war perspective.[31] In contrast, information about Vietnam produced outside the United States provided a broader and more critical picture. Whether that difference in reporting was significant enough to account for differences between the protest plays in America and those in Europe is open to debate.

Returning to the images of the war in the American media, doubtless some helped to prolong the war in some quarters, others to shorten it. The vast and by no means ideologically homogenous American public did not ignore what transpired thousands of miles away. It was relentlessly solicited to take a stand on the war, and while many supported it, wholeheartedly or reluctantly, significant numbers of others took part in mass protests against it, left the country, went underground, were put in jail. In spite of a reporting bias and censorship, enough upsetting images slipped through the various control systems to leave an increasingly sharp impact on "the American mind." Eventually these images were to leave a stronger imprint on American history than the supposedly "objective" day-to-day coverage of the war. The question remains, what type of images had that extraordinary power? What did they show that could survive the trivialization of most repeated media images? And how did live theatre respond "in a media-saturated environment" to the same mechanically reproduced image whose "shock value" is "progressively diminished" or "acquires the character of a stereotype"?[32] The questions that must be asked are if, how, and why live theatre is able to restore at least weak contestatory power to the dominant "anaesthetizing" trend of media images.

In the pages that follow, specific references will be made to the most "spectacular" and "spectacularized" images that initially appeared in photographs and on television. These images include the self-immolation of a Buddhist monk; a news report by Morley Safer showing U.S. Marines burning down a *South* Vietnamese village with Zippo lighters; the shooting of prisoners of war by South Vietnamese officers; the image of a napalmed naked girl running helplessly toward the camera of an American journalist; and of course the images from Tet and My Lai.[33] It must be noted that verbal statements operating as clichés, and filtering through various levels of mediation, also seemed to convey such lasting "images." When, in the Mekong Delta, "artillery and air strikes levelled half of My Tho, a city of 80,000, and the provincial capital of Ben Tre with 140,000 inhabitants, was decimated," the offered justification was, "as an American colonel put it in one of the most widely quoted statements of the war, 'We had to destroy the town to save it.'"[34] (That this quotation was repeated frequently in broadcasts was more crucial than the fact that it first surfaced in a newspaper story.)

The visual horror compressed into such verbal images made them particularly suitable for adaptation to theatre, yet also difficult to stage. In many cases, they too are conveyed verbally, not visually, in Vietnam Protest Theatre. Whatever their nature, however, they elicited a strong public response when they did re/appear on stage. Jean Baudrillard, in *The Evil Demon of Images*, claims that the public's taste for violence paradoxically derives from a reaction against the "nuclear" nature of television, which "cools and neutralises the meaning and energy of events."[35] By this post-McLuhanesque logic, viewers craved explosions of violence as a compensation or overcompensation for the trivialization of the Vietnam War on television: "For an explosion is always a promise, it is our hope . . . let it reassure us as to the admittedly catastrophic presence of energy and gratify us with its spectacle" (Baudrillard 1984, 20). Baudrillard's views are surely pertinent to our understanding of properly theatrical violence. Indeed, arguably the most scandalous images of Vietnam on stage were precisely those of explosion, heat, fire: the monk pouring gasoline over himself and burning, the GIs burning huts, the young girl's flesh burning with napalm, and the explosion of brains shot by a gun. But it is still not clear why these violent images would keep their power intact after their transformation into "civilized" or "stylized" scenes onstage or into merely verbal evocations in theatre dialogues. For theatre (Snuff Theatre aside) cannot show actual burning or violent death, only their simulacra. Of course, this is true of film as well.[36] So perhaps our fascination with the images of the Vietnam War does stem, after all, from a more general appeal of the image in our society, an appeal manifested in *all* media—television as well as theatre. On the other hand, however, theatre does hold—perhaps to a *degree* that television does not—the sense not only that "you were there" but that "you are here." And that is to say the intolerable sense *both* that you can do nothing about the (television) war *and* that you must do something about it.

3

Critical attention to Vietnam Protest Theatre has been long in coming. Social and cultural historians of the war still commonly ignore theatre, and the literary scholars who have begun to describe and analyze it have yet to expand their scope beyond the national borders of the United States. Yet a comparativist contextualization is crucial to understanding both this specific genre of protest plays and more general problems of political theatre.

No claim is made in this book that Vietnam Protest Theatre was great or even *good* theatre, nor even that it was politically *effective*. But, like all *interesting* art, it does provide eye-opening glimpses into the relationship between culture and politics, theory and practice. True, historically, the Vietnam Protest Theatre was a very ephemeral phenomenon. However, its very existence shows that it is possible for artists and intellectuals (and, as Gramsci says, everyone is a potential intellectual, though each in her or his own way)[37] to have the capacity to forge a *community* of response, a resistance to war across national and linguistic borders, an artistic protest independent of other forms of protest and yet in solidarity with them. Furthermore the existence of this theatre as a genre is not only a retroactive projection by contemporary critics. Political playwrights in the 1960s, such as Daniel Berrigan, were keenly aware of the tendentious nature of their craft. They knew that living theatre was ephemeral and had a limited effectivity in an increasingly technologized and mass-mediatized age. They were equally aware that the community of antiwar response that needed to be forged between languages and cultures (between antiwar activists in the United States, Europe, and Vietnam) certainly had to *include* theatre, but also that it must extend far beyond the stage—not only in space but in time, into the future. Subsequent world events, including U.S.-led multinational interventions in Latin America and the Near East have confirmed the accuracy of Berrigan's politically engaged vision of "staging protest," "staging the television war."

Today, when regionalism and nationalism are back with a vengeance on the global agenda, cultural as well as political, Vietnam Protest Theatre may still provide some reason for hope. The fact that such a community response has occurred in the past (we may think also of the international community of response to the Spanish Civil War) means that it might occur in the future. In 1937 Brecht wrote to friends about his plan for "a small society of *productive* people" around the world, tentatively called "The Diderot Society," designed to combat the growth of national fascisms.[38] This international society was not *realized*, needless to say, by the Vietnam Protest Theatre. Nonetheless, implicitly, that theatre kept its spirit alive.

The task at hand is not to criticize the plays retroactively for any general historical or theoretical blindness. At the same time, since complete neutrality is neither possible nor perhaps desirable, it is necessary to express here the hope that this book, with its documentation and criticism, is not merely academic in nature, though it is surely this, too. The additional aim in teasing out deeper structures or constellations that might be unknown to the playwrights, to their plays, and to their contemporary critics and audiences is to provide some sort of basis upon which other playwrights and critics tomorrow might provide us with more profound, precise, and progressive plays, criticism, and perhaps theory than has hitherto been provided either by Vietnam Protest Theatre or its critics—as similarly complex historical, aesthetic, and political situations arise in the future.

4

Vietnam Protest Theatre: The Television War on Stage is not intended to be a book of theory by some current standards. Rather, it is informed by a set of theories that may help prepare a theory of the way that cataclysmic events and wars such as "Vietnam" come to be re/presented on stage and elsewhere. To this end, I understate rather than overstate literary and cultural theories relevant to living theatre: for example, its relationship to other media, its internal tensions between documentary "fact" and "magical" fiction, and its struggle to represent historical events effectively while at the same time influencing them. To understate theory entails that one allows the historical evidence to speak in its own terms as much as possible. Vietnam Protest Theatre has not yet been grasped by critics as a coherent genre, and I place rather more emphasis on theatre reviews written at the time of the war than on subsequent criticism. In that sense, too, my focus is historical. This does not mean, however, that this is a book of history in any strict sense, either. No attempt is made, for instance, to provide an overview, let alone analysis, of all Vietnam Protest Plays in their empirical plentitude. A main argument of this book is comparative: namely, that in order to grasp the American theatrical response to "its" war critically and in its full complexity one must step outside the national and linguistic borders of the United States and look at the response that came from the rest of the world. But, again, "the rest of the world" is not intended here to cover all international responses by dramatists to the war. I focus mainly on the United States, England, France, Austria, and Germany, rather than, say, on Italy, Spain, Northern and Eastern Europe, or Central and South America. In part, this restriction is due to contingent factors, such as my own areas of expertise; in part, it is because the most complex and extensive restaging of the Vietnam War abroad arguably came from the former imperialist countries France and England and from the Germany that had been the Third Reich. Certainly many other plays could and should be taken into consideration. To take but one example, I have not included careful analysis of Dario Fo's play *Una madre,* even though it uses the issue of the Vietnam War and the protest movement against it as a way of coming to terms with Italian "terrorism."

A more specific remark about methodology. Just as the reader should not expect an exhaustive discussion of all the relevant Vietnam Protest Plays, nor should she or he expect a detailed close analysis of each play that I do consider. Instead, I tease out common threads woven out of interconnected thematic and formal relationships. These include tensions between fact versus fiction, propaganda versus documentary evidence, past versus present, the search for causation versus awareness of continuing responsibility, the representation of unrepresentable atrocity versus aesthetic value, and living theatre versus technological reproduction. Walter Benjamin might have called this contested deeper structure or generic norm of Vietnam Protest Theatre a "constellation"—of the kind that cannot just be discovered within texts but must also be created by active criticism. This generic norm or constellation is seldom if ever made explicit in the plays under discussion, though I argue that it is more or less unwittingly broached by each playwright. Hence the reader is further forewarned that the type of analysis required here sometimes disregards the context in which a particular line in a play is uttered—who is speaking, when, and so forth. This procedure, unusual or inadequate in most formal close analyses of texts, is more acceptable when one is searching for—and producing—deeper patterns of meaning slightly beneath those either intended by a playwright or consciously received by an audience. In short, these deeper structures are ideological.

Writing of American imperialism in the twentieth century, including in Vietnam, Edward W. Said has stated: "Granted that American expansionism is principally economic, it is still highly dependent and moves together with, upon, cultural ideas and ideologies about America itself, ceaselessly reiterated in public."[39] This remark cuts two ways for my book. It opens up the possibility and necessity for the analysis of cultural objects and practices—theatre among others—to contribute to our understanding of U.S. expansionism, the relationship between imperialism and culture, and the overdetermined complexity of human experience. The danger, however, is that this leap from the economic to the cultural tends to become self-legitimating in cultural studies when the economic is simply taken for granted and when intellectuals—artists or scholars—speak exclusively of cultural phenomena, never returning to other determinations on expansionism and its representations.[40]

I would hope that my understated use of theory, my principle of selecting texts, and my critical method will help us to be critical of this perhaps inevitable leap to culture from other social determinations as it occurs on the Vietnam protest stage in several theatrical forms and national languages. Although in Vietnam Protest Theatre there are many allusions to matters of political economy and its contributing responsibility for the war, this basic ideological problematic is more typically downplayed or even ignored by playwrights and their critics. Perhaps the most that playwrights and cultural critics can do is to be aware of the boundary conditions on their work posed by ideology. To point out some limits of a complex genre like Vietnam Protest Theatre is not necessarily to propose radical ways of transcending them, only to make this effort as best we can.

5

Finally, in this preface, a word about the way *Vietnam Protest Theatre* is organized. Following an introduction, "Visions of Vietnam and Protest Theatre"—which establishes some of the key terms and concepts to be used around the category of the "vision," and lack thereof, possessed by playwrights and scholars with regard to the war—the book has two main parts.

Part One, "Negotiating National History through Vietnam," analyzes symptomatic examples of Vietnam Protest Theatre in four chapters dealing with the United States, Britain and Austria (brought together as two "contestations from the periphery"), Germany, and France. The common thread in this part is the way different national cultures attempted, while referring to Vietnam, to work through certain problems in their own national past (including the destruction of native populations, and the postimperialist, postfascist legacy). The United States is represented by Megan Terry's *Viet Rock*, Barbara Garson's *MacBird*, and Daniel Berrigan's *The Trial of the Catonsville Nine*—illustrating different forms of critiquing, but always on the verge of "playing imperialism." England is represented by Peter Brook's *US* and Austria by Gerald Szyszkowitz's *Commander Carrigan*; Germany by Rolf Hochhuth's *Soldiers* and Peter Weiss's *Vietnam Discourse*—plays with the task of "documenting" the present along with Germany's recent past; and France by Armand Gatti's *V comme Vietnam* and André Benedetto's *Napalm*—plays in which colonialism and techno-culture are broached from two different perspectives. These dramatic negotiations are characterized by compromise solutions, the degree of success and failure of which varies widely, depending not only on the content of these plays but also on their formal structures.

Part Two, "Mis/representing the Inappropriate/d Other," takes its title from Vietnamese filmmaker Trinh T. Minh-ha, specifically from her attempt to construct a notion of "Otherness" that would be clearly "inappropriate" for the forces of global domination but also "inappropriateable" by them.[41] This part, in two chapters, is particularly concerned with the intersecting matrix of several problems in Vietnam Protest Theatre. First, "Performative Sub-Missions" considers avant-garde theatre of George Tabori and Tuli Kupferberg, struggling to subvert the war by highlighting various submissions to power. "American I-Witnesses" returns to the particularly American issue of "subjective imperialism" discussed in chapter 1, but now in terms of two particularly problematic playwrights, David Rabe and H. Wesley Balk, who threaten (with sexism, among other things) the genre's otherwise progressive impulses. The synthetic conclusion, "Re-Acting to the Television War," deals explicitly with the ambivalent response of the living theatre (including some new plays) to the mediatization of the war and indeed, increasingly, of all aspects of everyday life by TV and its equivalents. Live theatre predated and anticipated significant aspects of current postmodernist debates about the mutual and often contradictory imbrication between mediation and immediacy, and yet this theatrical anticipation has been ignored by cultural critics. Vietnam Protest Theatre of the 1960s significantly contributes to our understanding of "the condition of postmodernity" in technoculture and "the cultural logic of late capitalism."[42] Finally, the Epilogue—"Antimedia: Vietnamese Theatre as Pacific Resistance"—explores the possibility, suggested by a Vietnamese, of nontechnological opposition to the Vietnam War and post/modern warfare.

ACKNOWLEDGMENTS

I would like to thank Allen Riedy, assistant curator at the John M. Echols Collection on Southeast Asia, Karl A. Kroch Library, Cornell University, Ithaca, New York, and the staff at the Münchner Theater Museum, Munich, Germany. I am grateful to the Mellon Foundation for a Postdoctoral Fellowship in the Humanities at Cornell University, 1992–93, which gave me time to work on my project. Additional funding was provided by the German Academic Exchange Service (Summer 1991) and the National Endowment for the Humanities (Summer 1992). Initial preparation of the manuscript was facilitated by Elaine Dawson at Old Dominion University. An earlier version of my epilogue appeared as "Vietnamese Theatre of Resistance: Thich Nhat Hanh's Metaphysical Sortie," in *Imperialism and Theatre*, ed. J. Ellen Gainor (London: Routledge, 1995).

Several playwrights generously provided me with unpublished materials and other information relevant to this book: André Benedetto, Tuli Kupferberg, Gerald Szyszkowitz, and George Tabori.

I have benefited over the years from intellectual exchanges with colleagues, advisors, and friends at the University of Pennsylvania and Cornell University. Among the people who have given me support and encouragement in my work are David Bathrick, Russell A. Berman, Susan Buck-Morss, Michelle Caroly, JoAnne Dubil, J. Ellen Gainor, Sander L. Gilman, Peter Uwe Hohendahl, Anton Kaes, Ruth Klüger, Paul J. Korshin, Dominick LaCapra, John A. McCarthy, Gerald and Ellen Prince, Azade Seyhan, Peter Stallybrass, Debra J. Thomas, Frank Trommler, and my friends in New York City, Bavaria, and Rehoboth, past and present. The readers and staff at Indiana University Press have been most helpful at all stages of publication, including Robert Sloan and Timothy Wiles. Particular appreciation goes to Loris Mirella for his intellectual acumen and faith in my project.

Special thanks go both to Maria P. Alter for all her encouragement (whatever *Sitzfleisch* I may possess I owe to her), and to Jean V. Alter, who provided enormous patience, critical insight, and sense of perspective. Above all, my deepest gratitude goes to Geoff Waite.

VIETNAM PROTEST THEATRE

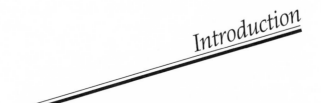

Introduction

VISIONS OF VIETNAM AND PROTEST THEATRE

In his room he had all the posters of the big heroes of
the moment: Mao Tse Tung, Che Guevara, Ho Chi
Minh. Vietnam . . . Vietnam. . . . I remember in particular one poster that you must all remember seeing—A Vietnamese. A young Vietnamese girl holding a submachine gun standing in front of a gigantic
American pilot with his hands up. Goliath toppled
by a young girl.   —Dario Fo, *Una Madre*

1.

The 1980s saw an explosion of American visions of the Vietnam War. Images
and words previously repressed or suppressed burst open with increasing
frequency like unwanted time capsules, even bombs, in the cultural and
political imaginary. In the nineties, with the war receding once again in the
dubious depths of collective memory, and the Gulf War having replaced it
for a time as the focus of national attention, the proliferation of new
publications about Vietnam has hardly abated. Nor has the committed,
often critical, and sometimes militant spirit of these responses diminished
over time, all across the ideological spectrum. It seems that the Vietnam War
still needs constantly to be revised and, not only for an older generation,
relived and fought again, no longer as it might be remembered in bits of
individual memories, uncertain about its meaning, but as if it could one day be
cast in History Itself in the form of a dispassionate and stable representation.
Even the younger generations, who did not live through Vietnam, appear

strangely drawn to its story told in historical reconstitutions, prose fiction and films, sometimes as if they were seeking the surrogate experience of a truly controversial war that might help them understand and assess, through similarities and differences, the less controversial Gulf War and any potential future conflicts. Indeed, what happened and did not happen during the Vietnam War clearly remains, after twenty years, a most sensitive issue for American society—itself suspended historically between an uncertain (modern) past and an equally uncertain (postmodern) future. Accordingly, the Vietnam War continues to be a source of more or less consciously mastered and unmastered emotional reactions and more or less tentative moral judgments. Some people feel equally as guilty not to have fought as not to have resisted; few know for certain what they would have done had they lived "back then." Often those who did are not really sure what their positions back then were, either.

Deep ambivalence about the Vietnam War at times breaks out in the form of public "debate" such as that which, during the last two presidential campaigns, was triggered by the widely mediatized reports first about Senator Dan Quayle and about then Governor Bill Clinton's alleged evasions of Vietnam combat duty. No doubt political considerations largely inflated the ultimate importance of now President and Commander-in-Chief Clinton's "resistance" to the war years in the past, but the acrimonious polemics unleashed clearly demonstrate that the Vietnam issue is hardly settled or worked through and it still grates on raw nerves.[1]

The continued topicality of the Vietnam War—fought over and over again in American minds with determination but seemingly without possible resolution—may well be unprecedented in the history of the perception of American twentieth-century wars. True, World Wars I and II and the Korean War also generated interminable series of written and pictorial representations. But these wars were more solidly backed by the American population before they were widely concluded in near euphoria, in the case of World War I, and with a sigh of relief, in the case of World War II and Korea. The vast majority of the representations of these earlier wars, whether scholarly or fictional, in historical studies or novels or films, systematically sustained and perpetuated their canonical image as "right" wars, which were somehow justified and legitimized despite their more or less repressed horror. The Vietnam War never benefited from such a benevolent support. But then it was unique in many ways.

This was a war that had no specific beginning in a dramatic official declaration—in sharp contrast to the "official" beginning of the Gulf War in January 1991, which was synchronized with U.S. evening television. Long before the Tonkin Gulf resolution (1964), America was sliding into war in Indochina through a series of escalations that, for many years and up to its abrupt end, seemed to turn it into a "permanent war."[2] It was also the first recent war that, in the general public judgment, ended with American defeat. Defeat was all the more traumatic because, for the first time in the century, the war had not been waged against a strong and threatening military power but against a small and supposedly weak enemy (uncannily similar racially to the once-defeated but now economically powerful Japanese) in a divided "Third-World" country on the opposite side of the globe. For many Americans, it was a profoundly disturbing war, consciously *and* unconsciously, neither glorious nor necessary. The first phrase heard today when war looms (Granada, Panama, the Gulf) is, "We don't want another Vietnam." This means a number of things: defeat and deaths, the splitting of the U.S. society, quagmire for years, and foreign entanglements. Vietnam was a war that became increasingly unpopular at home as its escalation resulted in increasingly high casualties among drafted U.S. youth. It was a war that eventually cleaved America in two: obviously between those who supported the war and those who opposed it, those who approved the government policies and those who resisted them; but less obviously fissures also occurred *within* members of both camps. As the tension increased, it became evident that the cause of the Vietnam War, now a national issue, had to be primarily won in America against the antiwar protest movement. Thus, it became also a home-front war for the hearts and minds of Americans, waged largely in the realm of the media: on the one hand in support of the war, with official releases, government sponsored reports, widely disseminated press photographs and TV images; on the other hand against the war, with writings that exposed and censured it, dissenting public speeches, mediatized protest marches and student demonstrations, and, not least, staged anti-Vietnam War plays. Often the propaganda—pro *and* con—was effective; sometimes it backfired and was counterproductive. The "real" war was nearly masked for several years by an inconclusive war between multiple conflicting representations, and in that form it is still fought within and between individual and collective memories as well as in the manifold scholarly and fictional postwar representations. Jean Baudrillard sardonically notes:

> It has been said that war is the continuation of politics by other means; we can also say that images, media images, are the continuation of war by other means. Take *Apocalypse Now*. Coppola made his film the same way Americans conducted the war—in this sense it is the best possible testimony—with the same exaggeration, the same excessive means, the same monstrous candour . . . his film is very much the prolongation of war by other means, the completion of that incomplete war, its apotheosis. War becomes films, film becomes war, the two united by their mutual overflow of technology . . . this film is part of the war. If Americans (apparently) lost the other, they have certainly won this one. *Apocalypse Now* is a global victory.[3]

Among the representations of the war, a certain number have sought to recapture, and historicize, the way that Vietnam was—or might have been—perceived during the war or shortly thereafter. They reconstitute and/or deconstruct the visions of the war offered to the public while the war was still fought on the fields of and in the skies over Vietnam and, for a few years longer, in the media. Inspired by a critical perspective or simple hindsight, some of these recent representations promote their own vision of the war in fictional forms—novels, songs, plays and films—which propose perceptions of the war that compete with, and revise, the perceptions in visions promoted in the past. Coppola's *Apocalypse Now* (1979) in that sense was indeed a cinematographic "continuation of war by other means," a revised continuation of official images of the military operations that were shown during the war on television screens.

But most postwar recreations of the past perceptions of Vietnam have been carried out by historians.[4] While their works cover many topics, a respectable number of them deal specifically with concrete contemporary visions of war found in a variety of mediatized sources: in fictional accounts, ranging from Hollywood movies to private poetry readings by Vietnam veterans, but also in the press, in photographic documents, in debates about the Vietnam memorial in Washington, D.C., in radio broadcasts, and in television news releases about troops "missing in action." And this diversity of primary sources is matched by a parallel diversity of critical approaches used by professional historians. Many of their studies of Vietnam images also serve them as vehicles for the promotion of more or less tacit theories and ideologies of historization, gender or culture. The resulting wide range of historical perspectives thus provides perceptions of the war in Vietnam that seem to reflect not merely inevitable historiographical biases but also genuine concerns for the various groups that were involved in it: soldiers and civilians, men and women, mainstream Americans, African Americans and Native Americans, even—though rarely—Vietnamese.

The total combined coverage of representations of the Vietnam War is thus quite comprehensive. It is also coherent despite its diversification. Whatever their methodological and even ideological differences, there is little question that most approaches today share a comparatively dispassionate and removed attitude both toward the war and toward its images. (One significant exception, of course, is the MIA/POW lobby.) Part of this common perspective derives no doubt from the temporal distance between the postwar studies and the war events and images reconstructed in them. For the historians, and their intended readers, Vietnam is no longer a direct experience, or a meaningful memory, but a construct to be elaborated within their own contemporary cultural context as an alternate past reality.[5] This distance may legitimate a claim to greater objectivity, i.e., to a cold, analytical, almost scientific vision, but it also prompts the release of more subjective and harder to detect subconscious intentions that may color that vision. In particular, the very drive to revise the images of the war inevitably sets up its own prejudicial and paradoxical goal: making these images sufficiently compelling to draw the attention of the American public and to force it to face anew the festering unresolved memory of Vietnam. Looking back at the past pro-war documents, John Carlos Rowe and Rick Berg note, "When we failed to sell America to the Vietnamese we tried to sell Vietnam to America" (Rowe and Berg 3). It would seem that Vietnam studies today, not excluding my own, are trying in turn to sell Vietnam as a cultural commodity and that they tend to adopt a single marketing strategy: producing jolting images that have a shock appeal to consumers. This does not mean that the resulting revised representation of the war is totally homogeneous. Even critical judgments a posteriori may vary and differ in their assessment of discrete features of the past. As noted, television played a significant role in shaping the vision of the Vietnam War, but the actual meaning of TV influence, and its positive or negative impact on the image of the war, is still undecided. There is little doubt that the television images of Vietnam, received by a growing audience, formed an increasingly familiar visual landscape that competed with any "objective" vision of reality; they were even viewed as original models in which reality seemed to be reflected. Thus, reporter Marina Warner notes: "I saw this old woman coming down the road with a child in her arms. The child's flesh was falling off. I said to myself, 'My God, I have seen this before.' I had. On television."[6]

Yet not all topics are given equal treatment in historical surveys. One particular category of public representations of Vietnam has been almost completely neglected: the Vietnam Protest Plays. There are surprisingly few articles on the Vietnam War drama, and they are limited either to a cursory view of some of its most basic themes or to the assessment of a single playwright.[7] No systematic study has yet been published about the development, meaning, and role of Vietnam Protest Theatre as a major art medium of antiwar dissent. This lacuna in collective memory creates an empirical but also theoretical gap in the current global picture of wartime representations of Vietnam. It is necessary to fill that gap to further a "full" understanding of the war that media waged about Vietnam on the home front and also to discover why that "gap" exists in the first place.

2.

The neglect of Vietnam Protest Theatre by the historians of the war cannot be explained, or justified, by any lack of plays that criticized the war. On the contrary, the range of performances generated by the Vietnam Protest Theatre is impressive, not only in the United States but in Europe as well. The first well-known antiwar play produced in America was Megan Terry's *Viet Rock* in 1966—a time when few critical visions of Vietnam appeared in other forms of fiction (Norman Mailer's better-known *Why Are We in Vietnam?* came out a year later). The same year, inspired by this spirit of Vietnam protest, Peter Brook staged his *US* in London. In 1967, barely a few months later, two French playwrights, working independently, produced their own Vietnam plays: André Benedetto staged *Napalm* in Avignon and Armand Gatti *V comme Vietnam* in Toulouse. Then, in 1968 in Germany, Peter Weiss's *Vietnam Discourse* was performed in Frankfurt am Main. Several other European plays followed over the next years. Meantime, back in the United States, Jean-Claude van Itallie wrote *TV* (1966), Barbara Garson achieved some notoriety with *MacBird* (1967), and Tuli Kupferberg wrote *Fuck Nam* (1967), but the latter was not performed. During the next few years, the Vietnam Protest Plays multiplied with, among others, Grant Duay's *Fruit Salad* (1968), George Tabori's *Pinkville* (1968), David Rabe's *The Basic Training of Pavlo Hummel* and *Sticks and Bones* (1969), Daniel Berrigan's *The Trial of the Catonsville Nine* (1970), and John Guare's *Muzeeka* (1970). Some were better received than others, but nearly all were reported and discussed in the media. By 1970, when the war reached its full development, at least twenty plays had been staged. At that point, most of the American Vietnam plays turned to the problem of returning veterans, but several still dealt primarily with what was happening, or had happened, during the actual war: for instance H. Wesley Balk's *The Dramatization of 365 Days* (1972) or, much later, Amlin Gray's *How I Got That Story* (1979). I shall not be specifically dealing here with plays written by and about veterans and about the problems of their reintegration into American society.[8] What concerns me primarily is theatre as a direct and immediate response to the war at the time it was being waged. Altogether, in America and in Europe, the Vietnam Protest Theatre directly resulted in between fifty and sixty plays, most of them written and performed between 1966 and 1976, also influencing dramatic works that, explicitly or implicitly, allude to the war but are not overtly concerned with it.[9]

The heterogenous American "street," "guerrilla," or "combative" theatre protesting the war was a key player in the circulation between "high" and "low" theatre culture, thus providing a fuller context within which to situate its more mainstream cousins—my main focus. "Street" theatre provides a major limit condition for this book. Insufficiently recognized is the extent to which "street" theatre has its own theory and logic, its own tradition and canon, its own historical roots. These roots are multiple—indigenous and foreign—and thus properly "inter/national" in intent. Besides the well-known Bread and Puppet Theatre and El Teatro Campesino, groups included Radical Arts Troupes (RATs) of the Students for a Democratic Society (SDS); the Pageant Players; San Francisco's Mime Troupe, Women's Street Theatre, and Red Theatre; Chicago's Rapid Transit Guerrilla Communications; and The American Playground.[10]

A common thread running through these troupes, beginning around 1965, is the insistence that their work was not theatre, including protest theatre. Sooner, it was simultaneously an imitation of military tactics employed by the Vietcong and part of a sweeping political and social agenda at home. Thus, for example, an anonymous programmatic note by The American Playground in 1969 stated categorically:

> The term guerrilla theatre is beginning to be thrown around quite loosely, referring in general to any form of political or avant-garde theatre from *Hair* to the San Francisco Mime Troupe; as such it is becoming more and more meaningless. I suggest restricting its use to that form of theatre which, like the Viet Cong, does not identify itself as such. Theatre which does not present itself as "performance." Theatre which IS a reshaping of reality. This type of theatre is peculiarly effective since it avoids being put into a box: "Well, it's only theatre"—the routine people go through to insulate themselves against change. It hits at an unguarded subject, itself unprotected by the sacrosanct mantle of ART.[11]

So it is that Vietnam Protest Plays, whenever they were published or appeared on stage precisely *as* theatre, were defining themselves over and against this militant "antitheatrical" stance. In an analogous way, Peter Schumann of The Bread and Puppet Theatre refused to define his work as "protest," explaining, "We are all sick of the Vietnam War. But the theatre must do more than protest" (cited in S. Brecht 483). Rather, it must aspire to be not "ART" but nothing less than the transformation of society. What the resulting "theatre" shared was twofold: first, a site—the street; and, second, a multiple antagonist—not merely the war and mainstream theatre ART but also television. Thinking primarily of Bread and Puppets, Stefan Brecht has linked its interventions both to the deep past and to television: "What Schumann and the Peace Movement carried into the streets of New York was the theme of war, and, to some—lesser—extent, its image" (S. Brecht 476). This image was directly related and contrasted to the mass media. "The populace was regularly notified by the media there was a war going on: here live performance was added to the airwave representation and the print" (476). Street theatre, Brecht continues, was "not like turning on tv, which, like smoking the next cigarette, is your choice, or getting the *Post* or the *News*, so that you can slip past the front page headlines back to the childhoodlike reassurance of the sports pages, or maybe hear it on the radio, packed in clipped or folksy accents with weather and the stock market quotations" (476). Paradoxically, then, when one reads or attends Vietnam Protest Theatre (in spite of its overt antipathy toward television and the television war, and from the point of view of guerrilla theatre) one is participating in an activity not entirely unlike switching on a television set. Unlike street theatre which is encountered willy-nilly, with Vietnam Protest Theatre "we" can "choose" which station or play to watch.

This is not to say that street theatre ever thought of itself as entirely new or unique. Indeed, it saw its roots in the tradition of European and Soviet but also American agitprop theatre, including the "Workers Theatre" developed in the 1930s by the Communist Party of the United States of America (CPUSA) (Lesnick 419-37). The Vietnam protests of both The Bread and Puppet Theatre and El Teatro Campesino were also part and parcel of a much larger social critique which had included protests against African American and Latino housing conditions, beginning in the early sixties and continuing well after the Vietnam War was over. Particularly noteworthy in this regard is El Teatro Campesino's "Vietnam trilogy": *Vietnam Campesino* (1970), *Soldado Razo* (1971), and *Dark Root of a Scream* (1971). As Edward G. Brown has shown, these plays exhibit a clear logical progression, chronicling three aspects of the Chicano Vietnam experience: "the draft, the pre-combat anxiety, and the return of the fallen hero" (Brown 29).[12] Ironically, in terms of the generic norm of Vietnam Protest Theatre, the bloodletting that came with riots following The Chicano Moratorium on the Vietnam War (Los Angeles, August 1970) and the death of leading Chicano journalist and spokesman Ruben Salazar led El Teatro Campesino to turn away from militancy directed against the war and to the position that "the fight is here"—in U.S. society as a whole.

Stefan Brecht notes that the theory behind puppet "parades" was not only modern but archaic, even quasi-mythic.

> A street parade is . . . like the messenger that comes stumbling in out of breath to tell of the approaching enemy, the battle lost or won: it's upsetting. . . . If, for instance, there were more or less regular television coverage of hell, on-the-spot reporting from there, with the cameras focusing on new arrivals, this or that routine of torture, the flames leaping on the screen, shots of Beelzebub back from a conference, speaking a few words into the upheld mike, even the elderly sinner . . . would not be overly disturbed watching from the couch. (S. Brecht 476-77)

But the most immediate historical precedent for American street and guerrilla theatre was European, both theoretically and generationally. As formulated by Michael Brown of Pageant Players in his "Some Dynamics and Aesthetics" (1971), "Reading Artaud, Brecht, and others showed us we had been on the right track. We were going back to where Western theatre got lost, and picking up the loose threads, bypassing the printing press."[13] Schumann, who had emigrated to the United States from Germany, explicitly situated his Bread and Puppet Theatre in the context of European agitprop, even though he was less concerned with the Vietnam War specifically than were the majority of guerrilla groups. Schumann's context is summarized by Stefan Brecht:

> American involvement in Vietnam, as overt paradigm of the XXth century form of the class struggle, the transnational exploitation/oppression/repression of a proletarian component of humanity by a technologically advanced one, was a godsend to a man of manichean vision, and, because of its inelegant

heavyhandedness, that is, the use of air power in the tradition of the World War II bombardments of civilian Germany, not only of intense personal relevance to him (conditio sine qua non for art) but the perfect foil for a visually oriented moralist response to the simply meaningful image. (S. Brecht 480)

In short, the problem of defining both street "theatre" and more main-stream theatre in any national terms is that, "American" or "foreign" though they may seem, they are always already part of an inter/national project extending across time and space. Just as Vietnam was not just America's war, so also Vietnam Protest Theatre was never just American, even on American streets or stages. With it, the national definition of theatre, and indeed of all borders, is both reconfirmed and called into question. This is not to say that the division of its plays into "American," "German," or "French" is wholly invalid or useless, only that it is problematized by the plays, consciously or not.

The minimalist, low-tech strategies of "street" theatre should be con-trasted with the most famous and high-tech American protest production of the Vietnam era: *Hair* (1966) with its hyperbolic subtitle *The American Tribal Love-Rock Musical*.[14] Widely perceived at the time, and still today, as a rare example of genuinely "popular" protest against the war, largely by people unaware of Vietnam Protest Theatre, a closer retrospective look finds mainly a few catchy tunes (which pale in comparison to the best antiwar music);[15] a feeble (if well-intentioned) attempt to tackle racism, classicism, and homophobia; an ultimate "feel-good-about-America" ide-ology directed largely at a white male middle-class audience; and, in any event, none of the conceptual or political depth of the Vietnam Protest Plays. As with the Hollywood monolith which it subverted only to a very modest extent, the basic plot of *Hair* reduces a complex historical moment to a love story—recalling film critic Raymond Bellour's famous thesis that Hollywood, and its mass-media equivalents, is a relentless machine for the production of the (heterosexual) couple.[16] This is true a fortiori of the far more elaborate recent musical *Miss Saigon* (1989) with music by Claude-Michel Schönberg and lyrics by Alain Boublil and Richard Maltby Jr. A restaging of *Madam Butterfly* begun in England, this production required a huge financial advance, not least because a real helicopter was brought on stage.[17] It was inspired by the image in Saigon (April 1975) of the last helicopter as it was about to lift off from the U.S. embassy roof, dripping human cargo. Revamping *Madame Butterfly*, *Miss Saigon* offers yet another reduction of a turning point in the history of Indochina, indeed the world, to a love tragedy. A G.I. (Chris) is helplessly trapped within the American compound; the pregnant Vietnamese prostitute (Kim) he swore to marry is trapped outside. Arriving home safely but alone, the G.I. marries. Eventu-ally put in contact through a veterans' group with his Vietnamese family (the woman has delivered a son in Thailand), the G.I. travels to find them, planning to honor his promises, and unwittingly brings about the psychological and physical destruction of his former lover, who sacrifices herself for her son's future. The accompanying music is sometimes catchy, sometimes melodramatic, sometimes campy. The musical ends:

> KIM: The Gods have guided you to your son.
> CHRIS: Please don't die!
> KIM: Hold me one more time.
>   (Chris holds her)
>   How in one night have we come . . . so far.
>   (Kim's embrace becomes lifeless. Chris sobs, holding her.) THE CURTAIN FALLS

All this with an advance of $8 million dollars.

3.

In terms of sheer numbers Vietnam Protest Theatre is a weighty corpus indeed. It is also remarkable both by its cohesiveness and its diversity. As dramatic forms of committed dissent, intended to express and influence political judgments, and perhaps elicit direct, even violent action, all these protest plays clearly target the American war in Vietnam; and this common aim provides them with a distinct identity as a significant theatrical movement. Their shared topic, as well as a shared critical spirit, creates a strong unity that to some extent transcends national or individual variations. Taken together—whether they focus on the war itself, on its origins or on its consequences, on events in the United States or in Vietnam or even in other locations affected by the war—the protest plays thus display a remarkably unified vision of the "tragedy" of war, evoke similar scenes of atrocities, and testify to a similar need to assign responsibilities. They form a coherent theatre, politically and ethically militant. I will attempt to re/construct what can be variously described as the "discursive order" or "generic norm" or "deep structure" of this theatre.

But, within this cohesive ensemble, there is little uniformity in other important respects, and this might have been a major reason for previous neglect of the plays as a "genre." From one play to another, sometimes by the same playwright, the mood may change from optimism to pessimism to nihilism, from a playful approach to an acerbic satire, from sober analysis to gross obscenity. Different theatrical approaches produce different types of dramatic texts and/or different performance styles ranging from traditional to avant-garde, with different stress on dialogue, or pantomime, or mixed-media devices. Thus it is undesirable, if not impossible, to reduce this variety of individual achievements to artificially derived stable categories. Each play—or moment in a play—can make its own stand in its distinct way (without much evidence of mutual influences). And it is this diversity that is compelling: for it endows the Vietnam Protest Theatre with much of its moral and political force before it ever congeals into an academic topic.

There is one particularly significant exception, however, to this resistance of the international corpus to be structured in categories. It is not so much in matters of form, nor in the overall topic, nor even in the mood but rather in the assignment of *responsibility* for the war, and in the *degree* of severity with which the guilt is censured, that one best observes a definite split between, on the one hand, American plays-which lean toward a close-up, many-sided vision of the United States and its complex, "American," role in world events—and, on the other, European plays—that tend to show America as a monolith and are harsher in their judgment of it. This first basic and perhaps "normal" (in the sense of genre-defining) division is further accentuated by an equally natural tendency, in European plays, to project specific national concerns onto the dramatic canvas of the Vietnam War. American protest plays usually have but one goal: to protest against the war. But French, British, or German plays, while sharing that goal, seem also to have a second agenda, more or less open or hidden: to settle a sensitive issue in their own past. In Germany, for obvious reasons, that national issue most often originates in World War II: the Nazi war crimes, the systematic murder of Jews and others, the defeat and occupation by Western powers. For France, by a similar historical logic, the obsession with guilt and defeat has its roots in the bloody wars that France has lost since World War II: first in Vietnam itself, then and especially in Algeria. And the unpleasant issue of the colonial past of Great Britain, surviving the traumatic unraveling of its empire, and fueled at that time by the debate over the Suez Canal, surely was shadowing its representation of the Vietnam War as an imperialist "American" adventure. A comprehensive picture of theatrical visions of Vietnam cannot disregard these variations based on geopolitical regionalism. The insights these similar but different visions offer may not be directly relevant to the American perception of the war, but, in the world community, "Vietnam" was not viewed as an exclusively American problem and thus its full meaning, even in America, was at least indirectly affected by a certain internationalization of its theatrical and spectacular vision. And surely one way of dealing with our current fascination with "national identity" is to ask what forces of genuine international vision exist, however weak or exclusively "cultural," for contesting the worst excesses not only of nationalist fundamentalism but of liberal democracy.[18]

The pressing question then is not *whether* the Vietnam Protest Theatre ought to have been better noticed by American historians: obviously, both on its own as an impressive cultural movement, and as a testimony to the many ways in which the war was perceived in the United States as well as abroad, the Vietnam Protest Theatre certainly deserves much closer attention. The question rather is *why* scholars have failed to meet this need, if not demand. Part of the answer, visible especially in the case of European plays, lies in an unconscious or conscious ethnocentrism of American scholars. For many of them, even today, the war in Vietnam does indeed remain a primarily *American* story or trauma that therefore must be surveyed from an *American* perspective. Logically enough, many such academics are principally interested in the visions of that war which, whether favorable or critical, indicate how the Americans perceived a war in which they were "directly" involved, and how this perception might have modified its course. For linguistic reasons alone, foreign comments, or representations, offered outside the United States, obviously could not contribute much material to the study of the American mood or to the knowledge of the war that American media waged over Vietnam. On these terms, the American scholars' indifference toward the European protest theatre is both understandable and negligible. However, in terms of a more general empirical and theoretical assessment of the war, and a sharper appraisal of its American representations, the policy of discarding the European representations of Vietnam virtually a priori is surely regrettable. Not that the foreign perspectives could be expected to yield a more exact or "correct" vision of the war, one better informed or more objective.[19] French, British, or German writers who chose to represent Vietnam had no more, and probably less, information about the war than American writers, and were certainly influenced by their own idiosyncratic prejudices including an always problematic anti-American bias. Yet their European visions ought not to lack interest "even" for American historians. For the European perspectives inevitably differ from the American perspective on one crucial point: only they could see the Americans as the latter see their own "others." The degree of alienation from one's "others," or solidarity with them, obviously could and did vary widely, but nonetheless the European portrayal of Americans, and hence their vision of the Vietnam War, was bound to contain features that simply could not be found in works written from the perspective of the American "us." These features, which we will encounter and analyze in European texts and then find to be virtually absent in the American ones, reveal some specific blind spots in the American vision of the war and hence the limits of that vision. More important, a sustained comparison between American and European representations of Vietnam, whether converging or diverging, can yield a more balanced and at the same time complex picture of the war, combining the perceptions of participants and observers, and hence lead to a more diversified—and open-ended—judgment about the entire Vietnam story.

Protest plays accounted for a minute fraction of theatre shows performed during the war. But cold numbers do not yield an adequate understanding of a society as complex and divided as the United States. The protest plays, even though dwarfed by a much stronger commercial theatre, constituted a vital form that matched the feelings of a dissenting, but irresistibly growing, section of the general population and not just a marginal avant-garde. Their significance for that larger group may be compared to (though not equated with) the impact of televised Vietnam reports on the so-called "silent majority" of the American public. For, similarly, Vietnam reports on TV only accounted for a tiny fraction of television programs at the time, and yet they have long been acknowledged to be a major factor in forming public opinion. One might object to this comparison on the grounds that television reached many more people than theatre, and hence even a small fraction of its programs had an incommensurably greater influence. If only statistical averages were at issue here, this objection would certainly be valid. But any serious survey of American attitudes toward the war cannot be limited to studying the impact of mass media on the majority of the population; it also must present the full diversity of these attitudes and pay attention to the more restricted media that influenced and conveyed them. Television, for example, appears to be "commonsensical" or "second nature" only because of the existence of other competing and complimentary media of hegemonic and counterhegemonic influence: theatre for one.

4.

In mid-twentieth-century America the overall role of theatre as a political medium, and hence the power of subversive plays were often questioned in the medium itself.[20] Neither theatre critics nor even some of the protest playwrights themselves appeared to have placed much trust—and certainly not blind trust—in a wide-scale effectiveness of subversive messages conveyed on the stage. Thus Berrigan, author of the play *The Trial of the Catonsville Nine* (1970), strongly advocated Vietnam dissent in theatre, and yet he doubted that, in America, this dissent could have the same powerful and lasting effects as it ostensibly had in Europe except for "short periods and small numbers of actors":

> Maybe we're stuck with short-term efforts, being faithful to the sense of the moment.... (But maybe) we may be able to reproduce some sense of the depth, inwardness and communality that arises in a slower social scene over long periods. I am speaking again especially of the European dramatic experience and European teams.[21]

Yet not everybody shared these rather naively Eurocentric hopes, especially not the majority of protest playwrights who hoped to have a real influence on the American public and thereby to contribute to the antiwar movement at large. Surprisingly, the military authorities also seemed to believe in, and be remarkably concerned about, the potentially subversive effects of protest plays. It is reported that they denied to playwrights the access to firsthand knowledge of the situation in Vietnam. As Philip

Griffiths explains in an interview with Susan Moeller, "There was a little footnote in the application for your pass that said JUSPAO [Joint United States Public Affairs Office] is not in a position to accredit authors or playwrights. In other words, one had to be a bonafide journalist."[22] One notes that fiction or essay writers were also denied the press pass, but this was to be expected in view of the residual recognized subversive power of literature as a whole, if not theatre per se. The singling out of playwrights shows that *the military* was not convinced of the *total* futility of political theatre. In fact, the United States government under the auspices of JUSPAO used a traveling Vietnamese theatre troupe—Van Tac Vu—to spread U.S. propaganda. These dramatic "missions" are filed under the euphemistic titles "Cultural Dramatic Performances," "Cultural Seed Planting," "Civil Action & Information Propaganda," and "Leading and Organizing of People's Cultural Drama Activities."[23]

Until veterans began to write their own plays, even the most enterprising authors of protest theatre had to rely on reports and images of Vietnam conveyed by the mass media, i.e., made up with clichés that might be parodied with imagination but not counteracted with facts. A similar problem was noted by Martin Esslin about German war plays in the sixties:

> These plays no longer address an audience that knows war because it has experienced firsthand, but rather a generation which knows about it only through plays on war, movies on war of a former war. Also the authors of these plays are too young to have experienced war directly. So the rejection of war is expressed above all through the parodying of clichés of former war plays and war films.[24]

Similarly, Jean-Luc Godard, in the 1967 collaborative film *Loin du Vietnam,* and Harun Farocki in his 1982 film *Etwas Wird Sichtbar,* discuss the problematic of the representation of Vietnam. Comparatively few people have actually been to Vietnam or experienced the war firsthand; hence most rely on the mediation of reporters and journalists and their products: news reports and photographic or filmic images. This is, of course, not to say that even those who have actually been in a place experience it directly without any mediation whatsoever. Fredric Jameson's general claim about the postmodernist sensibility is that "historical" themes (in movies, etc.) are less about social history per se and more about when an audience was historically brought into the "loop" of mass media representation—e.g., the fascination with, say, Dick Tracy or Bugsy has more to do with comic books one read as a kid than with the Roaring Twenties, etc.[25] This ostensibly "postmodern" problematic was significantly anticipated by the Vietnam Protest Theatre.

For all these reasons, the American attitude toward protest plays was generally lenient, perhaps condescending. With an audience seemingly confined to the fringe group of avant-garde artists and their supporters, the Vietnam theatre might not have needed to be feared or regulated by censorship. Nonetheless, when it *was* censured, it was more for its potential power than for its actual subversive effect—at least in the eyes of the government, if not in those of the playwrights themselves.

The *relative* freedom of expression that America accorded to protest plays may be compared and contrasted with problems these plays occasionally faced in Europe. Political theatre has always been taken more seriously abroad, and European Vietnam Protest Plays, especially those produced by reputed and influential playwrights, did experience several serious difficulties with censorship.[26] In London, Hochhuth's *Soldiers,* an allusive critique of the Vietnam War, was shut down in 1967: the first case of theatre censorship in years.[27] Alternatively, Peter Brook's *US* was not allowed to be performed in Frankfurt am Main because the West German government was afraid of offending the personnel of a U.S. military base in the vicinity.[28] Peter Weiss's *Vietnam Discourse* had only one performance in Munich and three in Berlin before it was canceled because, immediately after the show, a collection of funds was made for the Vietcong.[29] No such drastic measures curtailed performances of Vietnam plays in the United States, though there might have been some isolated cases of effective intimidation.[30] No doubt the American belief in, and to a lesser extent even the fact of, the "freedom of artistic expression" explains much of this leniency. In the case of protest theatre, however, this general tolerance surely also reflected a genuine skepticism about the effectiveness of political action on the stage. As Andrew Ross laconically observes, "where live theatrical performance had once been subject to rigorous state censorship, its minority audience today guarantees its immunity."[31] It is perhaps in the same skeptical spirit that historians of the Vietnam War may have deemed that protest plays did not deserve serious attention.

But this lack of interest in Vietnam Protest Plays, and in theatre in general, might also have had a more paradoxical but perhaps more decisive cause: namely, a paralyzing fascination with more highly spectacular forms of modern public information. Most scholars of the Vietnam War, especially those who have surveyed its representation in mass media, tend to agree that its extensive visual coverage in illustrated press and on television turned it into a suspenseful "spectacle," indeed, into "the first television war." More recently, during the Gulf War and East European upheavals, this spectacularization was to be more generally acknowledged and more forcefully denounced for its misleading images, particularly with regard to the sensational television coverage by CNN.[32] Actually, the growing process of spectacularization has not been limited to reports on war or revolutions. Drawing on technological advances after World War I, mass media have been increasingly spectacularizing, and hence dramatizing, even events without a natural dramatic content or historical referent—public ceremonies, shows or games, or private lives of political, art, and sport figures such as O. J. Simpson—in short, everyday life. And there is no evidence that this trend is abating, nor that it constitutes but a minor aberration in the media's "ideal" function to provide "factual" information. It would rather seem that this problematic reflects a very basic fascination with spectacles in a society where, as Guy Debord claims in *The Society of the Spectacle*, mass-produced images, disseminated as market products, lose any mooring in reality, becoming consumed and valued for their own sake only as images:

> Wherever the real world changes into simple images, the simple images become real beings and effective motivations of a hypnotic behavior. The spectacle, as a tendency to make one see the world by means of specialized mediations (it can no longer be grasped directly), naturally finds vision to be the privileged human sense which the sense of touch was for other epochs.[33]

For Debord, the rapid proliferation of the "spectacle" is a dominant feature of contemporary culture. The exact scope of its impact on our society is difficult to assess, but it certainly has been exerting a capital influence on the visual media. Obviously there are many reasons for it but no simple one. As with most cultural trends, spectacularization inevitably derives from a multiplicity of factors, and these interact in very complex ways that discourage the search for a single primary cause. For example, when Jameson explains that, by "the cultural logic of late capitalism," spectacular images are severed from their traditional references and appropriated by the public for their sensational aspect only, his highlighting of late capitalism as the overdetermined source of spectacularization is a form of reductionism. Less controversial is his notion that we live in "a society of the image or the simulacra," wherein the "real" is constantly converted "into so many pseudoevents" (Jameson 1991, 48). But what is particularly interesting for us here, with regard to the problem of negotiating the past, is Jameson's related argument "that it is memory itself that has become the degraded repository of images and simulacra, so that the remembered image of the thing now effectively inserts the reified and the stereotypical between the subject and reality or the past itself" (Jameson 1991, 123-24). His identification of the power of images is quite persuasive and confirms aspects of Debord's diagnosis. Similarly, Theodor Adorno and Max Horkheimer had pointed already in the 1940s to an illusory promise of spectacle.[34] In short, the acknowledgment that spectacularization is a pervasive cultural dominant does not need to be supported by speculation about its ultimate primary cause. Whatever its origins, it stands on its own as a mark of modernist and postmodernist culture.

In this culture, one may then argue, the factual atrocities of the Vietnam War, spectacularized in sensational images of prize-winning photographs and television reports, were bound to become decontextualized in the media, split from their "natural" historical referents, and made to illustrate a "second nature" representation of Vietnam that removed the "real" war from general public awareness.[35] Emerging in a culture of spectacle, the Vietnam theatre had to pursue simultaneously two distinct but interlocking goals. On the one hand, most consciously and explicitly, it sought to wage an antiwar protest; on the other hand it was bound also to take on the spectacular media that supported the war. In that sense, the staged representations of Vietnam not only fought at home against the war, trying to win over American minds; it also fought against a more general and massive impact of mediatized images on the American society. Both fights (the one against a real event, the other against a medium) were potentially subversive ideologically: the antiwar protest in the strict area of politics, since it aimed at resisting and perhaps helping to overturn a policy of the American government; and the anti-mass-media stance in the less clearly defined area of consumer culture, where it tried to undermine the institutionalized power of mediatized images.

Animated by that double thrust, the Vietnam Protest Theatre was both "optimistic" and "idealistic." It expressed a commitment to a principle, an ethical, political, and/or artistic cause, rather than a strong confidence in pragmatic results of its action. In fact, the chances of prevailing in this war on two fronts could not appear to be very promising to contemporaries. For neither the political situation in the United States, at least in the early years of the war, nor the overall development of the cultural environment offered much encouragement to small theatre companies striving to subvert dominant social and ideological trends. Their steady adhesion to the two goals of the protest plays and a remarkable dedication in pursuing them over many years disclose the full power of the ancient belief that theatre is entrusted with a mission that transcends entertainment: to be the medium chosen to tell the truth in a society that promotes illusion. Or, more specifically in this instance, the special mission of theatre was to offer a representation of Vietnam that would somehow reveal the true horror of war, expose the deceit of pro-war representations in other media, and ultimately lead to stopping war—if not this particular war then perhaps wars in the future.

This dual program of the Vietnam plays—a political protest of a cultural medium against the war and a cultural protest of a weak medium against a more powerful mass media—can be related to the main objectives of "political theatre" as it is understood today. This is the militant theatre that initially has been promoted in Europe by left-wing playwrights and directors, notably Piscator and Brecht after World War I, and that, after World War II, found some of its best-known manifestations in the German documentary theatre plays of Weiss and Hochhuth. In that modern sense, political theatre is supposed to stage representations of controversial historical events for the specific purpose of inciting the audience to get involved in direct social action. This theatre is defined not as a closed space but as a porous site of articulation between aesthetics and the rest of the world. (The old question arises: does it "incite" the audience in the sense of [a] *converting* some members to new positions and/or [b] *reinforcing* and *reconfirming* previously held positions?) And that was exactly what the Vietnam Protest Theatre was attempting to do. To that extent, then, its dramas fall within the much broader category of political plays. But such a vast category covers many variations. In Europe, where the tradition of political theatre was well established and alive, the playwrights were preconditioned, so to speak, to turn to the stage as to the natural medium through which to register their protest against the Vietnam War and against a massively mediatized culture. The problems they encountered, the means they used to solve them, reflected the traditions of the European political stage.

In the United States, on the other hand, political theatre had fewer or weaker roots in the past, and the Vietnam protest playwrights had practically to reinvent protest theatre and to impose it on a public that had little experience in that genre. The problems they met and the means they devised could hardly reflect an existing tradition of political theatre, but rather emerged from new possibilities discovered during the process of creation. Several important questions raised by the production of Vietnam plays were obviously bound to reach beyond the topical matters and to open onto issues concerning the very nature and limits of theatre as an aesthetic and political medium.[36]

5.

The political dynamism of antiwar plays owed much to the emergence of a new avant-garde in theatre in the sixties. Conversely, when the avant-garde eventually declined in the seventies, principally in America but also in Europe, so did the parallel drive toward political theatre. True, the end of the Vietnam War was bound to bring about a natural end to Vietnam Protest Theatre regardless of the role played by the avant-garde. But, since that time, various other political issues raised a vocal public controversy and yet, in the absence of a strong theatrical avant-garde that would take them up, they failed to generate a significant protest on the stage. It would seem, in short, that the fortune of political theatre depends perhaps less on causes, which are never lacking, than on the internal evolution of the theatre world that generates truly radical avant-gardes. Peter Bürger has argued that a basic aim of the avant-garde has been institutional, critiquing the world of art in order to push past its limits into other institutions, politicizing and changing them in novel, perhaps progressive ways.[37] To that extent, for a combination of external and internal reasons, Vietnam Protest Theatre might be called an "ambivalent" avant-garde: oscillating until it had run its course continually between success and failure.

Yet the constitution of a dynamic avant-garde, however significant it might have been, cannot explain everything about the Vietnam theatre. It does not account, in particular, for its primacy among the other forms of protest waged by the art media against the war. A comparable avant-garde was certainly at work in the literary and quasi-literary milieu of prose writing. Yet, at least in retrospect, surprisingly little committed antiwar prose fiction was produced until the 1970s.

There are exceptions, of course. Of particular note, in addition to the earlier novels of Graham Greene such as *The Quiet American* (1956) are a number of texts that crossed over from journalism into fiction. One thinks perhaps first of Norman Mailer and David Halberstam.[38] There was also an extensive body of "popular" fiction, including Nick Carter's contributions to the "Killmaster Series": spy-espionage thrillers such as *Saigon* (1964) and *Hanoi* (1969), or Bill S. Ballinger's *A Spy in the Jungle* (1965), though little if anything in this genre can be counted as antiwar. The interventions of antiwar poets (women as well as men) would also deserve recognition.[39]

The area of film is more problematic. While there were many independent protest films made during the sixties, they remained marginal and are still relatively unknown today.[40] Hollywood did make a few pro-Vietnam films, conforming to the prevailing ideas both in form and message, but it failed to produce overtly antiwar pictures until long after the war was over. There were two well-known exceptions to this general support of Vietnam: Chris. Marker's aforementioned *Loin du Vietnam* (1967) and de Antonio's *Vietnam: In the Year of the Pig* (1968), but they were difficult to access both in Europe and in the United States. The American public had to wait until the story of Vietnam ceased to be a Hollywood taboo topic in order to see the first arguably critical blockbusters: *Coming Home* (1977), *The Deer Hunter* (1978), and *Apocalypse Now* (1979). Even these barely qualify as true protest. They questioned little the responsibility for the war, let alone its geopolitical economic origins, focusing on less overtly controversial themes such as male bonding, the spectacularization of war, and the reintegration of veterans into U.S. society.

This absence of deeper analysis and protest by the cinema can be in part attributed to the commercial and political timidity of the film industry. In addition, because of the visual illusion of reality that is expected from cinema, a film with complex settings needs both considerable funding and real—or "looking like real"—material models for its pictures. Or so it does at least in the expectations of an audience indoctrinated by the conventions of Classic Hollywood Cinema and its various ideologies of mimesis, suture, and verisimilitude.[41] A film about the war "scene" in Vietnam could thus hardly be shot without the use of real war planes and weapons: military equipment that the army, especially during the war, could not be expected to release easily. A notable exception was made for John Wayne's pro-war *Green Berets* (1968): real army weapons were provided by the Pentagon, and Hawaiian actors stood in for Vietnamese. On the other hand, even long after the war was over, the shooting of the mildly subversive *Platoon* (1987) was held up for years because the U.S. Army refused to lend the necessary military equipment. Similar logistic problems impeded the filmic representation of foreign lands, say, a Vietnamese village or jungle, and ethnically distinct populations. For Hollywood, economic constraints delay the speed with which the cinema can respond as a medium to a historical event in terms of production, distribution, and consumption.

Theatre has a far greater flexibility with regard to time, expenses, human and material resources, and continuous control over production, even though its innate resistance to "mechanical reproducibility" certainly prevents it from reaching the mass audiences of films. In each of these areas (the important question of "distribution" set aside), theatre is theoretically much more suitable than mainstream cinema to function as a direct political medium. I do not mean that all forms of theatre are able to take equal advantage of that potential. In matters of time, expenses, and resources, there is little empirical difference between most films and most commercial stage productions on Broadway, especially musicals that are intended to draw large audiences and must turn quick and large box-office profits. These highly professional productions, like professional movies, require a long preparatory period of writing the dramatic text (and music), securing public or private funding, auditing and selecting the performers, building the sets, and rehearsing the performance. Their star actors, in great demand, can be very costly; and intricate sets, costumes, and props can also be expensive. In all these areas, it takes as much time and effort to stage a great Broadway show as to make a movie. Broadway had to wait years before the financial, ideological, and other climates were right before staging *Miss Saigon* in 1989. But more modest shows, especially by small companies that have no commercial ambitions, can be produced very fast and very cheaply. Thus, the text of a political play, whether written by a single inspired author or by an enthusiastic performing collective, rarely demands a long gestation; it rather tends to be composed rapidly, so as to provide a timely response to the historical events that triggered its production. Its staging is then urgently carried out by a dedicated ensemble of director, actors, technicians, and staff, willing to work for a cause either for little or for no compensation. And no protracted rehearsing is needed to polish the performances; indeed, while they demand hard and inventive work from the performers, they are more oriented toward a fast delivery of a clear political message than toward time-consuming artistic excellence.

Such plays are also seldom slowed down, or financially troubled, by the need to find adequate locations, build intricate sets, and acquire expensive or hard-to-get equipment. Many political plays take place in very simple settings; but there are no real problems in staging even those plays, such as the Vietnam Protest Theatre, that refer to exotic places, mass action, and heavy (war) machinery. For theatre has a more fluid capacity than cinema to free itself, when necessary, from the constraints of basic iconicity, and to exploit, with minimal means, what may be called the metaphoric power of stage signs: the ability of any simple sign on the stage to evoke, by dint of the poetic convention, a complex reality in the represented world. More important, unlike filmgoing audiences, theatre audiences are not programmed to expect and demand representational verisimilitude. In the imagination of theatre spectators, a single palm tree will stand for a jungle, a waved red cloth for fire, outstretched arms for an airplane, a detonation and falling bodies for a bombing raid. In that poetic realm, the freedom of representation in theatre is practically limitless, and at low cost.

Theatre also offers a suitable visual medium to meet the sense of antiwar urgency and to adjust political statements to fluctuations of historical events and circumstances of reception. The dramatic text is never totally fixed since, each time, it must be spoken by live performers who are always able, even liable, to alter it in response not only to criticism of performances but also to audience reaction even as the play is performed. As a rule, performances follow a rehearsed text with no meaningful improvisation; but, on their own or by previous agreement, actors on the stage may (and do) make ad hoc changes that transform the meaning: substituted or added words, different intonations, modified gestures, an accelerated or slowed down pace, etc. This flexible control (and also sometimes lack thereof) over the delivery of the message, and hence over its reception, is good capital for a medium involved in political issues. It enables the performers to play, as skillful orators do at political meetings, on the emotions of their audiences, nudging them in the desired direction with minimal spoken alterations of the written text. It allows them to update their message from day to day, inserting references to the latest news and maintaining the sense of pressing relevance. Most politically committed actors are aware of their responsibility for that continuous re/creation of meaning. They know that their commitment demands participation in the promotion of their cause, an active involvement in a communication that needs to be adjusted each time to new conditions. In the case of Vietnam Protest Theatre (often staged for sympathetic audiences, to be sure) this personal contribution of actors served to clarify their own feelings, to inspire spectators, and to bring to the highest pitch the shared political commitment. But for political theatre in general, whenever there might be reasons to expect the presence of censors in the audience, or to suspect that the audience may be prejudiced against subversive ideas, the same continuous control of performances enables the actors to modulate the strength of statements, elude censorship, or minimize hostile reactions. These pragmatic considerations no doubt played a role in encouraging the staging of Vietnam plays, especially in a general climate of uncertain and labile social opinions.

Emergence of a dynamic theatre avant-garde, faith in theatre's revolutionary mission, awareness of the suitability of theatre to serve as a political medium—all these factors explaining the vitality of Vietnam Protest Theatre have one thing in common: they stem from theatre as live medium. A medium animated by the enthusiasm of its live performers, committed mind and body to its survival and eager to assert its creativity; a medium that always highlights the performance of physically present human beings, at the center of attention and production of meaning; a somatic medium where communication with the audience remains always controlled by actors. But also a medium that, on its live stage, is better able than other live media (such as mime or dance) to tell a relatively clear story and to convey a relatively clear meaning. It is both this live nature and this ability to communicate messages that moved theatre to express dissent from the Vietnam War and from the cultural sway of spectacularized and techno-images.

6.

Vietnam Protest Theatre must also be linked as live medium to a problem addressed in the next section of this book. "Vietnam" has been used as a means to work through, to reenact, and generally to negotiate other kinds of history besides the war proper. In this regard, we cannot always simply assume that we know where "Vietnam" is, as an easily locatable and identifiable regional or temporal site. Instead, it can stand in for many other signifiers and referents. This problem of displacement was well captured by the documentary filmmaker Pierre Schoendorffer, who had fought during the fifties in the French Army in Vietnam. Returning to Vietnam in 1966 to film *The Anderson Platoon,* Schoendorffer quickly came to an unsettling realization: "I went back to rediscover the Vietnam I had left 13 years ago with the French Army, but except for a few poignant scenes I discovered above all America."[42] Discussing *"Vietnam* Protest Theatre," we must be alert to the possibility that other things are always uncannily at stake, in the present as well as the past.

Negotiating National History through Vietnam

It isn't that the past casts its light on the present or the present casts its light on the past: rather an image is that in which the past and the now flash into a constellation. In other words the image is dialectic at a standstill. For while the relation of the present to the past is a purely temporal, continuous one, that of the past to the now is dialectical—isn't development but image, capable of leaping out.

—Walter Benjamin

National consciousness, which is not nationalism, is the only thing which will give us an international dimension.   —Frantz Fanon

PART ONE

In a time of increasing nationalism and the collapse of international resistance to transnational capital, it is a perilous task to diversify the topic of negotiating the past on the basis of distinct national identities. Such national divisions are neither empirically stable nor homogeneous to begin with, and examples chosen for a given nation (or language), such as "French" or "German," are not necessarily, if at all, representative of what is commonly assumed to be "French" or "German"—or "English" or "Vietnamese" or "American."[1] In the case of Germany, for instance, one certainly ought to speak of regional differences as well as of national ones. I am using national boundaries only as a makeshift means with which to bring flexible analytic order to my work. I also want to show how, in the words of Homi K. Bhabha, an "ambivalent nation-space becomes the crossroads to a new transnational culture."[2] My national boundaries will thus be fluid, without necessarily having a clear inside or outside. I assume, as Michael Geyer puts it, that "there are no interior histories without exterior ones and vice versa. In order to understand the nation, any one national history, historians have to go beyond the nation."[3] For this reason, one chapter in this section, while focusing on German language plays about Vietnam, will move both temporally and spatially within and without German borders and back and forth through history. While I give close attention to German language plays, I will use these readings to engage in a Benjaminian "dialogic exchange with the past" that implies and implicates contemporary cultural issues as well.[4]

I have, in this process, to answer a preliminary question: Why would any nation not directly involved in the U.S. war with distant Vietnam choose to treat it with an affective charge as a topic of its own cultural production? For there is little question that Vietnam, though far removed geographically and culturally from the Western world, was at the time of the war thrust into the center of global attention, becoming a triggering sign with multiple meanings in virtually all political and cultural discourses. If, to quote Geyer again, there is a specific "European field of signs," and it is this specific "regime of signification which organizes the particular national identifications" (Geyer 328), then the Vietnam War played a major role, for nearly a decade, in the determination and formulation of the identity or identities not just of the United States but also of a number of European nations. In other words, while within the general Western semiotic field each European nation becomes associated with certain distinct significations, I argue that by extension Vietnam served as one of the major shared signs that various nations, often in very different cultural circumstances, used to construct their national identities and identifications.

One could claim, no doubt, that the ubiquity of Vietnam plays with their strongly anti-American slant merely expressed a surge in a more general sentiment of anti-Americanism that was sweeping Europe at the time.[5] An overall anti-American prejudice could help to explain why French, German, and British authors like Benedetto, Gatti, Brook, Hochhuth, and Weiss systematically—and seemingly spontaneously and independently—took up the theme of the United States as the aggressor in Vietnam. But such an approach would be both reductive and ultimately misleading. A close examination of European Vietnam Protest Plays indicates that a general anti-Americanism fails to account for most of their specific features. Although they certainly engaged in a widespread censure of America on Vietnam, a similar censure also marks all the American plays about Vietnam. Further, each European playwright seems to be more interested in following his own agenda, largely dictated by his own ideological concerns determined by different national contexts. (Unlike the American playwrights in question, all the Europeans are male.) Besides, most European playwrights do not indict America *as such* but rather specific American *policies*, not American *people* but the American *govern-ment*. Instead of a blind and undifferentiated anti-Americanism, then, these playwrights display a remarkably selective condemnation of specific American political decisions. Furthermore, their highly politicized depic-tion and appraisal of the Vietnam War is typically grounded in their own political causes and generally leftist political ideals. It is quite likely, in fact, that the political orientations of the European playwrights offer a more precise explanation of their shared anti-Americanism than a vague anti-American bias. The politization of their plays corresponds to a well-established institutional tradition of European theatre in the twentieth century: a skilled and respected manifestation of political commitment on the stage.

The question remains: why, within this general field of signs and significations, did the Vietnam War come to play such a crucial role? Clearly it offered at the time an exemplary instance, and hence a sign, of what one could call a "wrong war." By "wrong war" I mean a war that is highly controversial at home and abroad; a war waged by a strong power against a weak enemy and yet, paradoxically, either lost or in the process of being lost; a war that causes large-scale destruction and suffering among civilian populations; a war that transgresses the limits of conven-tional war set by the Geneva Convention and leads to saturation air bombing, the use of napalm and Agent Orange, and massacres of women and children as in My Lai. The war was viewed as such a "wrong war" in the United States and in noninvolved countries. Challenging consensus, it was not another "good fight."

Most of Europe questioned the fairness of a war fought by a clearly superior Western power against a militarily and economically inferior Eastern or "Oriental" nation—yet one seemingly superior in moral strength. Hence there developed a general opposition to the war and the urge, among intellectuals, not only to write about Vietnam, not only to reproduce it on the stage, but also to *produce* "Vietnam" as a powerful sign of critical and creative political commitment. True, as Schoendorffer sug-gested, writing about Vietnam inevitably involved writing about the United States. But it also led to writing about the West in general and specific European countries in particular. This self-reflective imperative was felt nowhere more acutely than in Germany, which of course had a particularly problematic past and present; but its variants in other Euro-pean nations are no less interesting in many respects. The resulting diver-sity of antiwar plays can be best grasped when they are projected on the background of comparatively more homogeneous American Vietnam Protest Theatre to which we turn first.

PLAYING IMPERIALISM
(AMERICA'S WAR)

History is a *process without a subject*. —Louis Althusser

I now focus on three of the five best known and most reviewed Vietnam Protest Plays produced in America between 1966 and 1971, i.e., during the height of the war and of the antiwar movement in the United States.[1] (Two plays by David Rabe will be discussed in chapter 6.) As noted earlier, many plays about "Vietnam" were to be written after the war either by veterans or about them, most dealing less with the war itself than with the treatment and reintegration of returning GIs back into American society.[2] There are also more recent plays that present the Vietnam War from a necessarily more mediated perspective than the earlier ones—tending to indict what is commonly viewed as a *former* U.S. policy rather than an ongoing reality. Only rarely, do any of these plays interrogate the overdetermining causes of the war—Berrigan's is the exception proving a rule. It is for this reason—their failure to ask questions rather than to give answers—that I propose that the American staging of the Vietnam War was a form of "playing imperialism." This term will refer not only to the implicit "impe-rialistic" perspective from which American plays tend to *view* the war, more or less consciously, but also to a similar perspective from which they *restage* it, more or less unconsciously—in most cases to the exclusion of other perspectives that might be *less* subjective, *less* complicitous with the dominant ideology of the United States.

1.

The war ain't there, it's right here, here and now in
this obscene, cancerous glare of the TV lights and
tranquilized television dinners. Television, the tremendous masturbator of the masses. . . . All you
studs got to stop smearing napalm on the genitals of
the weak.   —Megan Terry

Arguably the first major American theatrical piece about the war to
achieve both national and international recognition was Megan Terry's
Viet Rock (A Folk War Movie) (1966).[3] It took shape in Joseph Chaikin's Open
Theatre workshop, receiving mixed reviews that stressed both its highly
innovative experimental form and its bold political content. One reviewer
noted, "*Viet Rock* is protest without aim or very much art,"[4] but another
praised it for offering "a protest demonstration, set in the form of a revue.
As a result, it continuously makes a point without any disguise, using
fervor and theatrical invention for climax rather than peak of plot."[5] That
these reviews appeared in popular and disparate venues such as the *New
York Post* and *Women's Wear Daily* is an indication of how deeply into
American consciousness and discourse Vietnam Protest Theatre had begun to penetrate—as early as 1966.

In the spirit of the Open Theatre, *Viet Rock* involved only a limited
number of actors who did not stand for fixed characters but constantly
exchanged roles, improvising and addressing the audience pretty much
as they saw fit. The traditional proscenium stage was abandoned, and the
spectators sat in a circle around performers who encouraged "audience
participation." Instead of a linear progression of action, distinct character development, and a logical plot, the play offered disjointed scenes,
ephemeral characters, and a barrage of popular images and music. As a
result of what might be described as proto-postmodern theatricality, the
fragmented and mass-mediatized story on the stage seemed at first to
make no more sense than the story of the actual war in Vietnam. Furthermore, the play stressed action instead of explanatory words in the
dialogue, and in her production notes Terry instructed future directors to
follow the same policy: "The director must keep in mind that the visual
images are here more important than the words" (Terry 21). The content
was purposefully episodic so that the spectators, faced with a bewilder-
ing puzzle of symbols, realistic episodes, bawdy or vulgar songs, and
poetic images, would be forced to make sense of them on their own, at the
risk of making no sense at all. In sum, the audience encountered on the
stage, barely transfigured by the "magic" of theatre, the same complex
vision of the war as in the disorienting reports in the media. Recalled
Michael Herr two years later, "Conventional journalism could no more
reveal this war than conventional firepower could win it,"[6] nor could
conventional theatre be expected to represent it better. Terry explains,

"We used material that bombarded us every day from television and newspapers" (Terry 21). But images can be powerful "bombs," and one cannot just "use" them without paying a certain, often unexpectedly high price. Predictably, the multimedia performance of *Viet Rock* did not please viewers with traditional expectations, and hence it failed to influence them politically. Subtitled "A Folkwar Movie," this designation seems a pious wish. Clearly Terry's stage could not compete with the "real" movies; on the other hand the "real" movies were not addressing the war in the mid-sixties.

The political content of *Viet Rock* was clearly controversial, but criticism did not necessarily follow party lines. For some reviewers, the fragmentary nature of the play, while retaining a strong albeit unfocused anti-Vietnam War thrust, lacked a coherent antiestablishment message. As a critic of *Variety* noted at the time: "the play is not outright pacifist in sentiment. It is a howl of protest against a specific war and the motives behind it."[7] Another, writing in the *Village Voice*, felt that the play did not go far enough: "*Viet Rock* is crude and obvious; it lacks the kind of on-target wit and corrosive power needed to make it effective either as antiwar propaganda or as entertainment."[8] Because of its diffuse nature and its presentation of political positions on both sides, *Viet Rock* was faulted for not taking an aggressive enough stance, and Terry was even accused of not having authentic political commitment or being, at best, an anarchist. In his introduction to *Viet Rock*, Richard Schechner wrote:

> The theme and scope, the variety and density, of *Viet Rock* would have excited Brecht, just as Miss Terry's politics may have disappointed him. Despite the fact that those of the American Left who know *Viet Rock* have welcomed it, the play is non-political. It is a war play and as such it is an antiwar play. But it is not propagandistic or dogmatic. . . . For most of the play Miss Terry represents and disparages *all* points of view. (Terry 17)

To get a different take on the play, contextualizing its impact, one may turn to Western Europe. For *Viet Rock* was also performed in West Germany in 1968 by a local theatre troupe.[9] Appearing a month after Peter Weiss's *Vietnam Discourse* and Barbara Garson's West German premiere of *MacBird*, Terry's play invited comparison to both works. In contrast to its mixed reception in the United States, it received overwhelmingly positive reviews. While Weiss's and Garson's texts were criticized for their one-sidedness, German critics lauded the very feature that the Americans had found too wishy-washy: Terry's attempt to show two sides of the matter.[10] This difference in response likely expressed the special situation of Germany which, contrary to the United States, had no obvious reason to take a strong position about Vietnam and hence could be more "objective" about the issues of the war. Furthermore, given its own past, a German audience likely welcomed, subconsciously or consciously, the notion that there are two sides to the story of war. The highly energetic theatricality of *Viet Rock*, contrasting with Weiss's comparatively tame and, as it was perceived at the time in Germany, "boring" documentary production, was extolled by German critics.[11] The play's form, unlike anything many German spectators had seen—or at least in recent memory—boldly set it aside from traditional, conventional categories.[12] It was praised for its *anti*-documentary style, which, it was believed, showed true creativity and imagination. As often happens, this praise was based on a misunderstanding or misprision. In point of fact, the performance relied *heavily* on the use of documents: specifically giant war photos and posters projected on the back wall of the stage. But these documentary features did not seem to disturb those German audiences who registered them as such or who ignored them as inchoate parts of an unfocused political message. They preferred to concentrate on the features of the performance that showed the psychological problems of American individuals affected by the war. Unlike the works of Garson, Weiss, or Gatti, according to a reviewer who undoubtedly had recent German history in mind:

> Megan Terry's play *Viet Rock* is neither analytical nor historical; it says little about the method of fighting, and its background of finances, power-politics strategies. What the author shows are the psychological mechanisms, complexes and manipulations, that portray people caught in an unpleasant war.[13]

Clearly the play elicited different, often contradictory, responses. One must wonder therefore whether it was really as apolitical as some critics felt it to be. Was it only a psychological study, or did it also deal at some level with motivations for war? Did Terry really present all sides in equal light, or did she show preference for some positions?

While not directly or adequately addressing the *cause* of the war, Terry's play does assign at least some *responsibility* for it in two ways: first, by exposing part of the ideology behind the war and the official reasons for waging it; and second, by offering satirical portraits of those who promote and legitimate it. The play would be less complex than it is, were it clearly reducible to what we would call a problematic of "subjective imperialism," even though it is still *part* of that problematic. The puzzling observation that contemporary reviewers did not highlight the issue of responsibility in the play may simply testify that historical responsibility was too complex or volatile an issue for them to deal with, especially at the time.

In the first scene of *Viet Rock*, a voice on tape recites the following slogans: "Let us persevere in what we have resolved before we forget. Look out for number one. What you don't know can kill you" (Terry 28). These slogans evoke popular American maxims that have helped to indoctrinate the citizens of the United States in the belief that they must defend their position in the world at all costs, that the ends justify the means, and that communism is a stealthy, surreptitious evil threatening the security of America. A sign appearing over the gate of at least one military base in the United States during the war read: "Obedience to the Law Is Freedom." And this slogan was to become a central target of deconstruction in guerrilla street theatre.[14] In her play, Terry's cited slogans are followed by the eponymous theme song—"Viet Rock"—while, on stage, actors play like children: "Playtime material, especially of war games, cowboys and *Indians* [my emphasis], cops and robbers, should be allowed to come to surface and explode into sound, sounds of weapons, horses, tanks, planes, guns, troops, etc." (Terry 29). Terry suggests that the war mentality, inculcated already into small children, is basically a childish mentality with lethal consequences. Enacted in traditional American "games," it is a deeply ingrained trope of "the American way of life."[15] The specific reference to "Indians" then links the Vietnam War to the often repressed founding moment of the United States—the murder and deterritorialization of Native Americans. Which surely opens up the problematic of deep historical responsibility (though not causation), even if it closes off others.

From childhood, Terry moves her characters to young adulthood while maintaining the theme of military indoctrination. The induction process into the service is exposed as a ritual recruitment into the world of war. As one GI explains, alluding to the Bible: "This is the time when the young man puts away childish things, like childhood and Momma's voice so that he can step out into the world of a man" (Terry 39-40). The scene at the recruitment office evolves into an evocation of marine boot camp. It is there that the radical transformation from boys playing at war to men who are killing machines is completed. *Viet Rock*'s brutal documentation and scathing indictment of this process preceded by many years similar scenes in movies such as Stanley Kubrick's *Full Metal Jacket* (1987). It also parallels Brook's condemnation of indoctrination and brainwashing techniques in *US*.

A more original feature of *Viet Rock*, and one wholly missed at the time, is its remarkable charge that the boot camp's sergeant begins the process of the transformation of young men into officially sanctioned killers by *feminizing* them. His tacit function, it would appear, is to transform recruits not from boys into men, but rather from girls into men, and only then into killing machines.[16] In that overdetermined process of re/gendering-cum-robotization, he first attempts to make his recruits aware of their "female" nature:

> Come my ladies, take your rifles
> Here my bunnies are grenadies,
> Stand to battle,
> Little pussies.

War a go go
Is our game. (Terry 41)[17]

In *The Remasculinization of America: Gender and the Vietnam War* (1989), a comprehensive study of the fictional treatment of the war in all forms *except* for theatre and one of the best treatments of the war by a feminist, Susan Jeffords claims that, whatever the "real" causes and reasons for the Vietnam War, it served most narratives, in a remarkably concerted way, as a vehicle for reasserting the primacy of traditional patriarchal values in what had come to be perceived as a feminized society.[18] In Vietnam Protest Plays, however, perhaps because some of them were written by American women like Terry, the orientation is rather different and certainly more complex (though this hardly explains why Jeffords would wholly disregard theatre); instead they show that war—or "the war machine"—does not necessarily undergird but rather can mock and undermine all traditional values, including the patriarchal.[19] Derek Walcott and Gary Friedman's play "Heavenly Peace" characterizes war as an ultimate symbol of disruption and subversion—a "whore."[20]

At any rate, already in 1966, Terry had certainly unearthed some misogynist roots of the "male bonding" experience promoted in military boot camp. As boy/girls become men/machines in a space without women, the sergeant realizes that patriotism may not be enough to make men sacrifice their lives, and so he appeals to feelings of brotherhood: "We'll show your dead brothers in arms that they did not have died [*sic*] in vain" (Terry 49). This particular slogan, as manipulative as the earlier slogans voiced in the first scene, forms a part of war indoctrination incepted with the games of "cowboys and Indians." Male bonding is tied—and leads—to aggression against the "other," the enemy, the emblematic *Indian*. After the childhood games, the sergeant pounds the point home: "Go Back to U.S. History 101. Have you forgotten the Indian Wars? What country are you really from?" (Terry 45).[21] And when a few minutes later a GI responds, "John Wayne has faith in me" (Terry 51), he echoes the legend of the "Old West" that in its Hollywood version had actor John Wayne incessantly fight and kill Indians.[22]

The references to "Indians" in *Viet Rock* serve to draw attention to the way in which war supporters aggressively appropriated and manipulated the American past—a past of expansion, power, and conquest congealed into myth. In Walcott and Friedman's "Heavenly Peace," there is constant slippage between the Conquistadores and marines in Vietnam. The indoctrination of Terry's recruits prepares Americans to view the Vietnam War as a continuation of genocidal policies deeply rooted in American history and its mis/representation. The stage is set, as it were, to trace the infiltration of that mentality into every nook and cranny of U.S. society, reaching the point where, in John Hellmann's words, "when they thought about Indochina, Americans generally saw themselves entering yet another frontier, once again 'western pilgrims' on a mission of protection and progress."[23] This is also a dominant theme flowing through Norman Mailer's novel *Why Are We in Vietnam?* But the Vietnam War was not being won as decisively or with as much consensus (among whites) as the Indian wars, causing a dramatic confrontation between the myths and reality, or rather between the mythic aspect of reality and the realistic aspect of myth—broaching the nagging possibility that this time the United States was engaged in both a wrong war and a "lost crusade."[24]

The power of the myth of triumphant expansion in the West and against Amerindians—also cited in Europe by Gatti and Benedetto to support their indictment of U.S. imperialism and racism—is thus both confirmed and subverted in *Viet Rock*.[25] We might recall that Arthur Kopit's play *Indians* (1969) was a thinly veiled allegory of the Vietnam War.[26] In Terry's play, the myth of the West is used to prepare for the war, but its promotion also serves American males to uphold their patriarchal values, to seek unity and continuity in their historical heritage. And what is more, this strategy succeeds, according to Terry. Moved by appeals to American history and to male brotherhood, American men depicted in *Viet Rock* are psychologically as well as physically *predetermined* for the war. "Even" some of their mothers support their indoctrination. The mother of a boy who has just been inducted into the service not only uses the "defense of freedom" argument—the U.S. duty to help the rest of the world achieve a comparable freedom[27]—but also invokes brotherhood to rebuke another mother who does not want her son to be drafted: "He'll be protecting the freedom of your son. . . . He'll be fighting for your little boy" (Terry 34). On the level of direct human experience, which Terry clearly does favor over abstract global politics or theory, any responsibility for the Vietnam War staged in the play lies in the willingness of too many Americans, at several levels of society, to believe as they are commonly taught that only by protecting their friends, killing the "others," and sacrificing themselves will they make it possible for "freedom" to be enjoyed.

There are exceptions that undermine the socially conforming beliefs both depicted and reconfirmed in *Viet Rock,* and the very fact that psychological as well as "mere" physical indoctrination is required of all recruits implies that the assumed predetermination for war is not quite as total as Terry seems to believe. During the Senate Investigations Committee Hearing scene, a Native American prophesies at the witness stand:

> This is the end of the line for you—and all you white men. The red man and the yellow man and the black man are banding together. We will run you off the scorched face of the earth. (Terry 63)

His testimony is followed by a group of Vietnamese who do not speak but only weep. Paradoxically, the sergeant himself confirms, in a later speech, the racist charges made by the Native American witness:

The Jews are mad that we're finally fighting for a minority before the genocide; they don't want no fights unless it's for them. This here minority ain't Western European; they' our little yellow-skinned brothers with slant eyes and too small to tote our guns. (Terry 100)

The confrontation between the two positions, for and against the war, is not decisively resolved, nor can it be in the terms set by the logic of the play, in part because it does not delve deeply enough into the problem of historical causation. Terry's personal, subjective sympathy certainly goes out to the protesters, but in her play the voice of protest against imperialism is muted by a vociferous support of the U.S. policy and patriotism.

From the perspective of America's safety or even survival, it is implied, Ho Chi Minh and the North Vietnamese are exactly as threatening as were Hitler and the Germans—even *more* so, one suspects, since racism lurks in the background not only of the play but of America itself. Recall Jeffords's thesis that a "feminized" America turns to war in Vietnam in order to reassert its "masculinity." By the same logic, however, one might suggest another psychosocial scenario—one positing that, as the United States becomes increasingly racially integrated in the sixties, it "compensates" by turning to fight yet another racial "other" in Indochina. This theme is present not only in Terry's *Viet Rock* but in other Vietnam Protest Plays, including: Tuli Kupferberg's *Fuck Nam* (1967), Walcott and Friedman's unpublished "Heavenly Peace" (early '70s), Adrienne Kennedy's *An Evening with Dead Essex* (1978), and in various street and guerrilla theatre performances. In Terry's play, one "good war" deserves another.

Terry's vision of the GIs as victims of the almost irresistible military machine is reinforced in scenes that stage military action. In the first act, still placed in America, the protesters claim that "innocent people on all sides are being maimed and murdered" (Terry 45). But this vague distribution of casualties is distorted in the rest of the play, as Americans become the most visible victims. There are only three really physically violent scenes in *Viet Rock*, and each one focuses on the death of American GIs. In the first, a group of undercover North Vietnamese disguise themselves as South Vietnamese, win the trust of the Americans, and then slaughter them. This "sneaky" and "unmanly" way of waging war prompts the sergeant to repeat his appeal to patriotism and brotherhood: "I wish the people back home could see this sight. They wouldn't have any question any more of why we is here" (Terry 80).[28] The second scene occurs in a bar, where the GIs are relaxing and having fun. A bomb is thrown, and all are killed. The third and most gruesome episode comes near the end of the play: the Vietcong capture an American soldier and murder both him and his Vietnamese mistress. They shoot off his genitals, rip out and eat his heart. The Vietcong Commander orders: "Mine their bodies with grenade booby traps. Leave them on the trail for the next GI platoon to stumble over" (Terry 110). In all three scenes, Terry's Vietcong clearly act like the ruthless "savages" that many Americans believed them to be—an image of savagery first proposed for the Native Americans—a "big lie" that is hard to shake subconsciously, even when it is exposed to conscious light.

By much the same token, the official reasons for the war—defense of a free and civilized world—are partly *legitimated* in *Viet Rock*, and the issue of accountability and guilt for U.S. intervention becomes at best clouded in the process. But this tendency to justify the government's policy forms only *part* of Terry's total picture. Overall, *Viet Rock* does protest against the Vietnam War, even though it presents American GIs as its primary victims: victims of warlike Americans and warlike Vietnamese, both of whom are presumed to be equally guilty. This perspective was to change in later plays where the Americans became the victims only of their own authorities. In 1966, in *Viet Rock*, there is still a significant ambiguity about the assignment of responsibility for the brutality of the war.

All the voices of dissent in *Viet Rock* come from marginalized groups in society: women, Native Americans, African Americans, Asian Americans, and even from some Vietnamese themselves. In other words, Terry attempts to compensate for the actual marginality of protesters in society by increasing the numbers of the protesters on stage. Consistently women and minorities stand united for peace against a white patriarchal society that supports the war. Reserving for women the "right" choice, Terry no doubt tends to resort to a strongly reductionist gender splitting: men are pro-war, women pro-peace.[29] Is this only because Terry happens to be a woman herself? Some twenty years later, Jeffords indulges in a similar polarization and reductionism, focusing her critical eye only on versions of Vietnam produced by American white males.

Yet nothing is entirely simple or naive in Terry's 1966 play. While, as a rule, women stand for peace and truth, their most radical voice belongs to the notorious Hanoi Hannah, an obvious puppet of enemy propaganda. Hanoi Hannah's name and role evoke the memory of the equally notorious Tokyo Rose. With a good deal of verbal aggression, she castigates all "Yankee imperialists" (Terry 90), hoping to educate the GIs and perhaps the audience:

> Hanoi Hannah, back again for our educational talk, my tiny round-eyed GI. You must understand that everything is divisible—especially the colossus of the United States, especially the immoral giant of U.S. imperialism. It will be and should be split up and defeated. The people of Asia, Africa and Latin America can destroy the United States piece by piece. . . . Victory will go to the people of the world! It is inevitable. Long live the victory of the people's war! (Terry 91-92)

Is this voice to be believed, and does it necessarily have to be female? Does Hanoi Hannah stand in as a (rather masochistic) surrogate for Terry, expressing her own extratheatrical views?

Because no answers are given, one may conclude that the political message of *Viet Rock* is not quite as "crude and obvious" as some critics alleged. It manifestly assigns the responsibility for the war in Vietnam to the establishment of white American males and to the myths and traditions on which they were raised. But it does hedge on the depth of that responsibility, discounts its nationalistic connotations, and depicts the Vietcong as being as guilty of war violence as the Americans, if not more. It seems symptomatic of Terry's own ambivalence about her subject matter that she apparently could not come to terms with the most striking scene, namely, the aforementioned depiction, near the end, of the preternaturally bloodthirsty Vietcong. For Terry's notes suggest that this be "an alternate scene," left to the discretion of the director.

2.

Barbara Garson's *MacBird* was first produced in February 1967 at the Village Gate Theatre in New York City.[30] *MacBird*, like *Viet Rock* written by a woman, is a political satire loosely based on *Macbeth* and other Shakespearean dramas. Written in verse, it grossly lampoons the Johnson administration, first with Johnson appearing as MacBird, then later with Kennedy as John Ken O'Dunc and his brothers as Robert Ken O'Dunc and Ted Ken O'Dunc. The plot starts when MacBird/Johnson is hailed by three witches who tell him his fortune. In response, he arranges the assassination of John Ken O'Dunc/Kennedy. The performance of the play received lukewarm reviews: it was praised by some for its energy and potential, but dismissed by others as offensive and childish. James Davis summed up his negative critique in the *Daily News*: "The chief problem is that it is more nasty than funny."[31] He might have been pointing to a problem of American political theatre *generally*, namely, that it is always expected to be funny rather than nasty, which can entail never being radically critical of prevailing ideologies. This expectation no doubt ties in with the "place" attributed to theatre in a consumerist society irrevocably oriented toward entertainment. Avant-garde plays, self-supported or financed by small groups of dedicated spectators, could and did display nastiness and criticism, but commercial theaters could not afford the risk of displeasing patrons. As John Berger and others have pointed out, consumer society is grounded in the principle of "marginal dissatisfaction": one can and must be made dissatisfied to some degree (so as to buy commodities or other compensation), but not with the structure of the entire system, since that might lead to rejection of consumer capitalism.[32]

By the time *MacBird* was published and read as literature, the publisher was able to quote quite flattering reviews on the dust cover.[33] It was hailed by one reviewer in the *New York Review of Books* as being "the funniest, toughest-minded, and most ingenious political satire I've *read* in years,"[34] and *The New York Times* predicted that "it will probably go down as one of the brutally provocative works in the American theater, as well as one of the most grimly amusing."[35] Why would a play meant to be staged receive more praise in its written form than as an actual performance? The answer no doubt involves differences in audiences and in the a priori criteria set for live theatre and literature, as well as even wider differences between relatively "public" performance and the more "private" reading.

However disparate the various reviews of *MacBird* were, and regardless of whether they reported on the performance or on the written text, they had one striking feature in common: they strangely neglected to refer to the play's critique of the Vietnam War. With the exception of Richard P. Cooke's observation in the *Wall Street Journal* that "the author attacks him [Johnson] on *Vietnam*, particularly, but the thrusts are less well aimed than those of other critics,"[36] there is not a single mention of the war in any of the reviews I have surveyed. If one were to deduce the topic of the play only from theatre reviews, one might conclude that it dealt exclusively with the power struggles between Johnson and the Kennedy clan. This is all the more astonishing because Garson's play grew out of a particularly sharp 1965 anti–Vietnam War pamphlet.[37] Why then did the critics omit to mention the Vietnam issue? Was this omission warranted? Does the play really elude the problem of the Vietnam War? Or, alternatively, does the war form *such* a crucial background for Garson's story that it must be repressed, suppressed, and left as unrepresentable—as war ultimately is? As with Terry's *Viet Rock*, a convenient way of getting a grip on this problem is to see whether and how foreign responses differed from the American.

MacBird was performed in Great Britain, France, and West Germany.[38] In London, the play was censured and forced to relocate to a non-government-subsidized playhouse because it portrayed the head of an allied nation in unfavorable light.[39] The response of officials in Stuttgart was not much better. Peer Uli Faerber, the representative of the conservative Christian Democratic Union, wrote a letter to the culture minister threatening to have the performance closed down.[40] On the other hand, contrary to the American press, the West German reviews, as well as the performance's playbill, stressed the importance of the Vietnam protest. The program contained a forceful statement by Garson herself:

> My play *MacBird* is my personal means by which to protest against the immoral political climate which made the war in Vietnam possible. Many members of the American government are against the war in Vietnam but they are not thinking of resigning.[41]

One notices that Garson's political commitment is relatively weak. She wants to protest against an "immoral political climate," but she keeps it on a personal, subjective level. In point of fact, she was *reluctant* to have her play seen abroad, apparently not wanting to wash what she perceived as

American dirty linen in front of an international public. According to the German journal *Theater Heute:* "She seems also not to be much in favor to have the play performed outside the United States. When she was asked about a performance in France, she said that it is too easy to engage in anti-Americanism in France."[42] Vietnam, for her, was an American affair and ought to be settled within a United States that maintained a good image abroad.

But let us go back to the three witches, who first appear in *MacBird* at the Democratic Convention. The first witch is a female antiwar student demonstrator, the second a male "Negro," the third a male "old leftist." The three represent coalition forces that oppose MacBird/Johnson and his administration. The position of the female student is most clearly defined at the beginning. Asked where she comes from, the witch replies:

> A troop train taking men to Viet Land
> Came chugging, chugging, chugging through
> our town. "Halt ho!" quoth I, and stood upon the track,
> Then, tossing leaflets, leaped up to the troops:
> "Turn back, turn back and stop this train.
> Why fight for them and die in vain?" (Garson 7)

Her commitment to anti-Vietnam protest is evident and gets the desired response from MacBird/Johnson. On the other hand, the opposition of the other two witches is not taken seriously by any authority. For example, the "leftist" worker's words are dismissed by MacBird/Johnson with "Yeah, pops, yeah" (Garson 8). But the action of the student seems to bother him: "God damn! Those beatnik picketers all over!" (Garson 9). Only she appears to pose a direct threat to the government. Neither the working-class movement, symbolized by the "old leftist," nor the civil rights movements, symbolized by the "Negro," are viewed as potentially dangerous. Again it is a woman who has the greatest effect, slight though it may be.

After Ken O'Dunc/Kennedy has been killed, the Vietnam War is mentioned by a reporter during MacBird/Johnson's campaign. The president reacts as if he had never heard of it:

> REPORTER: Your majesty, how do you plan to deal with rebel groups that thrive in Viet Land?
> MAC BIRD: What rebel groups? Where is this Viet Land?
> Who gave them folks permission to rebel? Lord MacNamara, valiant chief of war, What is this place I've just been asked about? (Garson 54)

He is more concerned by his ignorance than by its object, the war. Garson's simplistic and dismissive portrayal of Johnson contrasts sharply with his treatment by Harvey Einbinder in *Mah Name Is Lyndon* (1968) and by Gatti in *V comme Vietnam* (1967). In both these plays Johnson emerges as a complex character caught in a foreign war he inherited to the detriment of his plans for social justice in America. It is interesting to note that Garson has "feminized" Johnson by calling him "MacBird," coupling him with his wife Lady Bird. Intentionally or not, Garson does to Johnson what the drill sergeant does to his boys in Terry's *Viet Rock*—he turns them into women before they can act.

In the final act of *MacBird* as the internal dissent over the Vietnam War grows in the United States, MacBird/Johnson reaches a state of militant panic:

> CRONY: Peace paraders marching.
> MAC BIRD: Stop 'em!
> CRONY: Beatniks burning draft cards.
> MAC BIRD: Jail 'em!
> CRONY: Negroes starting sit-ins.
> MAC BIRD: Gas 'em!
> CRONY: Latin rebels rising.
> MAC BIRD: Shoot 'em!
> CRONY: Asian peasants arming.
> MAC BIRD: Bomb 'em! (Garson 73-74)

Despite her domestic "political" plot, Garson implies that the power of people's protest movements will bring about Johnson's downfall. Gatti also has high hopes in the people's power symbolized by the primitive but effective weapon—"planche à clous" (board of nails)—but his people are the Vietnamese themselves whereas Garson puts her faith mostly in the Americans.

Why does Garson's Johnson pursue the war that he has inherited from Kennedy, especially if he disagrees with him in other respects? In the play, he is a ridiculous, sorry figure, a nearly mindless product of his environment. Garson stresses his Texan origins, parodying his drawl and cowboy mentality. He is a willing victim at first, and finally, as a kind of overcompensation, a promoter of an ideology that holds that "might is right." When MacNamara says diplomatically and euphemistically that the United States is "trying to subdue" Vietnam, MacBird/Johnson explodes with outraged indignation:

> MAC BIRD: What crap is this "we're trying to subdue"? Since when do we permit an open challenge to all the world's security and peace? Rip out those Reds! Destroy them, root and branch! Deploy whatever force you think we need! Eradicate this noxious, spreading weed! (Garson 55)

Garson's Johnson repeats here the official line that the United States fights in Vietnam in order to prevent a communist takeover and to preserve world peace, indeed "civilization" itself. But, paradoxically, it is also implied that sheer "might" may not be enough to win the war:

MAC NAMARA: The matter's urgent.
   It's touching on our war in Viet Land.
   That pacifying program we embarked on
   Did not compel surrender, as we hoped.
   A new approach is desperately required.
MAC BIRD: Are we, or are we not, the strongest power?
MAC NAMARA: Of course we are. (Garson 59)

Johnson's limited and parochial mind, it would seem, may be every bit as dangerous as the more calculated government plans to deceive the American people. Yet, ridicule and outrage combine to turn *MacBird* into a tragicomedy in which the president largely plays the part of a bumbling loudmouth, hardly befitting a real or dangerous villain, if villains are most dangerous when they are most complex. Ted O'Dunc concedes that MacBird/Johnson's influence on the Vietnam War is not total (Garson 64). The war, for Garson, tends to become the creation of the entire administration and not just the burden of a single individual, but this tack does not really make the guilt any more acceptable—it just distributes it onto a group of people.

Although the war is presented in *MacBird* as an American affair, there are several references to the suffering of the Vietnamese. But only two passages mention the protest at home or the fight carried out by the Vietnamese themselves. Interestingly, the first is embedded—and thereby demoted—in a dream of Lady MacBird that offers an overall vision of protest, stressing its manifestations in America:

There gleamed demonic flames and dire combustion.
A flickering draft card burned, and then a draft card.
Then horror, horror, horror, howling horror!
A human being set itself ablaze. (Garson 75)

Actually it is unclear whether immolation refers here to Thich Quang Duc—the first mass-mediatized image to shake the American public—or to the American Norman Morrison. But the ambiguity is clarified soon thereafter in another scene where the witches, cooking their brew and mumbling incantations, evoke the same image but pointedly relate it to the Buddhist monk:

Mac Namara's bloody crime
Sizzling skin of napalmed child,
Roasted eyeballs, sweet and mild.
Now we add a fiery chunk

> From a burning Buddhist monk.
> Flaming field and blazing hut,
> Infant fingers cooked and cut,
> Young man's heart and old man's gut,
> Groin and gall and gore of gook
> In our caldron churn and cook. (Garson 79)

Out of the caldron emerge then the figures of General Ky and Madame Nu, sadomasochistically collaborating with the United States in the destruction of their own country. This archaic image of a caldron bubbling with political events and personages is the low-tech "premodern" version of Gatti's postmodern image of a "supercomputer" that, in *V comme Vietnam*, will spew out information bites about the Vietnam War, including the same image of self-immolation. One is tempted to see both the caldron and the computer as allegories also for television: a magical power and a technological marvel.

The references to the monk highlight the role of media images that were circulating at that time—quick pictorial bites of evidence and partial testimony of the horror occurring in Vietnam. Using these images, Garson demonstrates that media may be a positive force in informing the nation about war. But what is the value of that information? One of Garson's characters sums up the quandary: "Let's get the facts. Let's go and watch TV" (Garson 34). In view of the supporting vision of the war that TV offered at the time, notwithstanding some flashing images of horror, this recommendation must be taken ironically. Like Mac Bird/Johnson, television is an object of ridicule for Garson: a silly, pernicious influence on society and on the war. By positing Johnson as a Texas rancher, implying that he was incapable of understanding not only hi-tech media like TV but also the television war, he becomes more like a stereotypical character seen on TV. Because the dominant trend of TV Westerns is to reduce complex historical problems to individual terms, Garson's work helps ultimately to figure U.S. imperialism as a purely subjective rather than a structural problem.

The scope of the protest in *MacBird* was limited, but the play did its part in spreading a general mood of dissent. Since everything is centered on the political scene in Washington, the Vietnam War has no independent existence of its own, no ideological sources outside "the beltway." Its cause seems to lie in a corrupt government and in its individuals, themselves an outgrowth of a corrupt Establishment. There are no indictments of imperialism, racism, patriarchy, or economic interests in Garson's play—all of which arguably were part of the overdetermining origins of the war. Sharing the idealistic hopes of the rebellious generation of the 1960s, Garson appears to trust that changing old establishment values will solve all problems. Paradoxically, although it focuses on a certain kind of politics, that "voluntaristic" or "subjective" spirit explains why *MacBird* may be the least political of the American protest plays. Despite its sharp satire, it did not communicate the possibility that the "tragedy" of Vietnam was a *symptom* of more tragic national malaise evoked in a remark of Baritz: "One GI in Vietnam believed that the 'experience of war revealed what men are made of and those that came out badly usually had problems going in.' Just so, not only for the individual soldier, but for the entire nation" (Baritz viii).

3.

Daniel Berrigan's play *The Trial of the Catonsville Nine* was published in 1970 and performed in 1971.[43] Unlike the two preceding plays (but akin to Peter Weiss's *Vietnam Discourse*), *The Trial of the Catonsville Nine* is openly documentary: it is based on the court proceedings during the trial of a group of war protesters in Catonsville, Maryland. On May 17, 1968, nine people—including Daniel Berrigan and his brother Philip—entered the Selective Service office there and removed 378 files, burning them in the parking lot. The play centers on their actual trial and conviction but, in so doing, deliberately blurs the line between reality and theatrical fiction. The stage action is set in Baltimore's Federal Court in October 1968. *The Trial of the Catonsville Nine* also inspired two unpublished plays: Colin Cameron's "The Berrigans: A Question of Conscience" (1971) and Derek Walcott and Gary Friedman's "Heavenly Peace" (1973).

One might wonder why Berrigan chose theatre to tell his story—the only time he did so. One possible answer (literary talent aside) is that he tenaciously believed in the power of theatre as a political medium, trusting that the police could easily prevent or stop burning of files, but protest on stage could not be easily silenced and might spill over into the street. And, if theatre were silenced, the violation of the principle of free speech would be dramatically spotlighted. The religious and cultural background of Berrigan, a Jesuit priest, prepared him to use a play as a vehicle for dissent. The Catholic Church (especially the Jesuits) had a long tradition of utilizing theatre as a teaching/learning tool: mystery plays, passion plays, didactic plays, etc. Berrigan's faith in the power of political theatre no doubt also drew heavily on his familiarity with the European intellectual tradition and its love for setting ideas on stage. Indeed, throughout *The Trial of the Catonsville Nine*, he quotes many European thinkers whose political views and aesthetics have coalesced into theatre: Sartre, Kipphardt, Brecht, Weiss, and Camus. These citations, as well as his own speeches, build a solid "classical" (not to say also "intellectualist") crucible from which Berrigan casts his sharp censure of the Vietnam War and the American judiciary system. The resulting humanist postmortem tonality of his accusation disturbed some critics, such as the reviewer for the "countercultural" *Village Voice*:

But is a testament of any use? . . . Is moral uplift in theatre any more lasting than the legendary efficacies of Chinese dinners on white America? . . . America produces the personal refinements of My Lai and assorted prison horrors for domestic consumption.[44]

There is some ground for this critique. Berrigan's concentration on verbal and ideological arguments against the war indeed tends to turn his play into an intellectual exercise that is not necessarily effective as theatre.

Berrigan makes three basic claims about the war. The first is the most topical: the war corrupts the entire American system, but particularly the *judiciary*. The main target here is the trial. The story starts when the defendants choose not to contest the jury selection in order to demonstrate how biased it is. It is revealed that all the selected jurors are somehow connected to the U.S. war machine, either through past army service or through present employment, business contracts, and other close interests. The fundamental American concept of judgment by impartial peers is thus discredited, as are other institutions since, in Berrigan's elaborate metaphor:

> The war machine, which has come to include the court process that serves it, is proving self-destructive. The courts, like the President (two, three Presidents), like the Congress, are turning to stone. The "separation of powers" is proving a fiction; ball and joint, the functions of power are fusing like the bones of an aged body. (Berrigan x)

The second issue on which Berrigan focuses is the *racist* character of the war. When the defendants describe their background and explain how they came to be antiwar activists, one learns that Philip Berrigan started his career in a black seminary where he "learned in a graphic way what it means to be black in this country" (Berrigan 23), and that another of the accused, Thomas Lewis, worked in inner-city ghettos. Berrigan links opposition to racism, including an allusion to class exploitation, as a major reason for burning the government's draft records:

> The draft records
> on which we poured blood
> were records of the inner city
> the ghetto areas
> part of the protest
> was to dramatize that the war
> is taking more cannon fodder from the poor areas than from the more
> affluent areas. (Berrigan 44)

Berrigan (the distinction between the character and the writer seems moot) further protests that a small elite are profiting from the war, while poor people of color are saddled with the burden of carrying out a "genocide" (Berrigan 47). Here, Berrigan develops an argument already presented by Terry. And, like Terry and other playwrights, another accused, Thomas Melville, ties U.S. racism to the Indian wars and a long tradition of American violence:

> Americans know
> that their nation was born in blood
> we have expanded our frontiers
> and pacified the Indians
> in blood. (Berrigan 59)

Racism is also the basis of a recurring comparison between the United States and Hitler's Germany. The Catonsville Nine, who want "to stop the genocide" (Berrigan 48), are protesting the war in Vietnam because they cannot condone the racist murders that the German nation accepted. Thus, Lewis didactically accuses the jurors on stage and, by extension, the audience in their seats: "You are accepting this as in Nazi Germany people accepted the massacre of other people" (Berrigan 49). Then George Mische, yet another defendant, draws an especially pointed parallel between racism in World War II and in the Vietnam War, reminding the American people that, through quiet acquiescence, "All of us Christians share the responsibility for having put those Jews in the ovens" (Berrigan 73). And the defense concludes that the defendants' actions were "a cry that could conceivably have been made in Germany in 1931 and 1932, if there was someone to listen and act on it" (Berrigan 104). In short, the play implies, protest is necessary, though it may lead to civil disorder. But the possibility of such disorder does not legitimate fascist "law and order." Berrigan includes a quotation from Hitler to ridicule the hysterical antiprotester reaction of the U.S. government: "'The streets of our country are in turmoil. The universities are filled with rebelling, rioting students. Communists are seeking to destroy our country; Russia is threatening us with her might.' —Adolf Hitler" (Berrigan 71). What is unclear is whether Berrigan was aware of the possibility that such remarks might backfire, might *confirm* at least some of the audience's deepest paranoias rather than inspire them to resist and transcend them.

The third thesis is that global *class* war is being waged in Vietnam. The wealthy capitalist United States is aggressing and exploiting a poor preindustrial country. Furthermore, Berrigan claims, appealing no longer to morality but to pragmatic cost/benefit analysis, the government and big business are spending billions of dollars on war while poverty still prevails at home. One of the defendants, David Darst, had come upon this realization while living in a ghetto where he

> saw many children
> who did not have enough to eat
> This is an astonishing thing
> that our country
> cannot command the energy
> to give bread and milk
> to children
> Yet it can rain fire and death
> on people ten thousand miles away. (Berrigan 36)

This scandal is not limited to the United States; it reaches across the world. Berrigan reports that, in Brazil during the devastating flood of 1966, he met a community organizer who complained about the insufficient and ideologically motivated American aid: "My friend[,] millions for the war in Vietnam and this for us" (Berrigan 87). Indeed, in Berrigan's (actual and staged) words to the judge, "the resources of America which belong in justice to the poor of the world are squandered in war and war preparation" (Berrigan 87).

The moral (humanistic) concerns are linked in these arguments to hard economics and social policies. For Berrigan, the United States is not only guilty of forsaking the poor of the world, it is also guilty of furthering rapacious global capitalism. So Thomas Melville details for the courtroom the history of Guatemala and the United Fruit Company:

> The United States government
> identifies its interests
> in Guatemala
> with the interests of American big business
> and with the Guatemalan two percent
> who control the country. (Berrigan 57)

When American troops were sent into Guatemala in 1966/67, the real mission was to preserve the peace for the rich. The Vietnamese intervention is part of the same worldwide economic imperialism and cultural hegemony of the United States.[45]

In this arena, the play reaches a political conclusion very similar to that of the European critics who also rooted the causes of the war, and hence responsibility for it, in American imperialism. As will become obvious, the French playwright Benedetto would have applauded, if he knew of it, the bitter irony informing Thomas Lewis's vision:

> We supply weaponry
> to more than 80 countries we have troops
> in more than 40 countries. These troops
> are backed up with our weaponry

So I was speaking not only of Vietnam
I was speaking of other parts of the world
The fact is
we produce more goods than we are capable
of consuming We must have new markets
We must bring our industries our way of life
into Vietnam and Latin America. (Berrigan 45)

American reviews of *The Trial of the Catonsville Nine*, predictably enough, minimized this aggressive politico-economic condemnation of the United States—although its real weakness probably was in being *too* overt to be effective theatre. By 1971, when the play was first performed, protesting the war had also become quite "acceptable"—to the extent that certain forms of protest were used to legitimate the ideology of a "pluralist" society—and only the most conservative still defended the war to the hilt. But in most public manifestations of protest, the war was treated as one dark spot on the otherwise respectable history of the United States and not as an integral part of its basic political tradition. Looking back, the only mention of Berrigan's reference to Latin America or the Third World appeared, remarkably enough, in a *Time* magazine review by Edith Oliver:

That is the burden of the testimony, and in each testimony is the story of their own lives—Some as missionaries in places like Uganda or Guatemala—and of their beliefs and, above all, of their disillusionment with the United States as it has moved, in their opinion, against revolutionaries at home and all over the world.[46]

In this perspective, looking beyond purely U.S. concerns, Berrigan is also closer to European playwrights than the other American authors. The possible explanations for this similarity include Berrigan's stance as a political activist, his articulation of theatre to guerrilla actions, his intellectual training, the tradition of Catholic protest and theatre, but also perhaps, to be more cynical, the circumstance that his play was written toward the *end* of the apex of the protest movement—when other Vietnam Protest Plays, some of them European, were comparatively well known. Yet *The Trial of the Catonsville Nine* was one of the few Vietnam Protest Plays to "forecast" future U.S. entanglements in Latin America. Berrigan showed that it was possible for Americans to break the mold of staging and playing the war overwhelmingly in subjective terms.

Unlike Berrigan (who does identify economic imperialism and multinationalism as a mainspring of American aggression), Terry and Garson tend to stress *psychological* motivations: education, historical myths, political corruption. This more solipsistic orientation is not surprising. As was the case for many other Americans at the time, playwrights, too, were "normally" concerned in the first instance with their own country, could not help but feel some "natural" degree of solidarity with their young countrymen fighting in Vietnam, and were hardly interested in even the possibility of "economic determination in the last instance" or the idea that "history is a process without a subject."

In the American paradigm of Vietnam Protest Theatre, GIs tend to be portrayed as victims of either the U.S. government or the Vietnamese, and rarely see themselves as aggressors. In that regard, perhaps, these plays were actually not "subjective" *enough*—which, dialectically speaking, is merely the flip side of not being "objective" enough in their grasp of imperialism as a complex economic, racial, political, patriarchal, and historical phenomenon. For surely real GIs were both victims *and* aggressors. And we will see in the Epilogue that at least one Vietnamese playwright was unwilling to blame Americans as such. Of course, these American plays were intended for an American audience, interested primarily in American problems—and so were both subjective and solipsistic in that sense as well. One must not forget that these protest plays coincided—or followed close on the heels of—the antiestablishment rebellion of the 1960s: the heady time of "hippies," "flower children," "communes," and experimental theatre groups—revolting more or less effectively, more or less helplessly, against "the American way of life" but only more rarely radically against the undergirding system of ideologies, politics, and economics. By 1970, however, that heady period was all but over. Which may explain, together with other factors, why Berrigan's *The Trial of the Catonsville Nine* was the only American play to raise some of the deeper questions of the multiple determinations on the war, whereas the earlier *Viet Rock* and *MacBird*, and many other protest plays, seem unintentionally, unwittingly, unconsciously only to "play imperialism"—echoing the anonymous taped voice in Megan Terry's *Viet Rock*: "Look out for number one."

2

PERIPHERAL CONTESTATIONS
(BRITAIN AND AUSTRIA)

The catastrophic condition of Vietnam has forced it
out its national boundaries and has international-
ized it, that is to say, our political interest has to a
large degree cut itself free from its pigheaded back-
ward orientation of specific German historical dates,
of Auschwitz, the twentieth of July, the seventeenth
of July, the German "partition" and has joined the
worldwide commitment against the American war
in Southeast Asia.   —Botho Strauß

In the spirit of West German playwright Botho Strauß's remark,[1] this
chapter focuses on two countries which at first glance had little or nothing
to do with the U.S. involvement in Indochina. They were typical "innocent
bystanders" on the periphery of the conflict, and yet the Vietnam War
triggered a response in them. In both cases, the motivations for this
response included an attempt to come to terms with their own "national
identity": their history and contemporary geopolitical status. These two
nations, Britain and Austria, had been dominant forces in the nineteenth
century (the Austro-Hungarian Empire and the British Empire). Their
borders and power have shrunk in the twentieth century, leading them to
a peripheral status—on the edge of Western European (and American)
hegemony for Britain, on the edge of German (or Soviet) hegemony for
Austria.

1.

Peter Brook's *US* (1966) was arguably the most powerful of earlier indictments of the Vietnam War offered on the stage in any country.[2] The Theatre Workshop's *Oh, What a Lovely War* (1965, filmed 1967) ostensibly about World War I, helped establish a general antiwar context for *US*. Since the specific topic of the Vietnam War was still new, and the English public could not be expected to be as familiar with its history as, say, the French, Brook's play provides more factual background information than the French plays. (The Germans provide the most, the Americans the least.) The need to clarify the dramatic action, to root it in historical causation, and to explain its relevance to Great Britain also accounts for the division of the drama into two parts: a "documentary" first act that recapitulates the history of Vietnam up to, and including, the war; and a more militant "didactic" second act that tells the audience how it should respond. But the two parts are not always clearly differentiated conceptually: the first "factual" or "documentary" act is actually quite didactic, and the "didactic" act has several documentary elements.

This formal duality corresponds to the coexistence of the primary targets in the play. As Brook makes it clear in his introductory statement, there are two main points in *US:* "a collective theatre presentation about the war in Vietnam and life in England" (Brook 1). Identifying (some of) the causes of the war, branding the aggressor, and assigning the guilt belong to Act I. It reaches far into the past. Inspired by Brechtian theories, Brook first has an actor or "chorus" directly address the audience with a short summary of the forthcoming scenes: "History of Vietnam. Here we see a series of tableaux, designed to impress on the memory of our shamefully ill-educated people the history of Vietnam" (Brook 37). An account of the mythical origins of Vietnam and information about its geography, population, and religion follow. It is significant that (in contrast to the American plays), this first "documentary" part of *US* does acknowledge the importance of the division between South and North Vietnam: "Today Vietnam has 32 million inhabitants—15.7 million live in the north, 16.5 million in the south" (Brook 38), and this fact is highlighted with stage dramatics when a symbolic map of the country is ripped in half by the actors.[3] Then Vietnam's history is presented as a "great wheel of invasion" (Brook 40), from the Mongol conquest in the early Middle Ages to the French occupation in the nineteenth century:

> The French invasion began in 1858. The French worked on three principles: divide and rule, isolation of the country and economic subordination. By 1884 they had established colonial rule. The French corrupted the Vietnamese people, by introducing the evils of opium and prostitution. (Brook 41)

One notes that Brook omits to mention the Dutch and Portuguese settlements in the seventeenth century, emphasizing instead French imperialism. Should one see in this "oversight" an unconscious, or conscious, anti-French prejudice stemming from a long history of political competition between England and France? Or is this simply a wish to focus on the foreign power that, shortly before the U.S. war in Vietnam, i.e., in Brook's own memory, had been actively involved in a comparable war against the Vietnamese? At any rate, "history" next moves to the end of World War II, the Vietnamese rebellion against the Japanese and French occupation, and the foundation of the Democratic Republic of Vietnam, on September 2, 1945, under the "wise" leadership of Ho Chi Minh. Anticipating a performance of *US* in the United States, Brook draws attention to the little-known fact that Vietnam's Declaration of Independence was modeled on the Declaration of Independence of the United States: "All men are created equal. They are endowed by their creator with certain inalienable rights. Among these are Life, Liberty, and the Pursuit of Happiness" (Brook 48).

More significant for the initial audience, however, is a later fragment of "history" that must have been specifically intended for the British public. It refers to a relatively obscure involvement of Great Britain in Vietnamese affairs:

> The Big Three at Potsdam agreed that Vietnam should be in the British sphere of influence, and a British General, Douglas Gracey, was sent to Vietnam to restore law and order. General Gracey's British and Indian troops collaborated with the Japanese to re-impose French power in Saigon. (Brook 51)

The Gracey episode has a special meaning both for Vietnam's full history and for Brook's play. It was one of the more significant turning points in the post–World War II reintroduction of Euro-colonialism into Southeast Asia after the defeat of Japanese colonialism. A reference to Gracey was likely crucial to the English playwright and his audience because it implicates Britain in continuing global colonialism—European and now American—after 1945. Clearly Brook strives to convince the public, very early in the play, that Britain must share the responsibility for all that is taking place in Vietnam, including the American war. From that moment on, the double-barreled aim of the title *US* becomes obvious: *US* should be taken to refer both to the United States in Vietnam and to a more general "us"— all Western audiences, but particularly the British, who are indicted for their complicity with the United States. In the same spirit, when asked in France whether his play should be translated into French and performed for a French audience, Brook replied tersely: "No, the French must write their own play about Vietnam."[4]

Nevertheless, the United States bears the brunt of Brook's most explicit criticism. As in the other European plays, it is shown to be an imperialistic power, posited as clearly the aggressor in Vietnam, interfering in a civil war. In a heavily ironic statement, echoed in France a year later by

Benedetto's deconstruction of the United States as "the policeman of the world," Brook alludes to the official American argument that intervention in Vietnam was caused by "communist aggression," then raises the ante of an absurd, counterproductive global world policy:

> Defending the Free World! The United States Government did not lie down before the Communist aggressors. The rapid increase in U.S. military strength from forty thousand in May 1965 to three hundred thousand today was a major factor in defeating the Viet Cong offensive. (Brook 58)

In this censure, Brook follows a rather expected line. More original, and more closely related to specifically British postimperialist concerns, is the stress on the racial undertone of the war. Like Terry and Benedetto, Brook draws a connection between the U.S. genocide against Amerindians and its current war against "Oriental" enemies by bringing together the "Geronimo" and "Gung Ho" war cries.[5] In a sense his real target is less the territorial dreams of U.S. imperialism but undergirding U.S. racism. Racism informs the collective mocking chant of American soldiers concluding a brutal interrogation of a Vietcong suspect, who is called a "worm" and "slopehead."

> EVERYONE: Zappin the cong
> Back where they belong
> Hide your yellow asses
> when you hear my song. (Brook 83-84)

In contrast, the portraits of two American "heroes" offer an ironically stereotyped image of the White Man: "I'm a mature man, medium build with a hard trim body, sparse close cropped sandy hair and ice blue eyes" (Brook 68); and later "Colonel White, mid-westerner, lantern-jawed, Burning blue eyes" (Brook 100). One gets the impression—appropriately reinforced by type casting—of a blond and blue-eyed Aryan army (the spitting image of the ideal German Nazi) saving civilization from a small, yellow, slit-eyed alien race. Attention to racism explains why, interviewed about the war, an African American character feels at loss about taking a side: "As a negro, I can't say whether I'm for the war or not" (Brook 66). In short, Brook would have concurred with North Vietnamese propaganda directed at American soldiers of color that they were fighting the wrong enemy.

It is difficult to ascertain to what extent American soldiers, in 1966, actually felt that racism was playing a key role in their war against the Vietcong, though there is some evidence that they did.[6] Racial insults, often carried over from World War II and the Korean conflict, such as "gook," "slit-eye," "yellow skin," were commonly used—and the effect on American troops of color must have been double-edged. The question, however, is not whether Brook was inspired by real racism but rather why and how he chose to stress racism in his play. With much the same available information about Vietnam, the French and German playwrights rarely deal with that issue and do not include racism in their indictment of American neocolonialism. Of course, in France and Germany, racism was mainly associated at that time with anti-Semitism and its horrific consequences in Europe before and during World War II. From that perspective, racism had little relevance as yet to colonial policies. In fact, France's own colonial past, however ruthless and exploitative, was not strongly marked by racial prejudice. Britain, on the other hand, notably in India, had a long history of color prejudice that would eventually feed racial guilt—or, at least, the guilt of those British who condemned racism and were disturbed by its more recent manifestations in their country. Did Brook seek to exorcise that feeling of guilt by projecting it onto the United States? It is significant that by 1966, various forms of racial unrest began to trouble British cities crowded by "black" and "colored" immigrants from the former Empire.

Yet, however pervasive in Brook's play, racism does not fully account there for the U.S. aggression: it encourages or even promotes it, but does not cause it. The aggression by the U.S. government appears to stem primarily from political, and perhaps economic, rather than racial motivations. Manifestations of racism are shown to take place not among the authorities but among American soldiers, representing a cross section of American people. But Brook avoids overall judgments. Not all Americans in his play are racists or ruthless killers. A scene of bombing and destruction is followed by a contrasting episode in which an American officer tries to help wounded children. This officer is actually guilty of misconduct, but he also proves to be good; for always, as Brook puts it, "Mr Hyde has a buddy called Jekyll" (Brook 122). The GI who says, "I am at the moment quite willing to sacrifice the entire South Vietnamese people for my principles," yet believes that this sacrifice will spare "the peasant in Thailand or Laos, the Philippines or Malaysia from future wars" (Brook 92-93), is both a victim and an accomplice of the U.S. "domino" theory, i.e., he is an ambiguous character. Altogether it is difficult to make general or final statements about Brook's views on the responsibility of the American people. Brook's call for caution in the reporting of the war explains perhaps why his judgment is so equivocating:

> So if you want to hold a clear, crisp, impressive opinion on the Vietnam War, stay far away. The war is so unpleasant it distorts all judgement, and morality apes those novels which the critics, in despair, say have to be appreciated on several levels simultaneously. Each of these levels is contradictory. (Brook 95)

On the other hand, no matter how ambivalent individual soldiers may be, no contradictions mitigate the guilt of the U.S. government, which is fully deceitful and ruthless in the pursuit of its goals. Brook's "history" of the Vietnam War is quite detailed and misses few occasions to censure the official American version. It pinpoints the Gulf of Tonkin incident as an example of governmental manipulation of public opinion, called by one character a "deliberate frame-up to prevent pressure for peace becoming too strong" (Brook 116). The frame-up is all the more criminal because it helps to launch the relentless bombing of North Vietnam. The horror of that bombing forms one of Brook's most pressing reasons to condemn the United States. It also provides him with the chance to evoke, once again, a tacit British complicity: "The British Government must dissociate itself from this bombing" (Brook 119). By the same occasion, he exonerates North Vietnam, and through it the Vietcong, from the American accusation that they have long conspired, with the help of communist countries, to start an armed aggression against the South: it is only after the bombing of its cities that the "Vietnam Democratic Republic has no alternative but to seek aid, chiefly from the socialist countries, in securing modern weapons . . . aircraft, antiaircraft guns, and missiles" (Brook 119). Does "socialist" replace here the more expected "communist" for diplomatic reasons or rather as an expression of Brook's own socialist sympathies?

But what are the exact goals of the U.S. government? What political considerations are at the root of the war? Not traditional colonialism, since the United States, in Brook's play, seems little interested in conquering Vietnam, even though such a conquest would fit in the chain of all previous occupations of that country by foreign powers. Nor is the United States moved by blind anticommunism to defend itself against the Vietcong: it has little to fear from them at home. The long-term "domino" theory does not provide Brook a significantly convincing reason. Rather, he suggests, the United States wants to protect its image as the leading world power, threatened in the region by the rival power of China. The United States sees the Vietnam War, including the bombing of North Vietnam, as a testing ground for an eventual future conflict with China:

> HENRY: Now with respect to China itself, should we find ourselves locked in a war with China, is it your opinion, General, that we could subdue China by an all-out bombing attack against them?
> BARRY: Nuclear bombing?
> HENRY: Well, let us say first of all, conventional bombing.
> BARRY: In my opinion, it would take nuclear bombs. (Brook 131)

Of course, the Chinese are also an "oriental" nation, and they already have the atomic bomb. From that perspective, the U.S. policies that emerge from *US* are relatively logical: dangerous, evil, perhaps megalomaniac and paranoiac, but logical in terms of the preservation of American international power. (We will return to other aspects of Brook's play in chapter 5.)

In sum, despite some comments to the contrary, Brook's *US* is not primarily anti-American. Indeed, he views anti-Americanism as an alibi for people who want to deny their own responsibility: "By being anti-American," he suggests "you can enjoy all the pleasure of race hatred whilst persuading yourself you are on the side of peace" (Brook 175). Besides, Brook is not blind to the similarities between Britain and the United States. As the British critic Michael Kustow points out, "We will always find American experience closer to our own" (Brook 141). If the United States were to be singled out, and systematically censured, as the only guilty party in the Vietnam tragedy, the British who are so close to the Americans would unfairly escape all blame; and Brook certainly would deplore such a whitewashing of Britain. George Farmer, chairman of the Governors of the Royal Shakespeare Company, was right when he wrote to the Lord Chamberlain that *US* was not anti-American but "criticized Britain as much as the USA" (Brook 145)[7]—that is, not only Britain's own past of racism and colonialism but also its current inaction and acceptance of the war.[8] The long speech delivered by Glenda Jackson in the second act makes this very clear:

> And at our parties everyone else will be doing the same, so life will really be quite comfortable—apart from occasional exercises of conscience, over something like Rhodesia or Vietnam. . . . I WANT IT TO GET WORSE! I want it to come HERE! I want to see it in an English house, among the floral chintzes and the school blazer. (Brook 178, 183)

2.

Why does an Austrian play deserve a separate place rather than to be bundled with German-language plays? However unified they may be by a common language, Austria has always been significantly different from Germany and defines in different ways its national and cultural "identity." The Austrian perspective on Vietnam may be expected to reflect some of these differences, even in the midst of similarities. One must especially take into account Austria's reconfiguration, after World War II, as a small central European country whose severely remapped boundaries resulted in its "downsizing" into a "demilitarized zone," so to speak. Located at the crossroads not only of the European North and South but also of East and West, the modern Austria has been viewed since the war as an ostensibly "neutral" political terrain, and this fluid, chameleonic "identity" has been inextricably linked with its cultural products.[9] The problem is that "neutrality" means many different things in politics, economics, and culture, especially with reference to more powerful competing ideological systems. How could postwar Austria define itself as a nation against neighboring powers, and how could that process of definition be negotiated through Austria's awareness of a distant international event—the Vietnam War? What role did Vietnam theatre play in this negotiation?

These questions, and the underlying problems of Austria's national "identity," may be addressed in terms of Benedict Anderson's concept of a nation as an "imagined political community—imagined as at once both inherently limited and sovereign."[10] This dialectical stress on something conflictually *imagined*—in this case an imagined nation—sets culture firmly as a crucial (not exclusive) base for the definition of a political community. From that perspective, Austrian theatrical discourse on Vietnam belongs to the set of cultural products, signs, and signifying practices that overdetermine "national identity." And the relation to Vietnam becomes imbricated as a discrete part of Austria that is identified as, or suspected of being, a *periphery* of Western Europe or of Germany. Thus, the Austrian Vietnam Protest Play tells the story of one small peripheral postwar nation writing about another small peripheral postwar nation: the one between the First and Second World, the other between the Second and Third.

This problematic informs Gerald Szyszkowitz's *Commander Carrigan*. Though written and performed in 1968, it was published only in 1991 together with his other plays.[11] Originally the play had only one act; however, for the collection, Szyszkowitz wrote a second act or sequel in which the action is supposed to take place thirty years later. This second act is quite short and takes place in Germany, at the Frankfurt International Airport. One could suggest that Frankfurt replaces Saigon because Germany looms large today in the forefront of Austrian public attention while Vietnam has faded and no longer holds its initial fascination and signification. Be this as it may, I shall concentrate primarily on the single original act of *Commander Carrigan* as it is found in the 1968 performance script.

This act is divided into eight scenes, which take place in a U.S. military office at the Saigon airport. That this office is housed in the Air France building is significant: Szyszkowitz wants to suggest that the United States inherited a war that the French had lost a few years before. It also might be a reference to the notion that commercial airlines are a part of what Eisenhower, in his farewell speech, had dubbed the "military industrial complex." At any rate, the geographical and historical setting of the play is a location that views Vietnam at war from behind frontlines that are anything but safe, subjected to their own terrors. An American commanding officer indicates the dramatic national and international stakes: "Here is a *model war*. We only have one more chance: either to win here or to lock up the capital and burn down the White House" (Szyszkowitz 1968, 16).

There are four characters: the American commander, Carrigan; his new assistant, Baines; an Austrian traveler, Slatin; and a young Vietnamese, Trong, presumably a student. The first scene opens with a discussion between the two Americans. Carrigan wonders why the army would send him someone like Baines, who is a musician, formerly a church organist. It is Carrigan's duty to instruct Baines on the ways of war. As he puts it: "I am a good teacher. You won't even recognise yourself" (Szyszkowitz 1968, 2).

The lessons start immediately. Carrigan brings in Slatin, whose traveling papers and visa have been confiscated. Carrigan interrogates the Austrian "prisoner" while Baines takes notes. But, halfway through the ordeal, Trong is also brought in for "suspicious behavior," and Carrigan's attention is temporarily focused on the Vietnamese. In the next scene, Trong and Slatin are left alone and begin to talk. Trong, who had previous experience with Carrigan, warns Slatin of possible tortures. He tries to get Slatin to contact a Vietnamese friend in case anything should happen to him. Slatin, afraid of being accused of complicity, cuts the conversation short. At this point, the Americans return and the questioning becomes more violent, almost an inquisition. Eventually, Carrigan leaves Baines alone with the two suspects. Trong tries to attack Baines with a knife, but Baines is warned by Slatin and manages to save himself and to kill Trong in the process. The play ends when Slatin gets back his papers and is allowed to leave; Baines is racked with guilt because he is now a killer. Carrigan comforts him, and the "lesson" is finished.

The play is *semi*-autobiographical. Szyszkowitz, like his Austrian character Slatin, had traveled extensively in Southeast Asia and had actually visited Vietnam, before eventually choosing Vietnam as the locus for his play. He was a small child during World War II and, by his own admission in the playbill, it was only in Vietnam that he first experienced war as an adult: "Vietnam in this case is not a geographical, but rather an exemplary place, the place where I met war."[12] For Szyszkowitz, the Vietnam War thus stands not only for a reencounter with his own suppressed or repressed childhood but also for all "wrong wars" that encourage brutality and the will to torture that ostensibly lie as latent potential in all human beings.[13] Another autobiographical reference, but only in the much later 1990/91 sequel, mentions that Slatin was beaten by the police in Munich during a political protest—as happened to Szyszkowitz himself in 1962.

Other personal references are projected onto the young American Baines. In the past, as a musician, Baines had used his hands only to produce music; now he uses them to kill Trong. Baines is devastated by this betrayal of his talent and, at the end of the play, he doubts he can ever return to his congregation and to his American provincial town, not unlike the provincial Austrian town of Graz, Szyszkowitz's hometown. We learn in Act II that he marries a distant relative of Trong and settles, an exile, in Southeast Asia as a kind of penance for his transformation into a murderer. This metamorphosis, too, has a personal relevance to Szyszkowitz:

> Friends were commanded to go to Algeria from the University of Paris, they then wrote of how they had become accustomed to tortures that they never would have thought possible;—today: American friends are commanded to go to Vietnam; i.e. Jerry Baab, with whom I shared an apartment when he was

still studying music in Vienna and New York; now, instead of playing piano for 8 hours, he plays with machine gun bursts already for 8 hours; also he has become used to atrocities, that he would have earlier never believed possible. (Program Notes, Baden-Baden)

Szyszkowitz seems to allude to (or buy into) the behaviorist logic that anyone can be turned into a killing beast under the right, or rather wrong, circumstances. But what specific conditions can transform innocent and peace-loving people—notably artists—into inhumane cogs of the war machine? The answer is the Vietnam War as a "wrong war," but also all other "wrong" wars including World War II of Szyszkowitz's childhood.

In contrast to Baines (a young man who, like Slatin, now experiences war for the first time) stands Carrigan, a veteran military careerist. He flew Pacific transports against the Japanese during World War II and later was stationed in Germany. These experiences have predictably shaped his brutal outlook on life. Again, it is *war* that serves as a global and temporal link between people, both victims and torturers. In effect, war is an "imagined community."[14]

For Carrigan, as an American, the world and the war are simple. His duty to fight for America and American "freedom" is equated in his mind with fighting the Nazis and now the Communists. Slatin, as an Austrian, is doubly suspect as a potential Nazi and "Communist." Thus Carrigan to Slatin: "Because you come from the Communist-occupied part of Europe and you are allowed to travel here, therefore you must be one" (Szysz-kowitz 9). But a little later, commenting on the Austrian's desire to see the Vietnam War in person, he adds sarcastically: "Wasn't your Hitler good enough?" For Carrigan, all Germans have been tainted with nazism, and the Austrians are hardly better than Germans since, as Slatin recalls, his family lied to American soldiers during World War II. (Unlike the Holo-caust Memorial Museum in Washington, D.C., in which Austria's substan-tial contribution to nazism is virtually effaced, Szyszkowitz freely acknowledges it throughout his work.) A paranoid patriot, blindly anti-communist, the added second act shows Carrigan to have become a pitiful drunk who no longer has a goal in life: the Berlin Wall has come down, and the Red threat appears to be over.[15] Carrigan is unable to survive without an enemy: "But against whom should we now be? Then I was a hero! But now?" (Szyszkowitz 1991, 356).

Commander Carrigan, the principal character in the eponymous play, could be seen as an embodiment of America. A militarized America that has become a major player in Europe, imposing its military bases and missile sites (though not in Austria) and threatening to make the cold war hot again. A powerful America that aspires to dictate its policies to European countries, if not yet the whole globe, and inspires intellectuals to fear a double Americanization of Europe: political colonization, with its military weapons, and cultural conquest, with its films and television.

From this perspective, "neutral" Austria and its cultural production stand as a political allegory of a successful resistance to that multiple threat.

But Carrigan is not the only American. There is also Baines. Why is *he* in the play? Dramatically, after all, the play would work very well with only three characters: the Austrian, the American commander, and the Vietnamese. What does Baines represent in the play's allegorical scheme? If the play is really about the dehumanization that occurs during war, then the presence of Baines illustrates how the dehumanization process actually works—Szyszkowitz's version of Brook's "Jekyll and Hyde." Carrigan has already been corrupted when the play starts, but Baines is still a gentle artist who must be taught the lesson of war and whose former neutrality must be militarized. Another reason for his presence is related to Szyszkowitz's own connection to Austria. At the end of the play, Baines reads a postcard from a friend who went to Salzburg to attend a summer workshop in music. Baines starts to cry, wishing that he, too, were away from the war, in a country where music has prevailed. Like the Vietnamese, he is a victim of the United States war machine, which destroys "genuine" culture and uses the culture industry to legitimate war. Creating the character of Baines, Szyszkowitz seems to imply that even the best Americans will be corrupted unless they choose exile—a notion that seems to echo the suspicion of many Europeans that America was once a generous "savior" of Europe but has turned into an imperialist power.[16] The sad fate of Baines may also be the fate of Austria.

The Vietnamese Trong, strangely enough, is quite similar to Carrigan. As yet another exile, he has studied in the United States (not France or Britain) but now is clearly linked to the communist forces of North Vietnam. As a result, he is as prejudiced as Carrigan, believing in his case that all Americans are enemies to be killed. For Trong, Slatin is not an enemy, because "you are a European, there they are different." Trong is depicted as a ruthless, shifty, lying, treacherous "Oriental." And so, when he attacks Baines, Slatin takes the side of the "good" American: West unites against the East because the Vietnamese are no better than the "bad" Americans. In other terms, Szyszkowitz seems to suggest that both communism and the American way of life (or capitalism) represent destructive forces, that ideological fanatics on both sides must be condemned. But what is the alternative (ideological, theoretical, or theatrical) to such apparently essentialistic binarism, which the play is deconstructing without suggesting a replacement?

The answer depends on how one reads the ambiguous Austrian Slatin, who in many ways is the most interesting character and certainly has parallels with Szyszkowitz himself. They are the same age, they are both teachers, and they visit the Philippines before stopping in Vietnam. By instinct (or habit), at first Slatin takes the side of the West. When he meets Carrigan, he is delighted that they can speak to one another as Westerners: "Because it gave me pleasure to speak and double pleasure to be understood" (Szyszkowitz 1968, 3). In contrast, his exchanges with Trong are full of misunderstanding: "and there I spoke and spoke and spoke . . . but obviously [he] understood nothing" (Szyszkowitz 1968, 3). Furthermore, at crucial moments such as Trong's attack on Baines, Slatin chooses the side of the Americans.

But this identification with the West through Slatin/Szyszkowitz, partial though it is, concerns less Western *politics* than Western *culture*. In the play, Western culture is embodied in Western art, especially music. Slatin is from Vienna (the clichéd home of the classical music tradition) and he teaches music; his American counterpart, Baines, as well as Baines's friend who evades the Vietnam War to attend a music conservatory in Salzburg (home of the Mozart music festival), are also musicians. Dedicating oneself to the fine arts thus becomes an exile's alternative to fighting a corrupting war—an "aesthetics of resistance" à la Peter Weiss, as it were. In contrast, both Carrigan and Trong—the "bad guys"—have no interest in art. They are not only enemies of each other but of culture. "When I hear the word *culture*, I reach for my revolver"—as the fascist saying goes.

How then is culture defined by Szyszkowitz? It is essentially High Culture, as nurtured in "musical culture." The Viennese Slatin disseminates Austrian classic musical culture through his teaching. As a Viennese, he enjoys, as part of his "imagined" identity, a "natural" cultural superiority, indeed cultural imperialism (since that is all that is left of the Austrian Empire). But this Viennese, or Austrian, superiority is not without its problems. When Slatin makes a phone call to the Goethe House in Saigon to ask for help, they hang up on him when they learn that he is Austrian, not German. The old tension between Austria and Germany surfaces at this point: Which nation defines the other? It would seem that Szyszkowitz wishes to sever the ties. Germany disinherited Austria, and Austria doesn't need (or want) Germany. Does this problematic relationship display a fear of a new form of cultural *Anschluß?* Or does a ghostlike Germany hover behind the negative image of America, that other "friend" from the West? As a peripheral and yet central part of Europe, Austria was once occupied by Germany; and now the peripheral Vietnam is occupied by the United States.

We are faced thus with a strong albeit strange juxtaposition of Vienna and Vietnam. It is hardly coincidental. Slatin accuses the Americans of occupying Vietnam just as they occupied parts of Europe after World War II. What started out as a cold war confrontation in Austria between the Soviets and the Americans, Communism and Capitalism, East and West, has metastasized in Vietnam into full-blown war. Saigon, in history and in the play, is being pulled, on the one hand, by American civilization and by "democracy" of the West and, on the other, by the culture and ideology of the East—by China and the Soviet Union. Austria, after World War II, was similarly situated between Western Europe and the Eastern Bloc. Now, at the time that Szyszkowitz was writing his play, Austria claimed to have chosen a "third (ideological) path" in between: the way of "socialism." But this claim had many problematic features, just as, by rough analogy, the Vietnamese have long had a very difficult relationship with China, including the People's Republic. The convergence of Vienna and Vietnam thus functions as what Fredric Jameson might call a "geopolitical allegory."[17] Explicitly, the play censures both the United States and the Vietcong, while condemning all past wars, especially World War II, as historical sources of brutality and atrocities. Implicitly, it places the Vietnam War at the center of the struggle for contemporary global dominance waged by two superpowers. But that conflict also threatens an Austria that is trying to elude this struggle by choosing a third way: a "socialist" neutrality that will preserve its national identity through culture, but at an (as yet) undetermined cost. Szyszkowitz proposes—for better or for worse—a cultural solution to ideological problems that remain central to the Austrian, indeed European, political debate today.

3.

Neither of the two plays just examined ought to be taken out of the context of its own nation's history. Their playwrights' indictment of American aggression in Vietnam, whatever specific causes they attribute to it, was clearly rooted in their memory of a national wound or trauma that, while historically repressed, resurfaces and is both worked through and acted out in their texts. Both Britain and Austria were facing crises of national "identity" (Britain had just lost the struggle over the rights to the Suez Canal). They were no longer the Imperial powers of Europe, and they sought to reclaim some dominance through high *cultural* imperialism. Brook is particularly critical of this cultural policy. He shows that neutrality is not a "safe" path, as Szyszkowitz suggests, but rather yet another dangerous road to complicity. For Brook, to be apolitical is to take a political stance.

It is within this ideological framework that "Vietnam" operates as a complex semiotic system or signifying practice. It is a sign that refers to Austria, Great Britain, and the United States: a congeries of peripheries and centers that parallel, overlap, and contradict one another. It is not easy nor even necessary to map all the references of such a multiplex sign. But a certain basic tension clearly polarizes them in two directions. On the one hand, there is the "Vietnam" that refers, especially for Szyszkowitz, to the autonomous role of periphery, local or exotic, as the locus of geographical and political deviation from the hegemonic center, i.e., as an ostensibly independent state of mind. On the other hand, there is the "Vietnam" that serves as an exemplary instance of a real peripheral event that is elevated to a level of universality and that raises more general cultural and ethical questions that risk losing specificity in abstraction. Thus, for Brook, "Vietnam" is a space of possible escape from the insular "island mentality," a space of commitment.

The symbolic or imagined space of Vietnam thus becomes a semantically empty site, even while remaining a privileged and specific historical space: a periphery that generates meanings for a world community. Or, as Jameson writes in his analysis of the multiple and sometimes contradictory meanings of the shark in the film *Jaws:*

> their very multiplicity suggests that the vocation of the symbol . . . lies less in any single message or meaning than in its very capacity to absorb and organize all of these quite distinct anxieties together. As a symbolic vehicle, then, the shark must be understood in terms of its essentially polysemous function rather than any particular content attributable to it by this or that spectator. Yet it is precisely this polysemousness which is profoundly ideological, insofar as it allows essentially social and historical anxieties to be folded back into apparently "natural" ones, both to express and to be recontained in what looks like a conflict with other forms of biological existence.[18]

Or as Bhabha proposes, "the 'other' is never outside or beyond us; it emerges forcefully, within cultural discourse, when we think we speak most intimately and indigenously 'between ourselves'" (Bhabha 4). In like fashion, Vietnam has served as a space within which various writers sought to find their own national identity by seeing it fragmented and reflected in various Others: political oppressors and victims, cultural invaders and corrupters. Its geographical and political location provided a unique locus for the intersection of a necessary British/Austrian reevaluation of history with a historical confrontation of international identities. Such reevaluations and confrontations need to be pursued into other languages and regions as well.

"DOCUMENTING" PRESENT AND PAST (GERMANY)

> The past can be seized only as an image which
> flashes up at the instant when it can be recognized
> and is never seen again. . . . For every image of the
> past that is not recognized by the present as one of its
> own concerns threatens to disappear irretrievably.
> —Walter Benjamin

> The war in Vietnam takes place not only in Vietnam,
> it is everywhere.   —Robert Havemann

The self-reflective Benjaminian imperative to see the past shining through the present, the present shining through the past, was felt nowhere more acutely than in Germany with its particularly problematic past and present. (France had its own past and present to "master" in this regard.) There are many metaphors for dealing with an intractable, elusive, or uncanny past: one can attempt to "master" it, "settle accounts" with it, "negotiate" it, and so forth. I will focus here on how two leading German playwrights attempted to come to terms with the Vietnam War, in their own context, by "documenting" it—showing "Vietnam" not as fixed once and for all in one region of the globe, at one time in history, but rather as virtually "everywhere" (certainly much closer to home than their country-men wanted to know). To "document" (as in its source *docere*) implies in this sense not only "to teach" (as a "doctor" does) but also "to warn." Involved in documenting the past and present, these two functions are conflated in the production of cautionary records and/or narratives (both more or less fictional, more or less objective, and thus more or less "doctored," as it were) about the way things were, are, and hence threaten to become again. For, following Benjamin, images from the past that are not recognized and do not become "dialectical"[1] do not disappear necessarily; they can return with a vengeance in other forms.

Among the several German-language plays written from 1967 to 1970 and involving the Vietnam War, four deserve special attention. Gerald Szyszkowitz's *Commander Carrigan* (1968) was already discussed as a play from the periphery; and the concluding chapter will consider Günter Grass's *Max* (1970) as it relates to the spectacularization of the war by the mass media. At this time my primary focus will be on the relationship between the German present and the past, a problem particularly well illustrated in Rolf Hochhuth's *Soldiers* (1967) and Peter Weiss's *Vietnam Discourse* (also 1967).

1.

Hochhuth's *Soldiers* was the first major German staged play to raise the issue of the Vietnam War.[2] Its main topic does not directly involve Vietnam, to be true, but rather Winston Churchill's responsibility in the Allied bombing of Germany, especially Dresden, and in the death of the Polish General Sikorski. Nonetheless, allusions to Vietnam form a very important subtext, which was not overlooked by the early audiences. As was noted in the *Theater Heute* review at the time:

> When Hochhuth began to write the play there wasn't yet any talk of bombardments; but the premiere will make the stage of *Soldiers* into a world political platform; it has become a Vietnam play.[3]

The playbill of the Berlin premiere of *Soldiers* had prepared the audience to see just that point. It included an analysis of the Vietnam War by Herbert Marcuse and a preamble by Martin Wiebel who, discussing the bombing of civilian populations, explained, "Hochhuth's Dresden means the destroyed cities of Korea, the Near East and Vietnam."[4] Wiebel implied that the concern with the cities of Vietnam in the process of being destroyed by the Americans must lead to a retroactive concern with the destroyed cities of Germany. When the play was performed in New York a year later, it was clearly acknowledged to be a Vietnam play that—fairly or unfairly—equated the burning Vietnamese villages with the cities of Nazi Germany.[5] Problematic analogies to the U.S. involvement in Vietnam were immediately noticed: "He wants us to draw a comparison between Churchill's bombing of Germany and the bombing of North Vietnam. . . . But the war against Hitler was quite different from the war in North Vietnam. No one burned draft cards over Hitler."[6] And, "*Soldiers* also takes up the responsibility borne by an airman or a bombardier for killing innocent women and children in the 1,000 plane raids over Germany—and by extension, the same responsibility that now is borne by those flying B-52's in Vietnam."[7]

The equation between the U.S. policies in Vietnam and the Nazi policies in Germany was a commonplace at the time for the Left around the world, including Germany. (This equation was also resisted by some on the Left, notably by Jürgen Habermas, who in the 1970s sharply rejected the attempt by the Red Army Faction to call itself West Germany's "Vietcong.") But more sympathetic was Erich Fried who, in his collection of poems entitled *Und Vietnam und* (1966), systematically linked the incipient New World Order of the United States not only with Hitler's New Order ("In the Capital city of Sodom [Saigon], rules a Soldier [General and President Cao Ky] who reads *Mein Kampf*") but also with continuing, apparently eradicable traces of nazism in postwar Germany ("Vietnam is Germany, its fate is our fate").[8]

Like many other Vietnam Protest Plays, Hochhuth's *Soldiers* employs a play-within-a-play device. As in Brecht's *The Caucasian Chalk Circle*, almost all of the action takes place in a quite theatrical inserted play but, also as in Brecht's play, it is within the embracing frame play that the contemporary political message is located. This is, of course, a time-honored way to convey disruptive messages, not only in the theatre but in heterodox and esoteric writing generally. In Hochhuth's case, the 50-page frame play, entitled "Everyman," presents a group of actors (comparable to Brecht's peasants) who, while getting ready for their opening performance of the "inserted" Churchill play, debate the world situation and comment on the Vietnam War. Hochhuth's point is that all of us ("Everyman," as in a medieval morality play) are always involved in and responsible for some "war." Not only Germany and the United States but also Japan, France, Russia, Britain, and Poland come under this censure. This topic is by no means new for Hochhuth, who made his theatrical debut in 1963 with his extremely provocative and controversial play *The Deputy*, which directly accused the Catholic Church generally and Pope Pius XII specifically for condoning and supporting the Nazis. The "scandalous" play sparked a worldwide debate concerning the limits and responsibilities of theatre.[9]

The frame play also serves as a rehearsal for the actors who will act in the main "inserted" play, i.e., as a rehearsal substituting for a real war, since "War is not like the theatre—It's the spectators who take the money" (Hochhuth 41). The shared responsibility is also underscored through the use of the same actor to play multiple roles of Nazis in Germany and American military in Vietnam (Hochhuth 48). In a similar spirit of general censure, an exchange between the Theatre Director and his Son stresses the hypocrisy in the implementation of the Red Cross and Geneva Convention prohibition against mistreating prisoners of war. Europeans and Americans want the Geneva Convention to be enforced with regard to U.S. pilots shot over Vietnam, whereas captured Vietcong are not accorded respect for their basic human rights (Hochhuth 37). Hochhuth's neo-Brechtian framing device could suggest that the Churchill play, dealing with tragic but past events as does the Grusha story in *The Caucasian Chalk Circle*, should be viewed as a parable for the frame play that discusses Vietnam as a current political issue. But Brecht's Grusha parable was clearly fictional, whereas the Churchill play deals with well-documented and relatively recent events that belong in arguably the same historical continuum as the Vietnam War in the frame play. It is hence hazardous to reduce the Churchill play to the function of a mere parable. Rather, the two parts of *Soldiers* must be seen, reflecting each other, as two very similar though distinct images of a single "tragic" history.

That history (that "story") principally concerns the bombing of civilian populations. *Soldiers*, as indicated by its subtitle, *An Obituary for Geneva*, was intended to be an ironic commemoration of the hundred-year anniversary (1864–1964) of the Geneva convention on the "acceptable" conduct of war—a convention now violated by air bombing of civilians in Vietnam. Hochhuth's point here is that the rules for ground conflict, established toward the middle of the nineteenth century, could not cover twentieth-century air warfare.[10] The frame play exposes a long history of wars killing civilians but culminates in the World War II Allied raids on Germany and the U.S. atomic bombs dropped on Japan. However, in a further attempt to distribute responsibility, Hochhuth also alludes to the German bombing of Britain by setting his play in the ruin of St. Michael's Cathedral in Coventry, which the Luftwaffe saturation bombed in 1940, killing some 380 civilians and injuring many more. If the documentary finger of guilt thus points in several directions, the real horror of bombings is made vivid with concrete visual references that translate a general moral outrage into specific scenes of suffering. To re/stage the theatre of criminal war, Hochhuth notably borrows the power of the photographic image to evoke the memory of a witness to the Nagasaki catastrophe—the "most photographed" and "publicized" victim of the atomic bomb (Hochhuth 16). The photographic resources of the media are then concretized by cross-reference through the slide projection of a photograph of a "dead woman sitting in a Dresden street, her skull mummified by the firestorm" (Hochhuth 24). The fictional theatre director in the frame play says of this woman (in which "he loses himself . . . , murmuring, overpowered"): "First my victim, now my persecutor, and—soon to be—my image" (Hochhuth 25).

This re/embodied image—which forges a powerful "dialectical image" out of archaic (Egyptian) mummification and modern incendiary bombs and napalm—works in tandem with other instances of formal and thematic reinforcement to inform the stage with "documents" both past and present. That overall strategy raises Hochhuth's indictment of air bombing to a much higher and more complex pitch than do most other

Vietnam Protest Plays. Brook's US (1966) also vigorously protested the bombing of civilians, but did not single it out as forcefully nor did it *show* documentary evidence of the horrifying mutilation of its victims. For Hochhuth's photographs are carefully chosen to grate on the raw emotions of the spectators. But they also serve more subtly to problematize and politicize the distinction between reality and theatre. Seeing, on the stage, authenticated images of the dreadful results of bombing, the audience experiences a strong association between "real" historical events and their "representation" in the play. Such fusion or blurring of the distinction between "fiction" and "reality" is particularly powerful at the end of *Soldiers* when an actor, costumed as a policeman, playing a "real" policeman in whom spectators are asked to believe, walks on the set and states that *Soldiers* has been banned in Britain. This statement refers to "reality" since the play was *indeed* censored there, but it is also a fictional statement made by a fictional character. Essentially, however, Hochhuth believes that "the relation of the document . . . to the fact is that of the fragment to the whole vase" (Hochhuth 124). That is, all documentary references contribute to establish a whole reality—whether past or future, "worked-through" or not, "mastered" or not. (By 1970, Hochhuth will have revised this faith in staged documentation.)

Yet, committed to the problematic of totalization, Hochhuth is not only an effective manipulator of real and staged images but also a didactic debater. In his play, men who bomb civilians must not be equated with other military personnel; they are not "normal" soldiers or even "normal" air force pilots; and their actions cannot be justified "even" by the hard necessities of war. As one character admits to another, "A soldier is a man who fights other soldiers," but not so a "pilot who aims at tanks, bridges, factories, dams, . . . as it was . . . over Dresden" (Hochhuth 37). No doubt British and German audiences could be expected to react to "Dresden" in very different registers, even with incomprehension in some cases. Still, moments of self-reflection, guilt, and the vicissitudes of audience response set aside, the great war crime remains clearly for Hochhuth the unjustified (and unjustifiable) killing of civilians—an atrocity that transforms a limited soldiers' war into a total modern war where, as Virilio and Lotringer years later were to write in *Pure War*, the armies, "no longer fighting among themselves, tend to fight only civilian societies."[11]

Next to bombing, the main target of *Soldiers* is the connection between war and business interests. This important articulation was more stressed by German playwrights than by most others (except Berrigan) because the still recent German past was catastrophically marked by the complicity of big business and heavy industry with nazism and its war. German intellectuals, including playwrights, were also influenced by a rather orthodox form of Marxism that denounced precisely this articulation. As a particular theme of German Vietnam plays, this business-war connection requires a closer examination before a further discussion of its manifestation in

Hochhuth's and eventually Weiss's plays.

One of the many contested topics prior to the so-called historians' debate (*Historikerstreit*) about the specificity of the Holocaust is the so-called Leader-State debate (*Führerstaatsdebatte*). At stake are issues such as the actual role of Hitler in wielding and maintaining power in the Third Reich (e.g., how much personal power did he really exert) and how was social and economic power distributed, both coercively and hegemonically?[12] Another aspect of the ongoing debate deals with the role of big business in bringing the Nazis into power and in keeping them there. This question is by no means of historical and academic interest only; it broaches the explosive issue of the continuity of the Nazi past into the postwar period, including the hidden reasons undergirding the remarkably quick recovery of Germany, its "economic miracle." Taking up that issue, Hochhuth was intervening, at a relatively early stage, in a hotly contested terrain with intellectual but also directly political meaning in the West German context.[13] This debate was played out in West German media and cultural production in various ways in the 1960s, but not only there and then. For not long thereafter, in the 1970s, the leftist Red Army Faction (RAF) was to carry out some of its most spectacular (and subsequently also most spectacularized) actions precisely because it believed that big business has been supporting a virtually unbroken Nazi continuity between 1933-1945 and the postwar period. Indeed, this was the argument behind RAF's decision to kidnap, on September 5, 1977, Hans Martin Schleyer, who not only had been a Nazi but also was currently chairman of Daimler-Benz. His October murder (or execution, depending on the perspective) precipitated the so-called German Autumn. This moment was taken up, in turn, by the leading West German filmmakers in their collective 1977 film *Deutschland im Herbst* (Germany in Autumn).[14] One contributor in particular, Bernhard Sinkel, stressed the compact between German industry and fascism, past and present.[15] Similarly, the 1967 French film *Loin du Vietnam* (Far From Vietnam), produced by Alain Resnais (director of *Night and Fog*), Chris. Marker, and Jean-Luc Godard, influenced Weiss and Hochhuth by its political left-wing stance. But Weiss's 1965 play *Die Ermittlung* (The Investigation) had already used the venue of Nuremberg War Trials, including actual testimony, to make the link explicit between German industry and nazism during the Third Reich.[16] This play, premiering simultaneously in seventeen German cities, had an impressive impact: some actors representing the accused and/or the witnesses (in some cases they were the same) were uncannily seated in the audience, representing the audience as well. It is also significant that the articulation of business and nazism continually is taken up again in recent films: not only in Steven Spielberg's *Schindler's List* (1993) but also in Harun Farocki's 1988/89 *Bilder der Welt und Inschrift des Krieges* (Images of the World and Inscription of War), in which the German chemical plant IG Farben in Poland in the 1940s is directly linked not only to Auschwitz but to its direct descendants:

the powerful West German firms Hoechst, Bayer, and BASF. It is within this persistent framework that German protest playwrights in the 1960s, and foremost Hochhuth and Weiss, take their historical place.

Following Brecht's well-known argument of *Mother Courage*, Hochhuth believed that the economy of war (both limited and leading to total war) primarily profits capitalists or their historical equivalents. This was true in World War II, he notes in *Soldiers*, and remains true for the American involvement in Vietnam:

> Oh yes—very good for business it is. We none of us object to making money: ergo then war they will make—it's only human, particularly if the enemy is not in a position to bomb my factory—General Motors is as safe as the vault of the Credit Suisse. (Hochhuth 41)

At least two seemingly minor developments in the play illustrate Hochhuth's staging of this politico-economic problematic: an American scrap metal dealer gets twice as much for his merchandise during the Vietnam War than before it, and drafting young Americans is explained as a profitable way of getting rid of hopeless poor, "unemployed, colored men, illiterates, and criminal elements" (Hochhuth 50). The United States is indicted for using the Vietnam conflict to get rich, and the American economic interests are considered to be the determining cause for the prolongation of the war. Yet, as this denunciation of war profits applies as well to other modern societies, Hochhuth's pointedly anti-American thrust is somewhat blunted.[17] In any case, the American economic establishment benefits from the war in his play, and no doubt supports it, but is not charged with prime responsibility for starting it.

Hochhuth's third target in *Soldiers* is the indifference of his contemporary German countrymen. They are accused of allowing the United States to stockpile its offensive nuclear weapons in Germany and of displaying a general lack of civil courage. In the absence of strong protest, the German acceptance of American bombs is judged to be as damning as was their acceptance of Hitler in the past:

> Because he [the German] had quietly accepted that West Germany, unlike France, should allow its "protectory power" to stockpile weapons, which according to Mr. MacNamara's [*sic*] Christmas message, have the explosive force of five thousand Hiroshima bombs. (Hochhuth 40)

Failing explicitly to oppose the U.S. war in Vietnam, Hochhuth implies, Germans tacitly approved it, and so must share with Americans the responsibility for bombing civilian populations. Here the distinction between *direct* and *indirect* support is intentionally obliterated (a move perhaps influenced by Georg Lukács's *The Destruction of Reason*). And of course, at the deep structural level, West Germany and the United States must be "the same" since they are both capitalist.

In all these ways, Hochhuth's "Vietnam" operates as an overdetermined sign that triggers simultaneous discussion of explicit and tacit relationship between the United States and Germany both during and after World War II. As early as 1967, *Soldiers* was "mastering" the past (*Vergangenheitsbewältigung*)—an apparently insoluble problem that many people today associate with an only later acknowledged need to give meaning to the Holocaust (or even admit to its existence). "Vietnam" also served Hochhuth to mask—i.e., to reveal as well as to conceal—an almost equally controversial topic: the treatment of Germany at the hands of the Allies.[18] But the specific points of comparison and articulation are inadequately worked through in this perhaps overly complex play. Such a failing, of course, is surely not—or not only—the "fault" of Hochhuth or of his audiences. It rather derives from the intractable nature of the aesthetic, political, moral, and historical problems that *Soldiers* attempted to "document." Hochhuth's later play, *Die Guerillas* (The Guerrillas, 1970), is enlightening in that sense. On the one hand, ideologically and thematically, it expands the argument of *Soldiers* now by linking U.S. imperialism to its economic interests in Central America, compared to Vietnam by statements of Che Guevara and Rudi Dutschke. On the other hand, *Guerillas* appears to disavow documentary theatre, indeed the use of any documents in theatre, and offers a good try at giving fantasy and the imagination an explicitly political role. For the Hochhuth of 1970, a stage that draws its style from reportage ends up "'documenting' nothing more than its own technical and spatial inadequacy," with the consequence being that "political theatre cannot have the task to *reproduce* reality, which is political anyway, but rather must approach it by means of the *projection* of new reality."[19] With this argument, Hochhuth not only opens the door, as he clearly intends, for fantasy and imagination as politico-theatrical weapons, but also, ironically enough, prepares to abandon the theatre for more powerful and influential media of "projection" that theatre had been holding in check: film and television whose overwhelming technologies had been so crucial for the "television war."

2.

More obviously and directly focused on Vietnam than *Soldiers* is Peter Weiss's play, *Discourse on the Progress of the Prolonged War of Liberation in Viet Nam and the Events Leading Up to It as Illustration of the Necessity for Armed Resistance against Oppression and on the Attempts of the United States of America to Destroy the Foundations of Revolution.*[20] As in the elaborately didactic title, the play covers two main topics in two parts: the history of Vietnam up to and including the war, and the American version of activities in Vietnam. In a sense, the noting of "discourse" in the title anticipated Michel Foucault's definition in 1970/71 of "discursive practices," defined as "not purely and simply ways of producing discourse." Rather, they are also "embodied in technical processes, in institutions, in patterns for general behavior, in forms for transmission and diffusion, and in pedagogical forms which, at once, impose and maintain them. Finally, they possess specific modes of transformation."[21] Weiss's title warns more obviously that he will use a historical perspective, i.e., that characters will be portrayed more as agents or objects of History than as individuals or subject-positions. Or, in Weiss's own words:

> The aim is to present figures bound up in historical processes, even when it is a matter of historical developments of which the participants were themselves not aware. An attempt is made to present a succession of social stages, with all their essential features and discrepancies, in such a way that they throw light on the conflict existing today. (Weiss 67)

In these remarks, Weiss clearly follows a foundational principle of historical materialism.[22] He announces he will approach the "liberation" war against the Americans in Vietnam as a concrete *Beispiel* (exemplification) of class struggle—as a late stage in the long, often nightmarish *series* of wars of liberation that the oppressed and exploited Vietnamese have been waging for many generations against occupying powers. As in Hochhuth (and again in Gatti's *V comme Vietnam*), the theatre is inextricably linked to the theatre of war as its cultural *exemplum*.

The oppressors may and do change, as well as the forms of exploitation, and not all Vietnamese are necessarily among the oppressed, but, from Weiss's Marxian perspective, these variations do not affect the fundamental class struggle that has been driving the Vietnamese people to revolutionary liberation movements. In fact, to draw attention to the structural permanence of the struggle despite permutations of class roles, Weiss divides his characters into two distinct groups, clearly marked on the stage with contrasting colors of costume:

> All figures from the early and late phases of the history of Viet Nam and feudal China wear simple black costumes of a uniform cut. Representatives of the colonial powers, as well as of their vassals in Viet Nam, wear the same white costume. (Weiss 68)

One might then deduce that all oppressors are clothed in white and all oppressed in black. But the black costuming of early Chinese conquerors, hence oppressors, seems not to follow the rule. Weiss's reason for the exception might have been that this particular Chinese conquest of Vietnam took place in feudal times (precapitalist mode of production), before the emergence of the middle class and capitalism, so the notion of a modern class struggle could not yet apply. But did he then postulate, against his own Marxian theory and master narrative, that the early

Chinese conquest was a mere matter of territorial aggrandizement of one feudal empire at the expense of another? Or does *Vietnam Discourse* even subtly imply that the Chinese oppressors were somehow "better" than others because class exploitation in the strict sense was not involved? No clear answer to these questions is forthcoming in Weiss's play. Besides, the costume system soon asserts its logic everywhere else. When the Chinese come back during World War II, they wear the same white clothes as the French, the British, the Americans. Of course, black was the color of the uniforms of the Vietcong soldiers, and hence had a much more immediate positive historical referent. Weiss's theatrical color system rather serves him as a convenient stage device that enables spectators to identify opposed groups in the quickly changing scenes in Part I.

This part is further subdivided into eleven rapid "phases." The latter correspond to successive major stages in Vietnam's history (in a manner similar to Brook's "framework" in *US*). Phase One tells how Chinese sailors opened the trade with the Vietnamese Funan empire circa 500 B.C., and Phase Eleven ends in 1953, when the French return to Vietnam and set up their ill-fated fortifications at Dien Bien Phu. The intervening phases cover various invasions of Vietnam and the resistance of the Vietnamese people. Conforming to a Marxian perspective, the manifold conflicts and battles are consistently grounded not, say, in race but in an underlying class struggle. Weiss's strategy is to tell the story from the (ostensibly) single-class viewpoint of the Vietnamese peasants and thus to favor the outlook of the oppressed. To start, in Phase Two, which tells about the fall of the Funan empire and the establishment of a Chinese protectorate, the voices in the dialogue are voices of "the people"—peasants depersonalized and identified only by numbers:

> 6: That's where the great lords live
> 4: The emperor's officials
> 2: We never see them
> 3: They send their delegates to us in the villages. (Weiss 83)

In the next phase, European colonialists introduce protocapitalist then capitalist forms of economic exploitation. Vietnam enters the stage of modern development as the Portuguese build a gun factory (1615) and the Dutch and the French establish trading posts (1637, 1680). The history of French conquest moves up through to World War I. Next follows the evocation of the Bolshevik Revolution of 1917 and of hopes that Vietnamese workers and peasants would eventually seize power. A series of subsequent scenes then show the Japanese invasion in World War II, the defeat of Japan, and the proclamation of Vietnamese independence based, in part, on the American model (an irony also noted by Peter Brook a year earlier).

But the French return, and oppression is restored. Up until Part II,

which is centered on the American presence in Vietnam, France is generally portrayed as the dominant foreign oppressor—perhaps a close reflection of historical reality but perhaps also, in a German play, a testimony to
an antipathy against the French stemming, among other things, from
Germany's defeat in two world wars at the hands of the French and their
allies. Yet the overall message in Part I of *Vietnam Discourse* does not clearly
single out for censure any particular nation; rather, it conveys the notion
that all invasions of Vietnam were ultimately motivated by economic
exploitation and that the long history of resulting class struggle will
explain the forthcoming American intervention as well.

Part II develops this argument in more detail, with a multimedia
recourse to contemporary documents. As the scene moves from Vietnam
to a secret meeting in Washington in 1954, the stylized characters in Part I
are replaced by concrete political figures such as Dulles, Eisenhower, and
Churchill—identified by enlarged slide projections of their photographs
and by loudspeakers that announce their "presence" on the stage. (This
move, to speak Marxian Hegelese, stages in theatrical terms the dialectical
transition from the universal and abstract to the particular and exemplary,
recalling the word *Beispiel* in Weiss's title.) Not only Americans attend that
meeting, but French and British delegates, demonstrating again that the
planned anticommunist action in Vietnam is not promoted by a single
nation but by an alliance or bloc of Western powers with similar class
interests. (This is an uncanny anticipation, or anticipatory caricature, of
the strange unity of Western great powers against Saddam Hussein's
threat during the Gulf War.) France appeals for aid to the United States and
Britain, and the United States proclaims its readiness to replace Britain as
the leader of the global forces of "law and order."[23]

On the surface, the Allies want to defend democracy, but their real goal,
Weiss points out, is economic exploitation of the world by multinationals
(in what a postmodern Marxist might call the "third" or "late" stage of
capitalism). In that light, Weiss logically ties the production of *weapons* to
the production of *television sets*, predicting, as it were, that postmodern
conditions will fuse cultural, military, and economic hegemony. Already
in the mid-1960s, weapons used by Americans in Vietnam clearly serve to
promote watching American television, and American television is used to
publicize the effectiveness of the weapons. The Chorus in *Vietnam Discourse* proclaims:

> Making war planes, rockets, bombs, tanks, automobiles, and television sets, on
> which you show us, day and night, generals and film stars, burning villages,
> piles of corpses, ruins and twisted metal. (Weiss 223)

Weiss implies that TV is itself a weapon and that war is a kind of filmic
production on TV—a theme picked up in other Vietnam Protest Plays and
a thesis that will be made explicit by Paul Virilio in his *War and Cinema: The*

Logistics of Perception.[24] But Weiss's evocation of total industrial mayhem was perhaps too strong for the U.S. public in 1970 when it was first performed there: the above quotation from the American version of the play, otherwise quite faithful to the German text, omits a pointed reference to napalm (based on a chemical produced by Dow Chemical) that was in the original German.[25]

Part II of *Vietnam Discourse* dwells for a time on the U.S. decision to help France in Vietnam. Weiss then covers the escalation of the American intervention, the Gulf of Tonkin incident, and the authorization that Congress gave to Johnson (on 5 August 1964) to pursue a full-scale war in Vietnam. Weiss focuses exclusively on the U.S. political and military establishment, never showing individual American soldiers in action. His take on Vietnam contrasts sharply with the main concerns of the American Protest Plays: he shows little interest in individual responsibility for the war, or individual guilt for its conduct, or moral exoneration. As an objective historical account of the "Beispiel" war, *Vietnam Discourse* tends itself to become an abstraction: a few concrete atrocities are mentioned, but none are staged. In general, its extensive documentation supports a political thesis and ideological polemics more than a theatrical vision of concrete reality. This is its weakness and its strength.

3.

As initially performed in Frankfurt, *Vietnam Discourse* was a didactic play, more anticapitalist than anti-American. The United States is exposed as the aggressor, but seems no more offensive than other aggressors before it. It merely "happened" to be the leading capitalist power after World War II and therefore the inevitable agent of economic aggression pursued by the entire capitalist system. Even more than Hochhuth, Weiss insists that war always benefits business (Brecht's "business is a form of war by other means"), and, like Berrigan, he points to negative economic consequences of war for Third World countries: Vietnam, Latin America, Africa, the Middle East (Weiss 200). From Weiss's perspective (in this case quasi-Maoist, although elsewhere, paradoxically, he is something of a Trotskyist, as when he makes assumptions about the leading role of the industrial proletariat in the First World), only the oppressed people of the Third World—such as the peasants in Vietnam—can be relied on to oppose the capitalist system, and only through a revolution of these people and their allies can the system be destroyed and history at once "interpreted" and "changed" as Marx demanded. This is also the hope expressed by Weiss's chorus of American protesters against the war. They look forward, with some optimism, to the peace that their protest will bring about, but they realize that this peace will mean real freedom from oppression only if the class war against capitalism continues. Unlike Berrigan, Weiss is no pacifist:

But what do they mean by peace? Will peace remove the cause for which they attacked us? Will peace bring freedom to all who rose to win it? We know as long as they rule with all the great power of their wealth nothing will change. What we have shown is the beginning. The fight goes on. (Weiss 228-29)

West Germany is also targeted. The audience is reminded that, just as Vietnam was ideologically divided by the 17th parallel, so was Germany still divided between East and West, with West Germany taking advantage of American aid and then developing its own separate—economic—might (Weiss 191). Under the guise of a topical Vietnam play, then, *Vietnam Discourse* offered a militant politico-economic manifesto directed not only against capitalism in the United States and in general but also, in particular, against the postwar capitalist *West German* establishment. This criticism of the U.S–West German connection via capitalism was also a way to protest against other forms of postwar Americanization, including the molding of German theatre during Allied occupation.[26] In any case, *Vietnam Discourse* appears to have been understood as a subversive cultural manifesto in that context and was therefore disliked in many West German circles. In Frankfurt, where the performance of Brook's *US* had been canceled earlier for fear it might offend the local "American colony,"[27] police forces were called to protect the production of *Vietnam Discourse* against angry German demonstrators. Although it was also blamed for being boring (*langweilig*), one-sided (*einseitig*), monotonous (*monoton*), and mediocre (*mittlemäßig*), its *potential* impact was tacitly acknowledged.[28] In fact, Weiss offered one of "the sharpest political polemics in decades to be presented on a German stage,"[29] stretching the conventional limits of political theatre. Concomitantly Weiss raised the vexing question of whether *theatre* was/is the proper medium for political action and whether documentary style, at least as practiced by him in this play, could ever be objective or effective. It remains an open question whether, as one critic wondered, "this propaganda piece is so boring because it lacks an opposing voice"[30] or whether preaching exclusively to the converted must be the burden for all committed artists. West Germany's own leftist youth movement in the 1960s had already moved away from the more orthodox Marxist thought of Brecht, Hochhuth, and Weiss.[31]

Another question that mainly concerns theatre is whether the critics of *Vietnam Discourse* might have been more disturbed by the *formal* strategy of the play than by its explicit didactic, political character. Or does the "documentary approach" have a *special* power to be unsettling? Critic Siegfried Melchinger, who had praised Weiss's *Marat/Sade* in 1968 despite its ostensible documentary features, limits his objections to *Vietnam Discourse* to its excessive stress on the *political message*:

A creator of theatre is committed; his profession is primarily theatre and not primarily politics.—A theatre spectator is also committed: his interest is primarily theatre and not primarily politics, . . . Why, as is generally said, is *Marat* a better play than *Vietnam Discourse*? Because *Marat* was primarily theatre and *Vietnam Discourse* wants to be primarily politics.[32]

On the other hand, it is surely the *documentary style* that irritated the reviewer who accused the Frankfurt production of offering an "antiplay," protesting that "it does not put any humans on the stage, instead speakers of ideas out of which theatre cannot develop."[33] One suspects that both critiques may have been disguising, with questionable theoretical arguments, a shared ideological prejudice against Weiss's subversive politics. There are no solid grounds to claim that theatrical and political goals are incompatible; in fact, from Shakespeare to Sartre and Cixous and beyond, explicitly political plays have enriched theatre. Nor are there good reasons for denying that theatre can develop in new directions through the adaptation of documentary forms and multimedia effects. In fact, at a theatre conference in Vienna in 1965, the traditional notion of "pure" theatre art forms had been found to be obsolete in the world of modern communication:

> One cannot imagine theatre in an audiovisual world, which is the world of communication of mankind with itself, as one imagined it a hundred and fifty or a hundred years ago. Our time is a time of syntheses of contradiction and of mutation. The traditional forms of theatre no longer agree with the perception of the world that is shared by audiences of all countries.[34]

Weiss's recourse to the documentary style to communicate his vision of the Vietnam War in 1967 as well as his persistent political views demonstrate that—like many other Vietnam Protest playwrights—he tried to adapt to the culture of new mass media, often indeed the deadly rivals of theatre. Obviously Weiss believed that this technocultural strategy offered the best hope to counteract the brainwashing influence of modern press, radio, and television.[35] He was willing to take the risk of a trade-off between appropriating on stage the popularity of the mechanical mass media and sacrificing some of the existential and phenomenological immediacy of living theatre. To be sure, Weiss was inspired by other German playwrights in this regard, notably Piscator or even Hochhuth, but when he introduced "documents" that are supposed to be somehow more "real" than the "documents" of media, he sought on his own to turn theatre into a persuasive channel of truth, to dispel false images propagated by all media, and to close the gap between the stage and history, between history's often theatrical aspect and theatre as a part of history. In Weiss's own words:

> Documentary theatre as it is brought close to us by the means of mass media, is a component of public life. The work of documentary theatre is hereby determined by criticism to various degrees. A) Criticism of distortion. Are the

news in the press, radio and television guided by the viewpoints of dominating interest groups? . . . B) Criticism of falsification of the truth. Why is a historical person, a period or epoch eliminated from consciousness?[36]

Yet Weiss's use of documents is selective in a paradoxical way, which limits the possibilities of Vietnam Protest Theatre as genre or medium. On the one hand, he trusts that documents have the capacity to reveal truth; on the other, he knows that one must be careful in selecting these documents because not all truths are equally true. Weiss explains, theorizes, and politicizes *Vietnam Discourse* from a (Maoist) Marxist perspective that views most documents and publicized truths as products of the ruling class or hegemonic powers in First World countries (and which must be opposed, at least in the case of Vietnam, by a Third World peasantry). In order to show a more objective or fuller truth, documentary theatre must then be comparatively "subjective," not only aesthetically but also politically, in its more or less "arbitrary" selection of documents and its commitment to a revolutionary constituency. In order to combat the "truths" of the dominant power, theatre must put that power on stage and on trial, and *produce* as well as merely *find* alternative evidences. It must purposefully choose the "documents" that both represent *and* create the other side of the story. In other words, Weiss promotes the use of "documents" that "document" not as much an objective reality as the process whereby theatre produces reality, not as much the Vietnam War "as it really is" as, quite literally, the *staging* of war. He wrote:

> Documentary theatre is subjective. Many of its themes can only be presented with prejudices. For such theatre, objectivity under certain conditions, serves as a concept that a power group uses to excuse its deed. (Weiss 1968)

Documentary theatre becomes, in effect, historically contingent, strategic and reactive:

> a critique of veiling. Do not press, radio, and television represent the perspectives of the dominant party group? . . . Documentary theatre is erected against any group whose politics are dark and blind, who supports the mass media which keeps the population oppressed in a vacuum of anaesthesia and ignorance. (Weiss 1968)

It is rather obvious at this point that Weiss and Hochhuth approach documents in a quite different way than did their great predecessor, Piscator, back in the twenties. Part of the difference involves a more critical attitude toward all representations; another reflects the quantum leap taken by technologies and their applications to media. Hochhuth and Weiss share growing doubts that Truth can be (simply) located in documents and represented (transparently) in order to be effective. They know also that History is manifold and cannot be grasped in just one image or just one document of evidence. And they believe that fiction, specifically theatre, can use visual data to manifest a truth close to poetic truth. In other words, whereas technological evidence was seen by Piscator as supplementing theatre, Hochhuth and Weiss now regard theatre as supplementing the technological evidence of truth.[37] In the absence of a stable representation of History or Truth, the question becomes whether theatrical and historical fiction can substitute for these lost or deceased gods? And at what cost? Weiss and Hochhuth, who feel they must raise such questions in 1967, are also aware that all answers will depend on the role of audience and on other cultural, political, and ideological factors in addition to the more explicitly theatrical.

There remains that, whatever its exact goals, documentary theatre must be able to galvanize, however briefly, the attention of the audience. And this was not quite the case, as some critics pointed out, for the "boring" Frankfurt performance of *Vietnam Discourse* staged by Harry Buckwitz. It might have been simply too long (three hours) or too relentlessly humorless: *panem* at the expense of *circenses*. At any rate, when the play was produced three months later in Munich, the new directors, Peter Stein and Wolfgang Schwiedrzik, heavily edited it to make it more entertaining and thus, they hoped, more persuasive.[38] In the added part of a cabaret MC, the popular actor Wolfgang Neuss briskly paced the audience through Vietnam's history while making witty asides. The strict documentary drama became a lively revue. A bold slogan painted on the backstage wall proclaimed, "Dokumentartheater ist Scheiße" (Documentary Theatre Is Shit), which the directors attempted to clarify by explaining, "Documentary Theatre is shit because it claims to be impartial and yet follows a party line."[39] At the same time, however, the Munich production was explicitly supportive of the Vietcong cause. Not only did it appropriately focus on the Vietnam history in Part I but also, at the end of the performance, a collection was solicited for the Vietcong—a common "Maoist" tactic in political protests of the time. It was that collection, netting about 500 Marks, which created the *real* scandal. It was found to have violated local theatre regulations, and the production closed after three performances.

The public reaction to the staging changes in the Munich production was remarkably positive, attesting to the capacity of live theatre, unlike film, to meet the changing demands of the audience. The audience liked the huge papier mâché heads that, made in the likeness of Eden, Dulles, and Churchill, reinforced the theatricality of the documentary play. As the director Schwiedrzik explained:

> I want to start with Weiss. He thinks that when he brings the historical trial of "Vietnam" on the stage he can count on resonance within the audience. We do not believe that. We have distilled the scenic material from Weiss, we try to mediate the story theatrically.[40]

The innovations were discussed in the press: "The play was theatrically enticing . . . full of energy and imagination . . . grotesque gigantic clown theatre . . . with wit and sometimes astonishing artistry the primitive forms of street theatre are transported back to the stage."[41] But the overall response to the production was overshadowed by the controversy about the collection of funds for the Vietcong.

This last circumstance suggests that theatre's greater potential power to disrupt—greater than that of other media—does not (only) derive from its fluid "textual" form but (also) from the full "context" or anthropological ritual of its production and reproduction. The lesson of the Munich performance of *Vietnam Discourse* comes close in that sense to Louis Althusser's observation in 1962 about the performance of a play by the late-nineteenth-century Milanese playwright Carlo Bertolazzi, which had been taken apart by the Parisian press for its admixture of fact and fiction, *verismo* and fantasy. Althusser favorably compared this production by the Piccolo Teatro of Milan to the theories and practices of Brecht, concluding that the true effectiveness of political theatre depends both on the formal elements of a staged play and the consciousness of the audience. Brecht would be right, Althusser wrote,

> if the theatre's sole object were to be even a 'dialectical' commentary on . . . eternal self-recognition and non-recognition—then the spectator would already know the tune, it is his own . . . if, on the contrary, the theatre's object is to destroy this tangible image, to set in motion the immobile, the eternal sphere of the illusory consciousness' mythical world, then the play is really the development, the production of a new consciousness in the spectator—incomplete, like any other consciousness, but moved by this incompletion itself, this distance achieved, this inexhaustible work of criticism in action; the play is really the production of a new spectator, an actor who starts where the performance ends, who only starts so as to complete it, but in life.[42]

This is a tall order for any theatre, and it is certainly an open question whether a Hochhuth or a Weiss (or *any* other playwright for that matter) can live up to the challenge radically to transform an audience into a more progressive one. Nonetheless, the German attempts to "document" Vietnam may be seen as caught up, successfully or not, in this noble attempt.

In January 1969, *Vietnam Discourse* reopened in West Berlin, where regulations about collections of money were more lax.[43] But it also had to close because the issue of collection, while still itself legal, might cause too much illegal commotion and disturbance outside the theatre.[44] The performance's run was even shorter than in Munich. Formally, it came even closer to the cabaret style, verging somewhat on street theatre; the papier mâché heads were replaced by giant plaster puppet heads reminiscent of the Bread and Puppet Theatre. Once again critical reviews paid more attention to the collection for the Vietcong than to the general political message of the play, let alone its intricate politico-economic argument.

The only productions of *Vietnam Discourse* that received relatively neutral reviews, without complaints about boredom or the collection "scandal," had been staged in *East* Germany, first by the Volkstheater in Rostock (4 April 1968), then by the Berliner Ensemble in East Berlin (4 May 1968). There are no indications of any special demonstration by the public. Predictably, the West German journalists attributed this general acceptance to the political solidarity between the GDR regime and North Vietnam.[45] It is also possible, however, that the East German performances did strike a more harmonious balance between political commitment and entertainment. For, as in Munich somewhat later, they toned down the most didactic and realistic features of documentary theatre, giving up slide projections and loudspeaker announcements, and arranged for an MC to interject humorous comments while telling the history of Vietnam. No collection of money followed East German performances of *Vietnam Discourse*. Support was given North Vietnamese by the East German government. (The West Germans supplied the South with military advisors and *Schäferhünde* to sniff out hidden Vietcong.)

4.

Hochhuth's and Weiss's comparable "documentary" styles raise significant questions not only about the Vietnam Protest Theatre but also about documentary theatre in general. The presence of a common "German" agenda is not particularly problematic in and of itself. It expresses a relatively natural concern with national issues that are projected onto the representation of a controversial global event. It was to be expected, in that general sense, that German theatre would approach the Vietnam War in the same spirit of self-reflection as the French and British theatres: i.e., as an excuse to "document" national past and present, although with different results corresponding to different national inflections, ideological commitments, and obsessions. More interesting is Hochhuth's and Weiss's shared interest in some of the same techniques of documentary staging. A common national origin cannot by itself account for such a converging formal development, though both playwrights clearly belong to the same theatrical tradition. Nor can the revival of documentary theatre in Germany in the 1960s be reduced to an "innate German character" of that theatre: it has had a comparable success in other countries as well (indeed all over the world and not just, say, in Europe). It seems that a couple of other factors were here at play, both individual and cultural.

In the first place, one must fully acknowledge the tremendous influence of Erwin Piscator. Piscator (to whom *Soldiers* is dedicated), along with Ernst Toller and later Brecht and others, began to use documents on the German stage in the 1920s, i.e., long before the emergence of the modern "documentary theatre." He continued that practice when he returned to Germany after years of exile in the United States. In a strict historical sense, therefore, the documentary theatre of Heiner Kipphardt, Hochhuth, and Weiss was continuing, long after World War II, a project that Piscator had set into motion already under the Weimar Republic at a time when political theatre was at its zenith.[46] It was also a time of experimentation and technocultural optimism. The use of "real" radio news broadcasts, photographs, and cinema newsreels was supposed to make more "truthful" the fiction presented on the stage. Directors and their public believed in the "truth" value of media images, even when these images were in fact mediated and reprocessed (as "even" in photography). Their authenticity was not as easily questioned as it is in our current "postphotographic era" when documents can be manipulated and synthesized almost at will.[47] In fact, media images were granted more reliability than a direct visual theatrical experience, and it was expected, as film critic Siegfried Kracauer noted in 1960, that they would "reveal things normally not seen . . . capture physical existence in its endlessness."[48] This somewhat idealistic trust in the revolutionary or "redemptive" power of objective "truth" motivated then Piscator to show "truthful" media images on stage, and plays with a high content in documentary evidence were assumed a priori to have a stronger political impact than those without. Almost forty years later, Hochhuth and Weiss were reverberating this message and using documents for a similar political goal—with rather less naiveté and optimism but with about the same effectiveness or lack thereof.

A second factor for the resurgence of documentary staging was more specifically technocultural in nature. There is little doubt that Piscator's early experimentation with documents and the later "documentary theatre" were both encouraged, even promoted, by a general climate of confidence in technological progress that prevailed in Germany in the twenties as well as in the sixties. The Weimar Republic was the time of the Bauhaus, whose technical and industrial art innovations spilled over from architecture onto the stage, opening it to the "real" world outside. The aim of a technologically informed theatre, said Walter Gropius, "is no longer to accumulate a collection of fanciful technical apparatus and gimmickry"; rather, "everything is a means to an end: [and] the end is to draw the spectator into the middle of the scenic events."[49] This instrumentalization and, it was hoped, democratization of theatre meant not only removing the "fourth wall" of the stage but also using documentary techniques to bring the outside world onto it, to provide the spectators with an image of the "reality" that, however illusory, would incite them to seek a change for the better. In Piscator's inspired words: "It is not mere chance that, in an age whose technical achievements tower over its achievements in every other field, the stage should become highly technical. . . . [I]ntellectual and social revolutions have always been closely bound with technical upheavals" (Piscator 189). After the Holocaust, and during the cold war years, that hopeful vision (not to say also its unquestioned technological determinism) certainly faded—replaced or displaced by pride in the German economic "miracle," which kept alive the faith in technical progress but no longer in the socialist revolution, to say the least. In the sixties, some dreams of revolution returned, but the reality of the German "success" story kept on dominating a documentary theatre dealing with audiovisual "facts," not ideal fictional words.

On both accounts—Piscator's influence and trust in technical progress—the documentary theatre was a properly "German" product, though it later came to inspire playwrights in other countries (e.g., Berrigan's *The Trial of the Catonsville Nine* in 1970). But problems it encountered, and the issues it still raises, concern the general cultural development of the Western world and not only Germany. The actual nature of the stage-drive to experiment and the technological resources may not have evolved very much after World War II, but the *perception* of the value of documentary media has changed radically, suspicion replacing reliance, cynicism replacing hope. Piscator himself became aware of the coming change when he staged *In Spite of Everything* in 1925, "the first production in which the text and staging were based solely on political documents." He used documentary film clips from Second Reich archives to convey the horror of the war, but he did so only because "war films had not yet come into 'fashion,' so these pictures were bound to have a more striking impact on the masses of the proletariat than a hundred lectures" (Piscator 94). As Benjamin and the Frankfurt School predicted, as Debord and Baudrillard would later confirm, both mass production and the spectacularization of documentary images were bound to reduce or erase any shock value that these images might have had initially.

In "The Culture Industry: Enlightenment as Mass Deception" (1944), Horkheimer and Adorno asserted that "the development of the culture industry has led to the predominance of the effect, the obvious touch, and the technical detail over the work itself—which once expressed an idea, but was liquidated together with the idea."[50] They shifted "blame" for this development to the basic mechanism of commodity capitalism, namely, "[t]he triumph of advertising in the culture industry is that consumers feel compelled to buy and use its products though they see through them" (167). One might say that it was a major task of Vietnam Protest Theatre to spotlight this problematic with regard to the advertising of war—but it had to make this attempt against all odds, against the full weight of the mass-mediatized culture industry. Nearly twenty years after *The Dialectic of Enlightenment*, Debord stressed the domination of spectacle over documented references to reality, arguing that the focus on spectacular representation rather than on the "real" is a necessary product of consumer society (Debord, Thesis 1). And Baudrillard brought this thesis up to postmodern speed—techoculturally as well as technologically—claiming that a "real" reproduced mechanically through film, photograph, or television produces a "Hyperreal."[51] When origins and totality are lost, everything becomes a sign and can therefore be re/produced as such, so that reproduction becomes part of "reality," reality a mode of production.

Yet, in terms of the impact of this argument on stage and on staging war, the shock and spectacle re/produced by the images remained crucial supports of Vietnam Protest Theatre. It is only through their interminable mechanical reproduction and reproducibility, in the Benjaminian sense, that the (progressive) political effects of these images would wear thin and the public would become numb to what they refer to, indeed, to their possibility of referring at all. At the time of Vietnam, some images did at least *initially* jolt *some* of the public into awareness about the war: as a return of historically repressed horror, as a continuation of business by other means, as a test of the United States, and so forth. Whether or not a Vietnam Protest Play could be restaged today with any effect, aesthetic or political, is not a question for the theatre historian or critic to decide, however, but rather for directors, actors, and audiences. The fundamental goal of creating effective counterimages to business as usual, theatre as usual, was summed up succinctly by Debord's definition of spectacle as "Capital accumulated till it becomes image" (Debord, Thesis 34), including images of images.

Just as historical documents were losing their shock value in the 1960s by appearing in mass media, these same documents could be expected to lose shock value, and hence interest, when appearing on a commercial stage. With such expectations, and in the general climate of growing distrust of media images, the later documentary theatre had no option but to undergo a radical (self)questioning (recall the slogan "Documentary Theatre Is Shit") that was not only "political" in a relatively obvious sense but also "aesthetic" in a less obvious one. That this theatrical (self)questioning can be seen as a prologue to our current postmodern problematic is not the least of the intriguing features of Vietnam Protest Theatre.

Anticipating the supposedly Derridian or Baudrillardian subversion of references to objective reality, suspicion had also been eroding confidence in even the most scientific documents. Does better technology reveal a greater truth, or does it only construct a better documented illusion? Already in the forties, Marcuse expressed grave philosophical and political doubts about the "relationship between technological truth and critical truth," since "the two sets of truth values are neither wholly contradictory nor complementary to each other."[52] Two decades after Marcuse, Hochhuth experienced and then subdued similar doubts in his theoretical and documentary practice, mixing in *Soldiers* both types of Marcusean truth—technological and critical—by the means of documents on the one hand and fictional dialogues on the other. Historical facts were rearranged in a special way that merely showed that Churchill *might* have ordered the death of General Sikorski. Whether or not this was factually true was irrelevant for the play; what was important was that it was *possible*. The British historian of the Third Reich, Hugh Trevor-Roper, initiated a public lawsuit against Hochhuth for "misrepresenting" his views on Sikorski's death in an article he published in the German weekly *Der Spiegel* (December 1967).[53] But Hochhuth himself admitted, indeed proclaimed, that his theatre, even when it claims to present history, is not a form of "Wissenschaft/Science."[54] Small wonder, then, that fiction and reality are blurred in (and by) most of his plays. Thus did the "science" of documentary theatre, and of "documenting" the past and present, undergo part of its own paradigm shift.

In the last analysis, and for better or worse, it would seem that it is not necessarily the epistemological "truth" of documents, nor even their "political" shock value, but rather the artifice of the playwrights that has endowed the German version of Vietnam Protest Theatre with its greatest dramatic power or at least potential. Hochhuth and Weiss turned to the documentary theatre because it was a culturally "natural" thing to do in the German political climate after the war, but their relative merits and successes were not bound wholly to that particular form. Nor, by the same token, was Peter Brook's *US* a relatively effective British antiwar play only because it also borrowed from the Piscatorian tradition a similar recourse to documents. Conversely, some of the best (or at least most remarked) Vietnam plays produced at the same time in the United States and France were not less effective because they substituted imagination and fictional freedom for documentary images and evidence. Formal and technological determinism rarely explains a phenomenon as complex as theatre history, though the latter is just as clearly overdetermined by such innovations and reappropriations.

The German Vietnam Protest Plays do raise *questions* about the nature and function of theatre generally and "documentary" Protest Theatre in specific. Was documentary Protest Theatre primarily a historical product limited to the German cultural tradition and to the special conditions of the Weimar Republic and of the 1960s? Was/is the Marxist or quasi-Marxist perspective of Weiss and Hochhuth adequate and effective as Protest Theatre in an increasingly (though not wholly) postmodernized and mass-mediatized age? Could the documentary model be followed only for a short time in other countries and without leaving a real mark on their traditions? And, more generally, is all Protest Theatre, if not indeed all theatre *tout court*, destined to have but an ephemeral life, sliding already always immediately into an archival past? Can (documentary/protest) theatre have only a passing appeal and a largely illusory effectiveness in dealing with the past and the present? Was Vietnam, as Robert Havemann suggested, really "everywhere"? Alternatively, precisely *be-*

cause both documentary theatre and Vietnam Protest Theatre have basically wilted today as distinct theatrical and political forms, perhaps it is possible at long last to give them their considerable due—which is to acknowledge them as one of the early and most interesting manifestations of increasingly radical "postmodern" contradictions between "staging war," in the broad and limited sense, and more explicitly mechanical and repressive forms of media dis/information and "entertainment."

Hochhuth and Weiss thus dealt with the Vietnam War not only in order to censure it but also in order to use it to critique Germany's present and recent past. They stressed major themes that served both goals—the actual horror of bombing civilian populations (Hochhuth) and the general danger inherent in the bellicose structure of capitalism, specifically the link between economics and war (Hochhuth and Weiss). But they also connected the two areas, Vietnam and Germany, by a formal combination of a Vietnamese war topic with a specifically German tradition of a documentary theatre. Of course, *Soldiers* and *Vietnam Discourse* were not their only response to the German past, and we could be disappointed because they failed to engage it in explicit terms. But we must remember that both Hochhuth and Weiss believed in, or at least certainly applied, the principle of a certain division of theatrical labor, addressing many central aspects of German history in other plays and texts. For a more evident, and perhaps effective, imbrication of national past and Vietnamese present in the Protest Theatre we must move west across the Rhine.

FROM COLONIALISM TO CYBERWAR (FRANCE)

War can never break free from magical spectacle because its very purpose is to produce that spectacle. . . .
And if memory is science itself for those who make
war, the memory in question is not like that of popular culture based upon common experience: rather it
is a parallel memory, a paramnesia, a mislocation in
time and space, an illusion of the déjà vu.
—Paul Virilio

The underlying theme of Brook's *US* was British imperialism and colonial past: more "us" than the U.S. He insisted in 1967 that the French "must write their own play about Vietnam." I now turn to the French response to this challenge, their *model* of Vietnam Protest Theatre.

Although it characterizes particularly well the specific French approach to the Vietnam War, the notion of model subsumes a more widespread way of viewing its exemplary function. The German Weiss's play
was subtitled *Example,* and the Austrian Szyszkowitz referred to Vietnam
as being a "model war." "Model" also had an "experimental" connotation
when it suggested that the United States might be preparing other ideological wars, or that the type of technowar waged in Vietnam would serve
as a template for all future warfare. But Vietnam was also a model for
Americans and Europeans in a more theatrical sense. Precisely because it
was so far removed from home, it was a "virtual reality" set in a nearly
abstract space and thus a "theatre of war" quite literally—a way of staging

and restaging it. Recall Sterne's Uncle Toby in *Tristram Shandy* who, wounded in the groin at the battle of Nanterre, is compelled to stage and restage his castration—as a toy model. These various notions of "modeling" are compressed in two French plays in which the model of the Vietnam War refers, in an overstated way, at once to a colonial past, to the repetition of that past, to an anticipation of future technowarfare, and to problems of "staging" in every meaning of the word.

Both major French plays about Vietnam were written and produced in 1967 when the war was already in full swing: André Benedetto's *Napalm* and Armand Gatti's *V comme Vietnam* (V like Vietnam).[1] Benedetto's was the first Vietnam Protest Play in France, and though initially produced in provincial Avignon, it received nationwide attention and some rave reviews in the press.[2] To what extent Benedetto's play might have influenced Gatti is uncertain. Both seem to have been written independently of the roughly contemporary plays of Brook, Hochhuth, and Weiss. The fact that, though quite different in many respects, the two French plays make similar political points could have been expected even if there had been no direct influence: they were written in the same period and from comparable left-wing perspectives. The comparatively "objective" organization of their material also leads to a significant number of structural similarities that need not be a matter of influence. Some of these parallels, such as the presence of a play-within-the-play, testify to a shared concept of staging strategy that is not particularly original. More interesting is the way in which political protest is tied, on both stages, to inventive theatrical forms, particularly concerning the dialectic of documentary "fact" and imaginative "fiction" as these relate to new technologies. There remains that both plays express a perception of the Vietnam War that is largely connected to the French situation and history—a perception all the more significant because its mode of ideological expression is not always explicitly textual.

1. SI(GH)TING VIETNAM

Obviously not all similarities between the two plays are equally meaningful. The observation that Gatti's *V comme Vietnam* and Benedetto's *Napalm* have the same two contrasting sets of characters, the Vietnamese and the Americans, is a mere matter of mimetic contingency: the war might not be expected to be staged without the presence of the two major combatants, even though, as has been seen, many of the American plays did just that.[3] Here, the choice of the same two main locales of action—Vietnam and the United States—may be equally expected but has a more significant connotation. For neither the German nor most of the American playwrights staged their plays *in Vietnam* where, after all, the real—killing—war was taking place. So Benedetto's and Gatti's focus on the Vietnam locale deserves special attention. Living in France, with painful memories of French Indochina, neither Benedetto nor Gatti had a pressing reason, as did the Americans, to trace the war's impact on the United States. This polarization of locales between Vietnam and the United States manifests rather a deliberate choice to show that the war opposed not only American and Vietcong troops in Vietnam but also two geopolitical sites on opposite ends of the globe; in other words, it was a war between two national, ideological, and cultural systems rather than merely an intervention of the U.S. military in the civil war between South and North Vietnam.

The two plays also focus on similar structural features within each of the two main locales. In both plays, action in the United States is clearly focused on the political scene in the White House, though Gatti also shows a military exercise on the West Coast. But the latter is a "rehearsal" for Vietnam, and hence an anticipatory image, belonging to the war sequence in Vietnam. In both plays, action in Vietnam involves not only war operations but also scenes from the everyday life of Vietnamese civilians. Both plays, in sum, propose a fairly narrow model of an America which, when staged, has practically no civilian population and a more balanced vision of Vietnam with peaceful peasants and militant Vietcong. As evoked on the French stage, the Vietnam War has thus no *visible* connection to the American people, no support or opposition among them, and no impact on their lives. Planned and carried out only by the government and the military in a techno-imaginary space, it stands as a virtual reality of war. Not America as a *site* is at war against Vietnam, but America as a *sighted* state—America as a threatening world power that wages war in order to promote its multiple interests. By contrast, the entire land of Vietnam and the Vietnamese population are directly involved in the war, collectively and spontaneously, without any perceptible decision made on their behalf by their government; they experience the war as lived experience and foreign curse.

Another similarity is the focus in each play, within the general framework of the White House, on figures standing for President Johnson and Secretary of Defense McNamara. In Gatti's play there are additional American officials present on the stage, in charge of propaganda, technology, or military operations. But—with a few exceptions, such as Dwight Eisenhower or John Foster Dulles—they represent types rather than specific individuals, bearing the implausible names of Docteur XXX, Général Bulldog, Théorème, and Amiral Pointu. It is also worth noting that, in Benedetto's *Napalm*, the fictional "Johnson" and "MacNamara" bear the names of the real Johnson and McNamara, providing an obvious link between History and Theatre.[4] Gatti, more subtle in this regard, formally conceals the identity of the two statesmen, but few French spectators could fail to see through their disguises.[5] The character "Mégasheriff" was obviously Johnson, widely pictured in France with his Texan hat, while the more enigmatic "Quadrature"—as in "quadrature du cercle" (squaring of a circle), a French expression for an insoluble mathematical problem—was referring to McNamara, reputed in the French press for his logic and rationality but in the service of an illogical and irrational cause.[6]

The overall reduction of America to the government-and-military complex is thus paralleled by a further reduction to its two best-known figures. The resulting impression is that the war in Vietnam is principally decided by the two political leaders, motivated by idiosyncratic ideological goals and/or by personal interest in the power of their office. This is the realm of conspiracy theory rather than structural analysis in the more Marxist sense of Peter Weiss. Johnson and McNamara hold the center of the stage in the French plays, and while they consult other officials and anticipate reactions by other politicians, they have final say about major policies. They barely allude to the "will of the people." Indeed, they dismiss it with a few terse words. As a state (rather than a country), America is ultimately identified with the president (commander-in-chief) and his secretary of defense (formally called the secretary of war), who bear enormous, if not full, responsibility for the American war.

This French "personalization" of the war is only superficially reminiscent of the American stress on individuals "playing imperialism." In this respect at least it is closer to the German approach, which tends to reduce the United States to the military complex. In the case of Gatti, this reductionism is linked to *technology* via a "dialectic of enlightenment," whereas for Benedetto it is linked to the larger problematic of *European* "civilization." One of my subtexts is the hypothesis that Vietnam Protest Theatre significantly anticipates what is regarded as "current theory," particularly the sweeping post-Enlightenment, post-Cartesian "critique of the subject." For example, Paul Virilio's obsessively reiterated theories about "pure war," the parallel evolution of technology of vision and postmodern warfare as "the logistics of perception," and the relations between "speed and politics" can all be found, at least in germination, on the earlier French stage. "Since the eighteenth century—since the Age of Enlightenment," Virilio argues,

> we have believed that technology and reason walked hand-in-hand toward progress, toward a 'glorious future,' as they say. It went without saying that we would find the solution: to sickness, to poverty, to inequality. We found it, all right, but it was final, not optimal. It was the solution of the world ending up in nuclear war, in Total War, in extermination and genocide. Thus, my intention is to say: no more illusions about technology.[7]

As part of this bleak historical analysis (anticipated by Gatti and Benedetto), Virilio attempts to show the deep imbrication of the mass media and warfare also exposed earlier on the French stage: "It's not by chance that the movie camera was preceded by Marey's chrono-photographic rifle and the Gattling gun, which was itself inspired by the Colt revolver. All these things are at the origin of war."[8] The consequences for the determination of human subjectivity—and hence responsibility for war—are deep:

Pure war no longer needs men, and that's why it's pure. It doesn't need the human war-machine, mobilized human forces. It was hardly a generation ago that we stopped needing assembled masses to provide an abundance, as Bernanos said of the troops in World War I who went to attack Verdun: "That troop of extras has been gathered here to provide death in overabundance." Now we no longer need the extras. (Virilio and Lotringer 1983, 171)

Theatre of course often does need "extras," and French Vietnam Protest Theatre in the 1960s struggled desperately to keep open the question of human subjectivity and responsibility in the face of already impending "pure" technowarfare.

The presentation of Vietnamese scenes offered other significant problems to the French dramatists. As a rule, Gatti and Benedetto solve them in different ways, each play being original in that respect. But here, too, they share one striking feature: a common discounting, practically to the point of a negation, of the historical—and crucial—separation between South and North Vietnam along the 17th parallel. Benedetto is particularly up-front about this issue, tying it to the concern for the ultimate responsibility for the war. His mini-chorus called *The First* and *The Second*, i.e., the voices of the Vietnamese people, asserts that all Vietnamese belong to a single nation, that no state borders can divide them, that they cannot aggress each other, which leaves the role of the aggressors to the Americans:

> THE SECOND: Here you are: who is the aggressor?
> THE FIRST: The USA, sir!
> THE SECOND: No sir, it is Hanoi!
> THE FIRST: In Hanoi the Vietnamese are the same as in Saigon.
> THE SECOND: But they are the bad Vietnamese!
> THE FIRST: How do you recognize these bad Vietnamese?
> THE SECOND: They infiltrate the South!
> THE FIRST: Between the South and the North, the border is fictitious.
>   (Benedetto 31)

With these words, a fictitious cultural production—a play—claims the power to intervene in History, radically altering—with its own logic and propaganda—the logic and propaganda of the U.S. government and media.

Similarly, in Gatti's Vietnamese village there is no difference between South and North Vietnamese but only between "the true and the false Vietnamese" (Gatti 47), prompting a character to wonder how one can tell the difference between a "true" Vietcong and a "false" Vietcong (Gatti 72). A publicized national and political distinction is transformed into a moral and ideological distinction between "good" and "bad" Vietnamese belonging to the same Vietnamese nation—the "good" being those who fight against the American occupation army, the "bad" being those who collaborate with it. From the perspective of the "national" war between the United States and Vietnam, the "bad" Vietnamese are viewed as traitors and hence as a minority. By the same logic, which both problematizes "national identity" and yet reconfirms it with regard to the United States, the "good" Vietnamese in *Napalm*, visibly approved of by Benedetto, are justified when they claim that "the American aggressors and the Vietnamese traitors are like the same person!" (Benedetto 139). Unlike "Johnson" and "MacNamara," we never catch sight of this composite "person" on stage, except metaphorically through his/her pointed absence.

Conversely, the "good" Vietnamese stand for the majority, the "true" population of Vietnam that resists the U.S. intervention. For Gatti as well as for Benedetto, no distinct group of fighters embodies the American notion of an aggressive Vietcong Army. All (good) Vietnamese can be expected at any time to take up arms against the Americans in self-defense. The Americans like to *call* them the "Vietcong," it is implied, in order to create the impression of a real difference between Vietnamese allies and Vietcong enemies of the United States; in reality (that is, in the two plays), all (good) Vietnamese, except for a few traitors, are potential Vietcong. Or, more dramatically, all Vietnamese killed in the war, even or especially unarmed civilians, are liable to be listed as Vietcong in the American military count of enemy casualties. Hence this cynical bit of cited U.S. Army wisdom: the very definition of a Vietcong is a "dead Vietnamese" (Benedetto 105).

In short, both Gatti and Benedetto use contrasting approaches when they deconstruct the two antagonists. On the one hand, they compress all Americans into two "personalized" characters who stand in for, and function as, ideological forces of historical causation. On the other, they collectivize the Vietnamese into a unified mass of human beings who oppose the forces of imperialism.[9]

Within such a complex but ultimately essentialistic scheme or model, the question may be raised why some Vietnamese would want to become traitors to their nation? The French playwrights appear to suggest that the choice between resisting the Americans and collaborating with them is not a matter of international politics, i.e., alliances with the United States or with the communist states, but an internal Vietnamese business. They imply, in *V comme Vietnam* more clearly than in *Napalm*, that ideological (and moral) differences among the Vietnamese actually antedated the American intervention (and, one must also imagine, the French occupation). A "traitor" in Gatti's play is thus identified as a former landowner who exploited the peasants long before the war. This approach requires, of course, a more complex socioeconomic presentation of the Vietnamese and their culture than is commonly found in the U.S. protest plays and rather less than in the German. In the American, the Vietnamese are shown only when they are involved in direct relations with Americans; they seem to have no life of their own; most often they are si(gh)ted and cited as fleeting images of stereotypes. In the French plays, however, the Vietnam scene is ostensibly viewed from the perspective of the Vietnamese, who are provided with distinct personalities, positive or negative, and often grounded in past history. In these plays the American scenes in the inner sanctum of the White House are being viewed, as it were, from an assumed "Vietnamese" perspective, which may help explain the otherwise curious dialectic between personalization and abstraction of the U.S. government. In any case, the shift to the Vietnamese viewpoint enables Gatti and Benedetto to get closer to their "imaginary community" of the Vietnamese and its ideological complexity. It also has a direct impact on their tolerant and sympathetic portrayal of the "oriental other" contrasted with the "occidental us."

The reasons why Benedetto and Gatti stage the Vietnamese as homogeneous people, and why they perceive Vietnam to be a basically single albeit currently divided nation, are rooted in French history, particularly in France's long involvement in Indochina. For many generations—roughly from 1850 till 1940—and then for several years after the Japanese withdrawal, France occupied and ruled what was to become modern Vietnam as a part of its Indochina possessions.[10] Numerous French families settled and prospered there, and many Vietnamese migrated to Paris, some as students.[11] Actually only Cochinchina, with Saigon, became legally a part of France, together with Algeria. But until World War II all of Indochina was ruled, with the status of colony or protectorate, by a governor appointed by the French Ministry of Colonies. Even Hanoi, though it was the center of the separate Tonkin protectorate, was considered French territory. During this colonialist period, the future of Vietnam was linked very closely to the French and vice versa, and the Vietnamese were perceived as familiar figures, each one endowed with a relatively individual character. Even after the French lost Vietnam, anything connected to it commanded a fairly high degree of informed interest, especially among the older generation with nostalgic memories. Neither Germany, Britain, nor the United States had a comparable experience.

For French of all ages, however, the most immediate reason for their fascination with the Vietnamese nation in the late 1960s was the recent experience of France's own war in Vietnam, ending in a humiliating defeat barely a dozen years earlier (1954). The loss of Vietnam was actually the second in a series of three dramatic and traumatic reversals for France: German occupation during World War II, the Vietnam War, and the Algerian War—three demonstrations that France no longer was a dominant world power either in Europe or abroad. Some historians argue that it all started when Paris fell to the Wehrmacht: "France was obsessed with its military defeat of 1940 as well as with its occupation by the Nazis; the loss of prestige led de Gaulle to make outrageous demands. France's need to regain its role as a world power was finally to lead it and the United States into the Vietnamese wars" (Baritz 49). Benedetto and Gatti were old enough to remember that series of defeats. They certainly recalled how, for ten years, the French Army had been fighting all over Vietnam a losing war against the self-described liberation forces, i.e., forces that drew their ideological principles, to a significant degree, from values of the Enlightenment and the French Revolution of 1789. They could not ignore that for the Vietnamese this was an ideological as well as a national war or that France was supported by conservative local groups and opposed by the communist DRV Army created by the Viet Minh under Ho Chi Minh's leadership. In fact, the military victory of the Viet Minh was viewed by the French as an ideological victory of the left wing. And this vision eventually overdetermined the French outlook on the American war in Vietnam, which seemingly was repeating the story of the war that the French had lost there. The awareness that this repetition, this return of the historical repressed, could be acknowledged in France when it was not yet admitted in the United States no doubt offered the French a certain more or less conscious feeling of compensatory intellectual superiority over the Americans.

Remembering how the French Army, well equipped and trained, had been decisively defeated only *after* the Viet Minh won over the support of most of the Vietnamese, Benedetto and Gatti were particularly sensitive to the importance of those ideological issues and internal Vietnamese policies that could lead the population to resist—often against all odds—a foreign occupation. Furthermore, learning from the French experience, they expected (and hoped) that the U.S. Army, despite its vastly superior armament and technology, would be defeated, as had been the French Army, by the Vietcong forces supported by the majority of Vietnamese people. From their perspective, the American war in Vietnam was as doomed as the French war earlier and for the same reasons. Any suspense, therefore, could only concern, as in a Greek tragedy, the dramatic progress toward that failure. This outlook, no doubt grounded in "realism," possibly benefited also from a form of national arrogance—if the French couldn't win, nobody could!—and from a need for self-justification—not even the United States, with all its military superiority, could achieve what the French could not! Indeed, though written in the middle of the war, when the outcome was very much in doubt, both *Napalm* and *V comme Vietnam* predict a final victory for the Vietnamese liberation forces.[12] By the same token, they expose the absurdity of the U.S. government's hopes, tactics, and strategies for the war. Given the "inevitable" outcome, the French playwrights could see no justification for the mayhem resulting from American military operations—the massive bombing, burning, killing, and maiming. And, following that logic, they denounce in their plays the stubbornness of a bellicose U.S. government which simply cannot read its (French) history.

The ambiguous blend of bitterness and derision that marks these plays was likely also influenced by the recollection of France's own mistakes in dealing with the Vietnamese, particularly the long and stubborn refusal of the French government and the military to negotiate an honorable end to a "wrong" war. The price for France was considerable, economically and politically, culminating in the shame of a final defeat that brought back the painful memory not only of the French collapse in 1940 but also of the division of France itself into "Vichy" and "Free," "traitors" and "collaborators." (The latter distinction is by no means as clear as many French have tried up until quite recently to convince the world and themselves.)

In fact, for several years, the French left wing itself was split on the Vietnam War issue. Only the communists denounced it from the beginning as "la sale guerre" (the dirty war, i.e., the wrong war), while the socialists (SFIO), in and out of government, supported it at least until 1953.[13] Many radical intellectuals were disturbed and frustrated by the failure of their political leaders to bring about earlier negotiations. Most opponents of the war, however, did not seem willing to assume their own part of the guilt for letting the war procrastinate. They greeted its end with relief, but did little to denounce concrete political French responsibilities for either the war's origins or its consequences. The lost war, in the dominant leftist perception, had been waged by incompetent generals, against hopeless ends, under a series of short-sighted governments. But no retroactive protest movement or trial in the media branded the direct or indirect guilty parties. It is thus quite conceivable that Gatti and Benedetto were tempted to project, onto a stubborn U.S. policy toward Vietnam, the long repressed frustration of French intellectuals with their own leadership, as well as with their diminished political role in French society—a feeling of futility dating back at least to the Napoleonic period.[14]

How, then, was this complex historical, ideological, and political problematic staged by the two playwrights, i.e., converted into concrete theatrical models? In Gatti's *V comme Vietnam*, the Pentagon carries out, in an imaginary California, a full rehearsal of the invasion of Vietnam (with American soldiers playing the role of the Vietnamese). For the United States, the audience is told, this war game "will be the introduction to our entrance into hyperhistory" (Gatti 13). Indeed, anticipating Baudrillard's "hyperreality," Gatti views "hyperhistory" as the production rather than the recording of events, yet under the guise of recording them. With that move, which conceals its mode of war production, so to speak, Gatti progresses from the specifics of the Vietnam War to the abstraction of "hyperhistory." Through the military exercise, the Americans prestage their own future history as a conquering global power, but also, as has been seen, one headed "tragically" for defeat. At the same time, in a different space and in alternating scenes, actors playing the Vietnamese are staging alternative visions of Vietnamese history and life.[15] The (possible) everyday life of humans is set in juxtaposition with the (possible) hyperreality of empires. An unresolvable dialectic of the particular and the more universal asserts itself here in theatrical terms.

Gatti's stage is cluttered with several large projection screens and a couple of smaller secondary stages. But this multiplication of traditional theatrical devices is undermined, or at least made obsolete, by the introduction of far more advanced modern technology. The Pentagon officials located on the main stage are actually supposed to be viewed by the spectators as if they were electronic images on a large television and/or computer screen. Then, during the military exercise, the audience sees the Vietnamese located on a secondary stage not only as characters played by Western actors but also as further images mediated and distorted on the screens of Western media. This post-Piscatorian technological framing alludes ironically to the claim of Western colonialists and postcolonialists that they colonized Vietnam only for the sake of progress. It evokes the American technosocial ritual of watching the coverage of the war on the nightly television news—as if Vietnam were just another spectacle worthy of prime time. Gatti's entire play is marked by the technologically updated theatrical nature of the rehearsed invasion of Vietnam—the play-within-the-play that becomes a televised play about the first television war, now restaged.

Benedetto's *Napalm* is theatrically self-referential in a different manner. It begins with this statement: "The play we shall perform for you tonight is a political play." This bold remark stresses the "theatrical" as well as the political nature of the play, for it suggests its own *self-conscious* politics *as a play*. And, indeed, *Napalm* shows a group of North Vietnamese acting out the Vietnam War from their assumed own perspective.[16] Remarkably, it is "Ho Chi Minh" who plays the lead role of Johnson, though not always willingly:

> Ho Chi Minh: Comrades! Why must I play the role of that despicable Yankee?—
>
> The Director: Come on, Minh, someone must play it! Am I not forced myself to play the role of an imperialist snake in the grass (Mac Namara)? They must be represented because they exist! (Benedetto 143)

This Pirandellian casting device enables Benedetto to tell the story of Vietnam as if he were a Vietnamese himself. In that sense, his play is the obverse of Gatti's where Americans are impersonating the Vietnamese. In both cases, however, there occurs what in German is a *Blickwechsel*: not only an *exchange* of glances *between* cultures—European, American, Vietnamese—but a more radical and disorienting *change of perspective* between "enemy" camps, so that one looks back on one's own position in an oscillatory *interchange* between "us" and "them." For Benedetto, such a variant of the play-within-a-play model is supposed to restitute the "reality" of the war as it is experienced by the victims, i.e., by the "other." Yet the theatricality of *Napalm* is not "realistic" in the common sense of the term. The audience knows at some level that the Vietnamese acting out the

Americans are in fact acted out by French actors. But since no real Vietnamese voices, speaking their own language, could be expected to be heard on a "normal" French stage, the artifice of the play-within-a-play offers at least the illusion of a truthful vision of war by the "other." That impression, yielded by the immediacy of living theatre, is reinforced by the use of documents, newsreels, and other presentations of historical fact. These ground the theatricality in external reality—without, however, diminishing theatre's "magic" power to be live action. On the one hand Benedetto acknowledges that his play may be too didactic and hence politically counterproductive: "You have reached an emotional impasse. You are clearly transgressing the limits of theatre. You are involved in politics!" (Benedetto 35). On the other hand, however, he trusts that inventive theatrical forms will blur the line between politics and theatre as they are conventionally perceived. Even as entertainment, theatre may have a subversive function, acknowledged and feared by the authorities, at least by the ones in the play:

JOHNSON: Theatre is entertainment, Mac Namara!
NAMARA: We too are . . . represented!
JOHNSON: Isn't it forbidden?
NAMARA: By the Geneva Convention? I don't know. (Benedetto 159)

Benedetto further uses self-reflexive humor to demonstrate that his own theatre is always "real" because it reflects a priori—and ontologically and temporally—a "real" situation. He proposes playfully, almost hopefully, that "a bomb could be thrown on our theatre with the pretext that it is situated in North Vietnam" (Benedetto 41). One is reminded of an old fable about the visual arts: the competition described by Pliny between Parrhasios and Zeuxis. The latter paints grapes so true to life that a bird flies up to the stage on which the picture is standing. Thinking he has won the contest by deceiving the birds, Zeuxis demands that Parrhasios in turn draw back the curtain from his painting, only to discover that his rival has painted that curtain, thus deceiving not merely birds but humans.[17] Benedetto's play about a play about reality has the same illusory power as Parrhasios's curtain. In the French plays we see a paradoxical parallel obtaining between two radically different strategies: the high artificiality of the theatrical play-within-the-play device and the display of those features of modernity that are usually contrasted with theatre, i.e., images conveyed by highly artificial technological media.

One of the best known of these media images, that of the self-immolation of Thich Quang Duc in 1963, is inserted by Gatti in *V comme Vietnam* as an emblematic exposure of the role of television. The image is certainly horrifying on its own, but its main function in the play is to contribute a spectacular example of the impact of *television coverage* on the war. The image is situated—or si(gh)ted—at the interface between a pretechnological "human" Vietnam and a technological "inhuman" America. As a televised image, it implicates the mass media, but it also represents an event—a human action—that dramatically supports the goals of the anti-war protest.

Actually, Gatti indicts not only television but all modern technology. The burning monk serves to condemn the entire American society run by information stored in a supercomputer, La Châtaigne (about which more later). When it becomes apparent that the U.S. Army is losing the war in Vietnam, authorities dismantle the computer in search of the piece of information, "the smoking gun" or "black box," that will explain why the war has been lost. They pull out the media news that had been fed to the electronic giant and, one by one, all sorts of characters appear on the stage, embodying the war stories reported in the press and on television. Among them is Thich Quang Duc, transfixed in the photo of his stoic self-immolation:

> A new bit is ejected. A bonze [monk] is shown in the background. Buddhist picture: Flames emerge from a human being shriveled by the fire.—His head is blackened, and turned into ash.—Thich Quang Duc is transformed into fumes of burned flesh.—Not a muscle twitches. No sound. (This immobility contrasts with the laments of the crowd.) (Gatti 114)

This image is followed by one of Norman Morrison:

> Another bit. Morrison picture:—victim of a duty that demands from him to state his belief concerning all that his country is doing. Especially when these doings cause distress, death and suffering. On November 3, 1965, he came up to the Pentagon at the time the offices closed there, poured gas on his clothes and set fire to himself. (Gatti 117)

Of course, as Dr. XXX (a Pentagon advisor) remarks, "The machine only spews out what it was given to swallow" (Gatti 117). If this is indeed so, then logically and paranoically *all* the bits of information (or disinformation) reported by the media may be held responsible for the loss of the war. Gatti offers here, already in 1967, an anticipation of the now familiar problem created by an excessive supply of information that humans cannot process: they are forced into the unattractive postmodern "choice" of either picking meaning at random or giving up the search for any meaning—a problematic echoed in contemporary Chaos Theory and information overload. Gatti seems to be implying that, parallel to the protest in the United States and the resistance in Vietnam, American media are also undermining the war effort by spreading anti-American news. This notion was not as far-fetched in 1967 as it might seem: both Johnson and then Nixon repeatedly, obsessively, blamed the press for their failures in Vietnam. The image of the burning monk, however, is probably intended to have a more universal impact. It anchors the play not only in the actual history of the Vietnam War but also in a more universal history where an eternally burning body stands synecdochically for the eternal horror of all war. For the image of body-become-flame is tragically overdetermined by a number of historical referents: the autos-da-fé of the Inquisition, the witch trials, the deaths of Joan of Arc and Jan Hus, the Shoah, and of course the napalmed thousands of "nameless" Vietnamese (i.e., names unrecorded by the mass media).

Gatti's giant high-tech TV sets on stage also are contrasted with human simplicity through the images they show of "the people." It is on these screens that the audience accesses the (imagined) quotidian life of the Vietnamese and learns the details and motivations of their struggle. All these images "happen" to be sympathetic toward the Vietnamese, supporting Quadrature's "paranoid" suspicion about the antimilitary influence of television. Surprisingly, Gatti asserts here his confidence in the beneficial potential of the media generally; at least, he implies, it can never be *totally* controlled by the government, for neither governments nor military can control *absolutely* what they might well desire to control. There is a hint in Gatti of the liberal Enlightenment belief that "truth will win," an idealistic position at odds with skepticism and political radicalism that Gatti otherwise espouses.

Besides—like the real Johnson or Nixon—the American authorities in Gatti's play also believe that not only televised but also photographic images may contribute to undermining the war effort to serve the interests of enemy propaganda:

> VENTRILOQUIST [U.S. ambassador to Vietnam]: We cannot identify our real enemies. Those whom we protect and those whom we fight look the same. That confusion could be even greater. Our photographers only photograph our atrocities, never the atrocities of the others.
> DAVE: And the propaganda services?
> VENTRILOQUIST: They published Ho Chi Minh's picture indicating that he was responsible for all the anomalies recorded in Vietnam. But his face of an old and underfed Father Christmas had everybody crying. (Gatti 49)

The point seems to be that even the U.S. propaganda machine cannot make Ho Chi Minh appear to be anything other than a benign and sympathetic old man. Yet the evocation of that photograph, for a French theatre audience, must surely have had a less positive connotation. Ho Chi Minh's reputation in France was that of an astute and ruthless politician who, French-educated, knew his enemy from the inside out. In his case, paradoxically, the Vietnamese "other" was, in part, one of Western "us." Does then Gatti insinuate that photographs can lie? In Ho Chi Minh's case, the lie would benefit the Vietnamese, but in other cases, publicized in U.S. mass media, lies could be used against them. As Roland Barthes showed in his analysis of the black French soldier on the cover of *Paris Match*, whereas photographs and other images may well be always infused with ideologically *coded* messages, their actual effects are unstable, unpredictable, and cannot be ideologically *fixed* once and for all.[18] It is possible, therefore, that free media can be simultaneously blamed *and* credited for the American failure in Vietnam.[19] More specifically, Gatti tends to be positive and optimistic in his presentation of the press: an American reporter in his play defects to the Vietcong.[20] And the all-pervasive, but essentially neutral, computerized media system La Châtaigne accomplishes at the end a remarkable transference of technopower from First to Third World: the supercomputer becomes a Vietcong propaganda tool. "Objectively Châtaigne was transformed into a Vietnam propaganda bureau. But you know very well that any objective vision is incomplete" (Gatti 99).[21] Thus, La Châtaigne may offer the most succinct illustration of the ideological trajectory of French left-wing theatre from a reflection on its own guilty past to the concern with transnational problematics of cyberwar.

In Benedetto's *Napalm*, the immolation image has a less globally and historically suggestive function. As a rule, Benedetto takes a less sanguine view of the media than Gatti. For Benedetto, the press and especially television are *always* used to disseminate dominant ideology. His view is similar to Joyce Nelson's belief that the media form the main colonizing tools of America:

> In this century colonization is accomplished through the eye. At least that is its more subtle and "peaceful" form. Through the power of spectacle, the powerful relation of images and the human psyche, the screen constitutes us as a globalized mass resonating to scanned pulses and impulses, of primarily one country.[22]

Yet, despite the harsh critique of American television in his play, Benedetto admitted in an interview that he had used television programs as his primary inspiration and information source:

> Last July, television had shown an entire series of films about American pilots, prisoners in Hanoi. The public opinion had been very moved. It is then that I got the idea to write a play about the story of a captured pilot.[23]

But *Napalm* was not quite as dependent as, say, Brook's *US* on contaminated U.S. sources; the film series in question was produced by the East German crew H&S. Benedetto also admitted that he "wrote this play on the basis of a large number of documents and writings by journalists of various nationalities and opinions."[24] And French spectators reacted favorably to the resulting "ring of truth." As one review put it:

> Each single minute of this play could be illustrated (or supported) with

photographs or articles: statements and testimonies, there lies the novelty of that work.[25]

Audiences may have been particularly impressed, among other references to television images, by Benedetto's evocation of Norman Morrison's self-immolation in front of his daughter on the steps of the Pentagon—a sacrificial image reinforced, in the next scene, by the self-immolation of Thich Quang Duc. As in Gatti's play, these two scenes enhance, and thus revitalize, the spectacularized photographs with a solemn tribute to all those who have given, or are giving, their lives to a just cause and who can say, with Morrison (not to say also Jesus): "I am the light of justice" (Benedetto 86).

Benedetto's use of television images was no doubt justified, despite his dislike for them on other grounds, by the desire to turn theatre into a more effective and up-to-date political tool and weapon. The "magic" of theatre, its allegorical power to evoke an absent world (in short, what is called its "illusion"), is supported in *Napalm* by public images that concretize a war waged far away and "bring it home," so to speak, with technocultural speed. The documents are used, as in other plays, to strengthen the belief in the objective reality of Vietnam, but at the same time they serve to sharpen the political message of the stage: "You are in an emotional blind alley! You obviously trespass the limits of theatre, you are involved in politics!" (Benedetto 35). The line that some critics draw between politics and theatre (or entertainment) is transgressed by Benedetto just as by Vietnam Protest playwrights generally; they all believe that theatre can and must aspire to be a subversive act, using subversive means.

Like other protest playwrights, Benedetto in 1968 exposes the horrors of the Vietnam War and assigns responsibility to those whom he sees as the aggressors; but he also is outraged by the way that official and commercial media have been (and still are) presenting/distorting the war. And he attempts to *counteract* that mediatized vision through a use, misuse, or abuse of the best-known media images—re-si(gh)ting Vietnam in the process.

2. UN/MASKING COLONIALISM

There is a common core of attitudes in the two French plays: sympathy for the Vietnamese people; faith in the victory of the Vietcong; distrust of aggressive policies of the U.S. government; the articulation of media, technology, and warfare. This similar perspective, however, inspires two diverging explicit explanations of the causes of the war and hence two different takes on the history and effects of colonialism. Benedetto is clearly focused, in a rather traditional way, on the concrete responsibility of American policies, while Gatti appears to be more concerned with broader human and cultural issues—seeing the war as a "problematic" feature of modern civilization *tout court*. Benedetto never directly indicts the American people as such, although his parallel censure of Johnson and imperialism could be extended to all of American society. And that is the way the play was understood by those French spectators who, as noted in a contemporary press review, saw it as an indictment of "a society which is infected with the cancer of its own death, and our death as well . . . made in the U.S.A."[26] The "cancer" refers here to the American dream of an ever-expanding imperialist conquest—the manifest destiny writ large that is said to have motivated the Americans long before it became the prime cause of the Vietnam War.

To drive his polemic home, Benedetto roots the imperialist impulse in a remote past when its first victims were the American "Indians"—a native population whose resistance, quite unlike what was happening or was assumed to happen in Vietnam, was relatively easily crushed by the superior military power of the white settlers. There is a trial scene in *Napalm* where a captured U.S. pilot named Charles Whitman (after the madman who opened fire on a crowd in Texas in 1961) brags to his Vietcong judges:

> I, Charles Joseph Whitman . . . I belong to the most powerful nation in the world. . . . We conquered the West with the Colt 38. (Benedetto 73)

The Colt ("How the West Was Won") stands for conquest and military violence—articulating conquest and war, big business and colonialism. One also might recall Virilio's thesis that the Colt revolver leads directly not only to the machine gun but also to modern media's technological and technocultural recording of war. Benedetto sees the Colt as a convenient concrete symbol of aggressive arrogance that goes hand in hand with the imperialist dream, and he returns to it, once again, in order to link the Indian Wars with the war in Vietnam:

> JOHNSON: Damn it, McNamara, did we conquer the West?
> NAMARA: Yes, Mr. President, with the Colt 38!
> JOHNSON: And now we have helicopters; don't tell me that a Vietnamese is more frightening than an Indian. (Benedetto 127)

This comparison between Native Americans and Vietnamese is by no means unique. It was picked up by several American writers at that time, including Daniel Berrigan, Megan Terry, Tuli Kupferberg, and George Tabori—all insisting that imperialist ideology is ineradicably ingrained in the United States even though, contrary to European powers, the United States did not build up a "real" colonial empire.[27] The blurring of any clear distinction between national imperialism and *economic* imperialism is the more dominant tendency in the Vietnam Protest Theatre.

Benedetto does suggest—ironically reversing and subverting the model of the "domino theory"—that, just as the United States did not rest after the conquest of the American West, it will hardly stop with Indochina. In the post–World War II era, American imperialism is also indicted by the French playwright for striving for a *global* domination by pushing the export of its consumer goods. A Vietnamese witness to Whitman's trial comments bitterly about the emblematic American airman:

> He will drop on us his bombs, his microbes, his bedbugs, his toxic gases, his chemical products, his supermarkets, his dollars! (Benedetto 79)

For Benedetto, in times of "global strategy," the United States wants to police the entire globe, not only Vietnam, and to force on "everybody" the superior "American way of life."[28] This modern version of the ostensibly archaic imperialist dream is presented as being as ruthless as the prior form of territorial conquest of the "Wild" West. Its current success, and hence justification, is guaranteed, explains Benedetto's Johnson, by American political gains after World War II—gains won by a hard-line power policy that must be continued to meet the goals of History made-in-the-USA:

> My opinion is that the only language that the enemy understands is a firm language. Let us show them that, unified behind their convictions, the American people will not yield, and they will become reasonable and capitulate. This policy has worked in Berlin, has worked in Korea, and sooner or later will work in Vietnam. (Benedetto 60)

Johnson singles out only a couple of international confrontations (and is hardly right about Korea), which Benedetto associates with a more general cultural imperialism conflated through the collective voice of a proud American crowd, with Johnson's leadership, his programs for *domestic* social justice, and the commodified American "way of life" in a celebration of national superiority:

> Long live Johnson!
> Long live the Great Society
> Long live high standards of living!
> Long live the refrigerator!
> Long live the television!
> Long live the United States! (Benedetto 60)

No wonder, then, that most American soldiers in *Napalm* are shown to support Johnson's war, or at least to carry it out without objections. Like Charles Whitman, they seem genuinely to believe in the imperialist and consumerist ideology that underlies government policy. True, four years later, in *Chant funèbre pour un soldat américain* (1972), Benedetto's attitude toward American soldiers changes from indictment to commiseration—from executors of governmental policy, they are transformed into its victims. By that time, of course, the war had taken on a more scandalously bloody turn, and the widely publicized My Lai massacre had sharply raised the question of individual responsibility: Was Lieutenant Calley guilty in My Lai, or was he but a tool of the U.S. government?[29] Thus, Benedetto's second Vietnam play leans toward sympathy for the American soldiers, but ironically it also dehumanizes them by depicting them as—literally and figuratively—empty shells. His main target, however, remains the U.S. imperialist dream.[30]

The obsessive indictment of U.S. imperialism, neglecting specific historical features such as paranoid anticommunism, can be partly explained by Benedetto's projection of French imperialist adventures in Indochina onto the American intervention in Vietnam. Attributing to both Western powers similar political motivations enables Benedetto to propose, through the censure of the U.S. policy, a belated parallel condemnation of the war that France had lost in 1954 at Dien Bien Phu. Several statements explicitly tie together the two successive wars in Vietnam, with the French bearing chronological responsibility for starting the entire sequence:

THE FIRST: Who began it? That is the basic question.
THE SECOND: If we try to find out who began it, then step by step we shall have to go back to . . .
THE FIRST: To the invasion of Tonkin by Napoleon's troops in 1860! (Benedetto 31)

Then, as Benedetto exceptionally seems to give up irony and to underwrite the statement of his character Namara, the righteous French who castigate the American imperialism in Vietnam are themselves accused of protecting their own economic interests, bearing their share of past and present guilt:

NAMARA: Ah, Mister President, there is also France! And its loud speeches that accuse and condemn us in the entire world! . . . but . . . we prevented . . . reestablishing colonization after World War II, . . . [although] there are about a hundred large French companies there, that all together they control a half of the industry, and that nine tenth of hevea forests belong to the French! (Benedetto 153)

This statement is particularly significant because, while solidly linking American and French policies in Vietnam, it also makes two points directed specifically at the French. On the one hand, it singles them out as the most vocal, if perhaps hypocritical, critics of the Vietnam War—a relatively flattering observation. On the other hand, it reminds them that their own *imperialist* policies, whether territorial or economic, were and remain *colonialist* in nature. *Napalm* offers here one of very few instances on the

Vietnam protest stage where European colonialism is explicitly identified as a form of imperialism that is worse than its modern American brand. Everybody in the play, even the representatives of imperialist United States, agrees to condemn a "truly" colonialist policy: i.e., a policy that reduces a conquered country to the status of a colony; a policy that led France to create its (botched) colonial empire in Asia and Africa, including Indochina and Algeria; a policy that became particularly anathema after the decolonization following World War II. Hence the following exchange with Ho Chi Minh acting the part of Johnson:

> MINH (AS JOHNSON): As if we were a colonial power who wants to keep its Algeria, its Indochina! What did Foster Dulles say?
> FOSTER DULLES: The U.S. does not identify with colonial powers! (Benedetto 144)

Not America, whose imperialism was not openly tainted with colonialism,[31] but France is targeted here and each time when colonialist policies are mentioned. To be sure, these references are sparse; and the precise relationship between imperialism and colonialism remains vague in the play, hinted at rather than exposed. Nonetheless, these hints suffice to invite a French audience to perceive, behind American imperialism, a shadow of French colonialism, to find them both censurable, and to move from condemning America today to condemning France yesterday.

The (self)critical function of *Napalm*, subtly shifting the focus from the United States and Vietnam to France and its former colonial possessions, could hardly be missed by European observers. Aware of a similar double edge of his own Vietnam play, directed partly at British society, it was for such a French self-criticism that Peter Brook was calling when he insisted that "the French must write their own play about Vietnam." Benedetto's *Napalm* was the first, and most significant, of such French plays, grafting a critique of France on the critique of America. No wonder, then, that Olivier Todd, the French journalist who interviewed Brook, hailed *Napalm*'s opening in Avignon as a fitting response to the English playwright's suggestion: "It is done. It has started. . . . The French, more remote in time, space, and responsibility from Vietnam than from Algeria, are coming."[32]

There remains to clarify Todd's pointed allusion to Algeria. He seems to assume that, in the minds of the French, Vietnam is automatically connected to Algeria and that this relationship must be based on a similar perception of the wars waged in the two countries, Algeria being indeed uncannily closer to home. But to *which* war in Vietnam is he alluding: the American or the French? Todd's statement is ambiguous. For Vietnam to be truly more remote in *time* than Algeria ("plus loin . . . dans le temps"), his reference must apply to the memory of the *French* war against the Viet Minh, concluded eight years before the end of the Algerian War. Yet in terms of a more remote *responsibility* ("plus loin . . . dans . . . la responsabilité"), and within the general context of the article, the American war against the Vietcong is a much better choice for the stage than the French involvement in Vietnam, for which France was as responsible as for the Algerian War.[33] Todd might have been carried away by his rhetoric without intending the ambiguity, but he also might have conflated the two Vietnam Wars on purpose to imply, as did Benedetto, that the guilt of the Americans and the French in Vietnam was comparable if not identical. In contrast, there is no comparable ambiguity about the reference to Algeria. It can only point to the traumatic military struggle of France against Algerian liberation forces, ending in 1962 when Algeria became an independent state. Whether linked to the American or to the French war in Vietnam, or to both at once, the Algerian War is clearly viewed by Todd as a haunting, if hidden, second source for the much needed French play about Vietnam: i.e., *Napalm*—a source that was still too close and sensitive to be overtly and publicly acknowledged.

Must one take literally Todd's suggestion? Did the Algerian War, five years past, really inspire Benedetto, albeit tacitly? Was it a missing piece that needs to be added for a full understanding of *Napalm*'s dual criticism of the United States and France? On the surface, Benedetto's play hardly supports an affirmative answer. It mentions Algeria only twice, and only once with an explicit reference to the American war in Vietnam, when a character bitterly observes, "Television didn't show as much at the time of Algeria!" (Benedetto 37).[34] The other instance takes place when he lists the sites that are watching what is happening in Vietnam; the last three are "Algeria, Tunisia, and Hanoi" (Benedetto 92)—all former French colonies. There are no other identifiable hints of an *intentional* disguise of Algeria under the mask of Vietnam. It is thus hazardous to speak of a conscious reference to Algeria in *Napalm*, or even of Benedetto's conscious conceal-ment of the influence that the Algerian War might have had on his vision of the Vietnam War. On the other hand, it is quite possible that the memory of Algeria has remained with him and with his audience on an unconscious level, suffusing his play with a frustrated and frustrating bitterness.

For the Algerian War was an exceptionally baffling and traumatic experience for most French, whatever their political opinions.[35] The military, the conservatives, the patriotic French, all viewed Algeria as an integral part of France (and not as a colony); and the support given by other French to the enemies of "Algérie Française" was judged by them to be treason that must be repressed by the government, by the police, and, in many cases, by terrorism. Dramatic manifestations of this conviction disturbed France for several years before winding down after the Evian peace agreement signed under de Gaulle's pressure in 1962.[36] Demonstrators were killed by the police in Paris streets; generals and army units stationed in Algeria rebelled and threatened to invade France; de Gaulle barely escaped an assassination attempt at Petit Clamart; militants of the clandestine OAS (Organisation de l'Armée Secrète) bombed the dwellings of supporters of the peace; and, after some semblance of normalcy was

restored, the mass exodus of French from Algeria created massive resettle-
ment problems. On the other hand, an increasing number of French,
especially those with left-wing sympathies, gradually came to accept the
"tragic" inevitability of Algerian independence. It was not an easy process
for many socialist leaders and intellectuals, among them many academics,
or for writers such as Algerian-born Albert Camus, who never could really
give up the idea of a French Algeria. But many others, including the most
prestigious, notably Sartre, opposed from the beginning a war waged
against a national liberation movement. It has been suggested that Sartre's
1960 play *Les séquestrés d'Altona* was more about the French situation in
Algeria than about Germany and that, as Henri Peyre writes in the
introduction, "a few implications in this story of torture, of an anguished
conscience, and of the soldier's conflict between his scruples and his duty
of obedience suggest that audiences may discover analogies between
Altona and Algeria."[37] As scandalous instances of French Army brutality
and torture became better known, left-wing intellectuals battled both the
right wing and a procrastinating government, denouncing the political
and human "tragedy" of the war.

The tense atmosphere in France endured for several years after Algerian independence. Although Algeria became a taboo issue, not to be
debated explicitly, the wounds it inflicted festered on. The suppression of
material about Algeria was so successful that documentary information
was still lacking in 1972, ten years after peace prevailed.[38] But the French
people did not forget what they had once learned or were still suspecting.
For Benedetto and Gatti, when they were writing their Vietnam plays, the
French war in Algeria was not part of a remote past; it was an integral
feature of their memorial experience, still meaningful and explosive precisely because it could not be discussed in public. Viewed from their
ideological perspective, it could only be perceived to have been as unwar-
ranted, unbearable, and "wrong" as the American war in Vietnam. One
understands why Todd, sensitive to the French political climate, could
assume a priori that *Napalm* must refer to Algeria as well as to Vietnam. In
fact, when one rereads the play in that light, and substitutes "French
colonialism" for "American imperialism," one discovers that many remarks on stage could apply to French Algeria as well as to American
Vietnam, and that Benedetto's ruthless censure of U.S. policies could
express very well a frustrated need to settle accounts with French chauvinism and colonialism. The correlation between the two wars is not developed in the play, but can be intuited. The question then is: What may have
prevented Benedetto from consciously following, or acknowledging, a
hidden Algerian agenda?

Part of the answer surely lies in the influence that the government's
constraining policy exerted on him, and on theatre in general, and in the
psychological fragility of citizens confronting the pressure of the state. The
censorship—external and internalized—that French authorities had been

imposing on reports on the military operations in Algeria was not perfect, working rather better in the visual than in the printed media.[39] But it did create a climate of restraint that, with tacit public approval, silenced for many years the discussion of what had taken place in Algeria. The Algerian-Italian-French coproduction *The Battle of Algiers,* perhaps the best known film about the war, shown abroad as early as 1966, was not seen in France till 1970.[40] It was a fiction disguised to look like a documentary, as well as vice versa, in part because few actual documentary materials were available. In 1967, when Benedetto and Gatti were writing their Vietnam plays, it was still embarrassing, even daring and illegal, to refer in public to the French atrocities in Algeria, to criticize French policies, and to display sympathy for Algerians, let alone to express solidarity with them. Like Americans for several years after the end of the Vietnam War, and like Germans after the end of World War II, the French needed time to allow their memory to heal—when it was no longer passively repressed and actively suppressed—before dealing with their Algerian past even in disguised forms.[41]

In the case of Benedetto, there was an additional reason why he and his audience would block any deeper feelings about the French guilt in Algeria. After all, he was living and working in Avignon, a southern city where practically everybody was closely related to some of the two million relocated *pieds noirs*—former French settlers in Algeria—who believed that they had been betrayed and victimized by the peace. To stage a play that could be construed as being sympathetic to the Algerian cause was unthinkable under these circumstances; it would have been received as a painful, tasteless, and counterproductive provocation. Even potentially illegal. On the other hand there was little risk in producing a French play about the ongoing American war in Vietnam. It offered Benedetto the possibility to hurdle the psychological block against an exposure of French war in Algeria and the external constraints of continuing censorship. In any case, even though *Napalm* certainly should not be *reduced* to a consciously coded esoteric political allegory about Algeria, one may assume that Benedetto's more or less conscious feelings of outrage about Algeria did nurture his staged denunciation of U.S. aggression of Vietnam halfway around the globe, tapping into similar feelings of his audience.

The title *Napalm* is deceptively simple. Two years earlier, near the end of Pontecorvo's *The Battle of Algiers,* French Army officers (depicted as having "served in Indochina" and as fretting that "Algiers will be another Dien Bien Phu") stage a press conference about a captured "terrorist" on March 4, 1957. It becomes clear on that occasion that "Napalm" is being used on the civilian and peasant population in Algeria. It is this horrific substance, this quintessential product of the multinational, but especially American, military-industrial complex that forms the international bridge—on the "stage" both of warfare and of the theatre—between the United States, Vietnam, Africa, and France. If, in the mid to late 1960s,

Erich Fried could si(gh)t—directly—"Vietnam as Germany," then the French could si(gh)t—indirectly—"Vietnam as France." Napalm is dropped from jet planes, and the Algerians, like the Vietcong, had none.

3. HUMANISM VERSUS TECHNOLOGY

In its main orientation, Gatti's *V comme Vietnam* follows Benedetto's line in *Napalm;* it too denounces the U.S. government as the aggressor in a war that the Vietnamese will eventually win. Gatti, however, is less interested than Benedetto in the politics of American imperialism, and perhaps for that reason offers a more complex image of the U.S. authorities. His Mégasheriff (Johnson) is not merely a tough imperialist totally dedicated to the pursuit of American domination; he has genuine qualms about the death and suffering caused by war and actually looks forward to the peace. Yet the true power behind most decisions is Quadrature— an intelligent, lucid, and persuasive man who has little in common with his counterpart in Benedetto's play, the more monodimensional and conventionally imperialistic McNamara. Quadrature is not motivated by imperialism nor by military ambitions. His approach is purely functional: taking the war as a given, somewhat as Mégasheriff does, without questioning its causes, meaning, and consequences, he sees it only as a problem to be solved in a technocratic fashion. In short, Gatti's depiction is closer to Weber than Marx. To the extent that it is Quadrature's war, the Vietnam War in *V comme Vietnam* seems to be, as he claims repeatedly, a very special war, unlike any other (Gatti 105). But is it really different? Or rather, what makes that war unique? What sort of war is shown on stage to result from Quadrature's Weberian approach? What sort of special war is waged by an America that is embodied in Quadrature rather than in Mégasheriff? What can be the reasons for a war that has no political or personal motivations behind it?

Some answers are not difficult to find in the play, others are. The specificity of *V comme Vietnam* among Vietnam Protest Plays lies in the portrayal of the Vietnam conflict as a struggle between two *cultures*, or types of *civilization*, rather than between two countries or states. On the one side, represented by the United States, stands a powerful, materialistic, rational, scientific, highly mechanized modern society that relies on the precise computation of data taken to be objective; it distrusts or disregards the influence of human input. On the other side, represented by Vietnam, stands a simple, quite primitive but humane society that lives close to nature and upholds spiritual values—much like Rousseau's noble savage, or at least his caricature. Gatti's staging stresses that opposition: the White House scenes display high-tech television screens and computer terminals while the Vietnam scenes evoke, with a minimum of props, rice fields and farming villages. Everything is calculated in America and experienced indirectly: The invasion of Vietnam is first rehearsed at a distance on

California's coast, then set in motion in Vietnam and reported by machines that are deprived of a feeling of reality. In contrast, the Vietnamese people (and a few Americans who participate in the military operations) are fragile, almost disembodied beings who, stepping out alive from the computer screens, convey another aspect of the tragedy of war. The overall theme is clearly the modernist antagonism between machine and man. Quadrature's war, whether he realizes it or not, is waged on behalf of the forces of the machine: i.e., on behalf of an American society irrevocably committed to build a technological civilization and to spread it to the rest of the world. In comparison with that overall techno-imperialist commitment, other goals—political conquest or defense against communism—must appear to be epiphenomenal or secondary.

The basic plot of *V comme Vietnam*—the story of Quadrature's war—is informed by this paradigm shift from (French) colonialism to (global) technology. In the White House, each available bit of war information is fed into the giant computer—La Châtaigne—which processes it into bites along with all sorts of other data, calculates the probable outcome of military decisions, and reduces costs in human lives to financial statistics: "Didn't our electronic brains compute that [in 1965] each killed Vietcong costs us 500,000 dollars?" (Gatti 12). La Châtaigne is the technical equivalent of Quadrature, and hence in a sense it is figured as the real protagonist not only of this play but of staging the war. According to La Châtaigne's computations, scientifically tested in the mock Californian experiment or model, the military invasion of Vietnam will succeed initially, and indeed it does move ahead more or less as predicted. Yet, warns Théo, a psychologist, no matter how perfect the blueprint, "there is always something in man that rebels" (Gatti 105). Because computerized planning does not account for "the human element," the conquest of Vietnam not only creates disturbing concrete problems but also projects their solution into an uncertain future, making their ultimate resolution problematic at best.

As *V comme Vietnam* progresses, American officials become more and more frustrated with Vietnamese (human) resistance, and even Pentagon experts, ironically falling back on their merely biological intelligence, begin to realize that something is wrong with a system that relies exclusively or mainly on artificial intelligence. "My instinct tells me," acknowledges psychologist Théo, "that the situation is different from what we get from our figures" (Gatti 111). The officials naturally seek a material explanation—a secret weapon invented by the Vietnamese—and identify it as the legendary "board of nails" which, as a symbol of resistance, immobilized the bicycles of the French Army at Dien Bien Phu (Gatti 76).

General Bulldog, perhaps speaking here for Gatti himself, summarizes the situation with a barely ironic formula: "Two weapons are competing: the hydrogen bomb of the civilized and scientific world—and the board of nails of the peasant in the rice field" (Gatti 27). But because Mégasheriff refuses to use the nuclear bomb, the civilized world, denied the full use of its technology, cannot prevail with conventional weapons against the moral superiority of the Vietnamese. (The argument that, without the use of full technology, notably nuclear weaponry, America always "fights with one hand tied behind its back" was not only often said aloud during the Vietnam War but also whispered occasionally during Operation Desert Storm in the Gulf.) In his role as human spokesman (and theoretician) of modern civilization, Quadrature is quite right when he complains: "I repeat that this war is not like any other—and [yet] we are doing what the others are doing" (Gatti 11). The reason why the machine fails to destroy man, Gatti seems to suggest, is that the Americans, including Mégasheriff, are not entirely devoid of human feelings: Much as they might like to impose Huxley's vision of a brave new world, they lack ruthlessness: a momentarily fortunate but not totally reassuring circumstance.

Gatti's contrast between a mechanical and a humane civilization is not very original. Related to the well-known opposition between "two cultures," scientific and humanistic, it has been criticized as a cliché. It could be significant that this reproach was most sharply couched in a review of the play in a mainstream German newspaper:

> He [Gatti] is not only concerned with denouncing an unjust war, he proclaims at the same time the victory of the simple man over technology. This however, is a false generalization. It results in a romantic and reactionary distortion, a denunciation not only of war technology but of technology in general.[42]

Germany was at that time in the process of completing its second industrial renaissance—its "economic miracle"—and hence perhaps was particularly sensitive to technophobia and criticism of technical progress. Whatever its inspiration, however, the review is largely correct: Gatti's protest against the American war in Vietnam tends to be overshadowed by his denunciation of an American civilization; he criticizes less the injustice of the war than its technologization. The war is "wrong" mainly because it is a technological war, as if war were ever really human. This theme and the staging it requires generate the significance of the play within the canon of Vietnam Protest Theatre.

The French concern for the preservation of a humane civilization in the age of technology is found not only in *V comme Vietnam*. In *Napalm* Benedetto also articulates the U.S. military imperialism with cultural imperialism, and he warns against the unchecked expansion of an American civilization that promotes and embodies modern consumerism. His Johnson is dangerous because he sincerely believes that the superiority of the American way of life justifies the war: "We are civilization, McNamara! And we are defending ourselves" (Benedetto 152). But Benedetto's Johnson is primarily motivated by political goals. Gatti's humanist argument is much more explicit. La Congrégation, a high official in his play who stands for the Church, specifically locates the cause of war in the American duty to defend the ideal civilization, i.e., American civilization. "The Vietnam War is a war in defense of Civilization. It was forced upon us; we cannot yield to tyranny. Any outcome other than victory is unthinkable" (Gatti 45). This is also Mégasheriff's belief, made all the more disturbing and ominous because of the apparently genuine goodwill and idealism of the American president who believes that the Vietnamese will "wake up" one day and say, "I give up because things are really nice on the other side" (Gatti 121).

The obsessive focus on "civilization" is not surprising in the French plays. It anticipates the notorious attacks against American cultural imperialism made a dozen years later by Jack Lang, then French minister of culture. Indeed, for centuries France has promoted its image as the most highly civilized country, excelling in arts and refined living. Bringing "civilization" to "less advanced" people has been a traditional French mission, notably invoked to justify former colonial conquests.[43] At the time of the Algerian War, even when the atrocities of the French Army became better known, many protesters "continued to express the greatest confidence in the fundamental benevolence and superiority of the French spirit and in France's role in the world as a disseminator of civilization."[44] This myth was only exploded in December 1991, when *Le Monde* finally disclosed that, on the 17th of October 1961, more than two hundred Algerians were killed by the police during a protest rally in Paris, and their bodies were thrown into the Seine. The 2.3 million returning veterans came home to silence, much as American's Vietnam veterans were to do years later.

The distinct French agenda in Benedetto's and Gatti's plays reflects in sum an ambiguous view of American imperialism, manifesting two diverging perspectives. On the one hand, assimilating American imperialism to French colonialism, the French playwrights are ready to share at least some guilt for war in Vietnam (and Algeria?). In that sense, their plays do settle accounts with their own national past. On the other hand, both playwrights (Gatti more than Benedetto) condemn American imperialism because, in contrast to French humanism, it is a manifestation of a technologically and mechanically aggressive "civilization." They defend "French" values, clichéd or not.

Such a duality is certainly not unexpected within the context of French culture and cultural criticism. It throws little new light on general French attitudes toward Vietnam and the United States. But it does throw some new light on the "American" war in Vietnam. The French Vietnam Protest Theatre helps us to assess that war because it highlights aspects that have not been stressed elsewhere. Two features deserve to be mentioned in this context. First, there is the thesis about cyclic history: their insistence that the American war in Vietnam continued a long sequence of European colonial wars, that the United States was more of a colonial power than is usually admitted, and that the entire Vietnam story should be viewed as an episode in the vast history of colonialism. Second, there is the thesis that the Vietnam War was only an episode of a much vaster conflict between the old humanistic culture and the new technological civilization—not a properly American or Vietnamese tragedy at all, finally, but rather a manifestation of a worldwide tension between the human-oriented past and cyberspatial, cyborg future. Thus, the French Vietnam Protest Theatre is proleptically broaching a crucial problematic ambivalence of postmodern warfare as it is fast emerging at the turn of the twenty-first century. At stake also in the cyborg problematic is whether warfare is significantly "gendered" or is moving "beyond gender." On the one hand, one still finds the seemingly archaic need to transform young human subjects into fighting machines and "hard bodies" that are explicitly masculine and masculinist in orientation (though they are expected to repress or suppress any homoerotic charge). Those are the bodies in the boot camps that were staged in Terry's *Viet Rock* and that will reappear with a vengeance in Rabe's *Basic Training*. There is, however, a common perception (including the one held by Terry and Rabe's armored bodies) that a more "feminine" and "feminizing" world of computers, with more "fluid" modes of operation, is displacing the old war as usual, along with business as usual. Boot camp is being replaced by "booting up," so to speak. This point is made by Iain Chambers when he asks, "What if what we call 'reason' is historically gendered?" And he continues:

> The construction of artificial intelligence is clearly not a mental process, nor is the potential flexibility of open-ended programming and interfacing necessarily acknowledged, in the patriarchal rationalizations and vocabulary of computerese: "slave," "abort," "boot-up.". . . [It] is also the paradox of computers removing much of the physical muscle from military affairs, of apparently demasculinizing the war machine when it is software, as much as hardware, determining the outcome of conflict.[45]

And so it was that not the least contribution of Vietnam Protest Theatre to the post/modern consciousness was the attempt to articulate this problem at a relatively early date—by staging the television war as a "postgender" problem of technoculture.

By contrast, the German focus on traditionally Marxist and modernist concerns with political economy seems old-fashioned, as might also seem the more "subjective" and "humanist" concerns of American theatre, shared by the British and Austrian stage. On the other hand, however, the French fascination with technology—alternating as it does between technophilia and technophobia—tends to make unclear the politico-economic determinations that they intuitively posit between such world-historical events as colonialization, imperialism, humanism, technology, and, not least, the *continued* threat of war(s).

Mis/representing the
Inappropriate/d Other

"All reification is forgetting." (Adorno) Art fights reification by making the petrified world speak, sing, perhaps dance. . . . Auschwitz and My Lai, the torture, starvation, and dying—is this entire world supposed to be "mere illusion" and "bitterer deception"? It remains rather the "bitterer" and all but unimaginable reality. . . . Authentic art preserves this memory in spite of and against Auschwitz; this memory is the ground in which art has always originated—this memory and the need to create images of the possible "other."   —Herbert Marcuse

PART
TWO

To be inappropriate/d does not mean "not to be in relation with"—that is, to be outside appropriation by being in a special reservation, with the status of the authentic, the untouched, in the allochronic and allotropic condition of innocence. Rather, to be an "inappropriate/d other" means to be in critical, deconstructive relationality—as the means of making potent connection that exceeds domination.
                —Donna Haraway

It is difficult to make a clear separation in most Vietnam Protest Plays between their assignment of guilt—who is to blame for the war and its horror?—and their representation of the horror that made that war scandalous and inspired the protest theatre in the first place. Simply to stage horror—often blurring the distinction between the illusion of actual horror and its ideological re/presentation—does not lead by itself to a clarification of the complex moral issue of responsibility. The latter inevitably involves not only individuals or even groups of individuals but also historical causes that can be staged only with extreme difficulty, if at all, due to their impersonal nature. Any theatre that exposes war takes the risk always to be somewhat at a loss about the precise nature of its target: Does it target one particular war or all the wars embodied in that one war? If war in general is targeted, then the concrete, historical specificity of the particular war in Vietnam may well somehow evaporate; and if Vietnam alone is

targeted, then its interconnections with the underlying social and economic causes of all wars could slip away. This tension, as well as other
often irreconcilable tensions—between morality and pragmatics, between
the particular visible and the abstract invisible—are of course endemic to
all representational art, perhaps to art per se (not to mention the writing
and criticism of theatre history).[1]

Here, I intend to pursue the specific ways that Vietnam Protest Theatre
struggled to negotiate the particular/general war tension and to stage it.
But, since that tension cannot be resolved, at least not on stage, it takes on
a "tragic" quality. Theatre faces the apparent failure to solve the
irresolvable, and yet it has no choice but to try again and again. This part
of *Vietnam Protest Theatre: The Television War on Stage* will pay particular
attention to the way that the representation of the "other"—i.e., "the
need," in Marcuse's words, "to create images of the possible 'other'"—is
staged in terms of atrocities committed against the "them" that sometimes
turn out, uncannily enough, to be "us." This part is divided into two
related but analytically distinct and contrasting chapters: "Performative
Sub-Missions" and "American I-Witnesses."

As has been seen, the indictment of governments and ideologies held
to be responsible for the war was hardly a mere exercise in historical or
academic justice; rather, growing from a painful awareness of the "tragedy" that took place in Vietnam, it was intended, directly or indirectly, to
pressure the guilty parties to bring an end to the war for which support
was dwindling. To achieve that goal, the protest plays had to show that the
guilt was indeed intolerable, that the horror in Vietnam could not be
dismissed as a regrettable but inevitable feature of any war, that the
responsible parties in Vietnam carried out activities that exceeded the
conventional "tragedy" of all wars. But did they really? Were these atrocities perhaps only better known than others because they were more
mediatized and/or staged than previously? In which case, the "first
television war" would be just another variant of general war and would
appear to be inevitable and hence "tragic" in the sense that it would seem
useless to try to prevent War ("the father of all things," as Heraclitus said).

We might then say that the Vietnam "tragedy" intersects more generally with, at least, three overlapping sets of distinction that are rarely made
clear in the plays themselves but that inform them nonetheless. One
distinction must be made between the representation of horror and the
assignation of responsibility for it. Another distinction concerns the already mentioned tension between war in general and a particular war that
is deemed somehow more excessive than others. And a third distinction
can be observed between references to more or less objective grounds
necessary to justify ending the war (or wars) and the more particular
references that produce propaganda rather than (or in addition to) factual
knowledge—in short, the basic distinction between "documentary fact"
and "creative license."

Keeping in mind these distinctions, I will try to determine what aspects of the Vietnam War were stressed on the stage as being particularly revolting, regardless of their ideological or political connotations. What scenes and images, in other words, were or may still be expected to cause the most effective outrage in a large number of spectators? The attempt to answer that question yields the observation that only a few selected features of the war were considered, consciously or not, to be dramatically objectionable. Indeed, the repertoire of "tragic" images and scenes proves to have been remarkably small—a veritable closed economy of possible signs that was rarely if ever identified as such in the plays or by their critics. The operation of such a relatively limited pool from which to draw illustrations of horror suggests the existence of an unacknowledged consensus among the playwrights, a kind of deep structure of quasi-archetypal images that cuts across otherwise very different plays and types of play. Identifying the most prevalent of these "tragic" images, and the reasons why they were selected by playwrights, helps explain not only why the Vietnam War was judged to be a "wrong war" but also what features could help in turning any war into another "wrong war" in the future. Of particular interest in this regard is that, very often, it is through scenes depicting atrocities against the "other" that the "we" are defined, and it is *only* through such scenes that the "other" comes to be constructed—violently—in the first place. A strange, even horrific thought: to be able to imagine "our" "other" only at the moment of voyeuristically witnessing that "other's" death or mutilation.

Shown as instigators much more often than as victims of the war, Americans are commonly assigned in the plays an active role that includes generating most forms of this violence. No doubt Americans, especially GIs, are occasionally shown as "tragic" victims, but the "evil" that victimizes them, most notably in the later plays, tends to originate among themselves, or among their leaders, rather than in the Vietcong. On the other hand, as obvious targets of the U.S. aggression, the Vietcong are systematically characterized as victims of violence inflicted upon them by the American war machine. Their own acts of violence, occasionally reaching extreme levels, are usually explained by some previous American violence and hence minimized; besides, they are rare. This diverging treatment, corresponding to the one-sided attribution of guilt, discloses the perception of two very different forms of "evil" in Vietnam. First, principally affecting the Americans, an *internal degradation* of the GIs, leading in some cases to their death; second, more exclusively affecting the Vietnamese, a violent physical destruction of their fighters and civilians— that is, *external atrocities* involving bombs, napalm, and so on. Both internal degradation and external atrocities illustrate the horror of the war but with a different impact on the audience, depending on where the play is performed. In Europe, playwrights and spectators could be expected to be more strongly moved by the atrocities carried out by Americans than by the internal degradation that they may suffer.

This dual approach expresses a dual perspective from which the playwrights viewed the two parties involved in the war. In the case of the Americans, a special consideration is given to the diversity of national images: active soldiers—idealistic and decent, or brutal and sadistic; victims—stultified, suffering, or dying; machines—marching or killing automatons; social rejects—angry, violent, despairing; objects of manipulation and/or active subjects of aggression. The composite picture—at least in the American plays but also in some European, possibly as a projection of their own military past—sometimes looks like an intimate self-portrait of America, sometimes merely a caricature. In contrast, the Vietcong, especially on the U.S. stage, are seen from the distant perspective that is traditionally reserved for the "other"—an "other" who, whether enemy or friend, always remains different, remote, somehow threatening yet usually also somehow inferior or "inscrutable." With the partial exception of some European plays, this "other" is viewed from the outside looking in at an imagined "inside," with neither real understanding nor true empathy, even when "it" seeks to evoke momentary sympathy. As "others," the Vietnamese thus tend to be portrayed as archetypal victims: tortured, shot, bombed, and burned with impunity, often without valid justification (especially in the case of women and children), or "simply" humiliated, exploited, corrupted into prostitution and drugs. Their role as stubborn, but worthwhile, enemies requires that they have a certain moral power, and indeed some plays attribute to them those aspects of strength that have been customarily granted to the "other": large numbers, stealth, cruelty, cunning, and other features of their "oriental *nature*." Other plays, however, stress their idealism and human decency, often in ironic contrast to the American veneer of "occidental *civilization*."

The issues of guilt and of the overall portrayal of Americans (or Europeans) and Vietnamese as "us" and "them," respectively, have a direct influence on the choice of images of horror evoked in and by the plays. Yet there is another and perhaps more significant factor that must be taken into account to explain that choice: difficulties inherent in any attempt to convey intense horror in a public art form. This problem has been much debated since the appearance of the first films about the Holocaust or Shoah: How indeed can an artist represent that which is believed to be fundamentally unrepresentable without oversimplifying and thus undermining its horror, reducing it to a more or less commodified banality?[2] For Edmund Burke, like Kant later, the fundamentally unrepresentable Sublime had its deepest root in *terror*, though not all terror was Sublime.[3] Many related objections to the filmic representation of the unrepresentable stem from moral issues: They protest against the distortion of the meaning of horror and its transformation into an artificial, and hence unreal, commercialized image.[4] Hollywood has no particular technical difficulty in showing (re/creating or creating) atrocities committed in Vietnam and thus in eliciting strong emotional responses from the audience.[5] All mimesis, notes Michael Taussig, operates in a dual fashion: it copies what it shows, but it also unites the viewer with the viewed, producing "copy fusing with contact."[6] But that same Hollywood audience sooner or later becomes jaded or anaesthetized by the very sight of horror against which it was supposed to fight.[7]

In theatre, the representation of horror is problematic in another way. Realistic illusion can be carried out by live actors only as long as it is confined to action that can indeed take place on the stage; in marginal cases, such as certain sexual acts or crimes, "tricks" normally serve to deceive the eye of the spectators.[8] Yet even the most successful theatre "magic" is more limited than films: no mass bombing, no flaming napalm, neither fragmented nor burned bodies can be simulated on the stage with any real or lasting pretense of verisimilitude. To be sure, these events can be stylized and/or transposed into more obviously artistic forms; for example, many protest plays, such as *Viet Rock*, conveyed mass killings with group pantomime. Nonetheless, the direct emotional impact of such scenes, filtered through aesthetic responses and/or intellectual understanding, risks becoming detached from their truly horrific source in reality. The ensuing loss of immediate reaction to staged horror would not matter much if Vietnam Protest Plays sought merely to tell the story of the war from a distance, as did much of the documentary theatre that, after World War II, re/created the story of the atomic bomb or the Nazi extermination camps long after the fact.[9] But Vietnam Protest Plays were intended to create a direct political response to an ongoing war here and now, and the stimulation of a strong reaction to the images of real horror was an important part of their strategy. In many plays, the stylization of horror was supplemented with photographs, newsreels, radio, or narratives chosen to intensify and galvanize the (potential) impact on the audience. Other plays, giving up on direct stimulation, obviously relied mainly on reflection and a thoughtful grasp of an overall poetic "truth" of the war, with a stress on the central part that horror must always play in it. Illustrating these and other strategies, the plays' manifold "Vietnam" always operated within these generic strictures.

The main theme, however, remains the complex dual articulation in these plays between "the other" and the way this "other" (not only the North Vietnamese and Vietcong but also South Vietnamese allies and the American military of color) appears—and sometimes appears *only*—in atrocity scenes, and the way that both this "other" and its mis/representation (through horror) generate ways of thinking about the *difference*, whether this difference could be racial, sexual, gender, national, ideological, economic, or whatever. The more specific problem here is the following: the supposedly unrepresentable "other" appears, and then immediately disappears, in scenes in which it is constructed in the first place, which means it is constructed only in the context of unspeakable or otherwise unrepresentable atrocities committed against it. In other words, no sooner do we catch a glimpse of an imagined "other" than it is destroyed or maimed, and so recedes back not merely into the (empirical) unrepresent*ed* but the (theoretical) unrepresent*able* as well.

PERFORMATIVE
SUB-MISSIONS

Atrocities perpetrated against the "other"—creating him or her only in
this process of submission—are staged differently throughout Vietnam
Protest Theatre. For example, in Brook's *US* they tend to fall into two
distinct categories: first, the tortures carried out by individual Americans;
and second, as somewhat later in Benedetto and Gatti, depersonalized
bombing.[1] The first instance occurs when, in silence:

> actors run to positions in groups of 3. Two grab the third and prepare to torture
> him . . . one group by holding his head underwater, another by battering his
> head on a wall, another by kicking him. (Brook 80)

The scene is followed by a reporter's question about the difference between physical and mental torture, and the torturers find no moral distinction. During the entire sequence, on the screen at the back of the stage, a photo is projected of a Vietnamese lying on his stomach and being brutalized. As could be expected, the silent torturers are all U.S. servicemen. A second, more violent torture scene, this time with an accompanying dialogue, is acted out a few minutes later. The two scenes are related not only by similarity but also by a progressive dramatization. Brook evokes torture in bits (a mime, an interview, and a photograph), then synthesizes it in the fuller audiovisual medium that increases its effect of brutality.

To hit his second target—bombing—Brook employs a character reminiscent of Benedetto's Charles Whitman: a pilot who gleefully describes his delight in chasing Vietnamese with his plane and dropping napalm on them. His one regret is "that he can't go into an area they've just raided and see the effects of the napalm" (Brook 84). In a sense, one might suppose that Brook's own *US* is expected, as theatre of representation, to redress this historical inability to show the audience truth, which TV notably failed to do or do adequately. This scene is probably derived from the infamous "Zappin' the Cong" song; it is repeated with variations four times, pounding the message into the heads of the audience. In a later sequence, a reporter comes back to the topic of bombing when he interviews an Air Force colonel:

> At Ban Sang, 55 B52s went in and dropped so many hundred tons of bombs, so many hundred tons of napalm, so many hundred tons of CS5 . . . and you do not know whether the VC were there or not? (Brook 100-101)

The reference to CS5, a toxic pesticide, originates no doubt in the (occasionally) publicized U.S. use of illegal chemical weapons. But it is also possible to detect in it a smoldering memory of heavy casualties that poisonous gas inflicted on British troops in World War I. (Since World War II was, surprisingly enough, relatively free of such poison gas used against humans, with the obvious exception being Zyclon B, Brook could be suggesting that Vietnam has leapfrogged back to the originary brutality of "the war to end all wars.") At any rate, as a result of the raid evoked in *US*, more than a hundred civilians were actually killed in Ban Sang, countless more wounded. The slide shows U.S. military standing and counting a mass of corpses, presumably as a "body count." The use of photographic evidence (reminiscent of photos taken by Allied troops who had liberated Nazi concentration and death camps) on stage each time Brook refers to an atrocity unmistakably serves not only to substantiate the validity of the reference but also to magnify its staged horror. The "seeing is believing" becomes in Brook's play "seeing is reacting." The slide brings documentary "reality" to theatre illusion and entertainment, in the perhaps naive expectation that the photographed bodies of the Vietnamese victims will rouse the British public in protest against the excesses of the American war machine.

Strangely enough, there are few typical "oriental others" in *US*. Vietnamese characters appear on the stage only in the beginning scenes that retell the early history of North and South Vietnam. The last Vietnamese physically on stage is a young woman who, in the role of victim, laments her husband's departure for war. She is obviously intended to be a sympathetic character. In general, albeit fleetingly portrayed, the Vietnamese are shown to be an appealing people, struggling to eke out their meager existence in a country ravaged by war: they bear no resemblance to, say, Gatti's "savages." Later in *US*, when the United States invades Vietnam, no further live Vietnamese characters enter the stage. This absence suggests not only figuratively that there are no longer any individual Vietnamese alive but also that an independent Vietnam no longer exists. Even more: It would seem that the United States has obliterated and effaced all traces of its "other" through its invasion. The only remaining Vietnamese now visible to the audience are *slides* projected on the back of the stage: i.e., mediated, mediatized, teichoscopic *images* taken from the battlements of the dead "other." With the use of disembodied photographs, it is as if theatre as a somatic medium had reached its maximum limit. It must turn to other media, perceived (rightly or wrongly) as more "real" or "truthful" or "effective," in order to push its political message forward. The consequences for Brook's attempt in *US* to link the "other" with "us" remains a vexed question for other playwrights staging the Vietnam War, informing their missions of protest and, often, their submission to the magnitude of the problem of "the other."

1. *PINKVILLE* (TABORI)

The linguistic/national roots of George Tabori's *Pinkville* (1970) are particularly complex.[2] Born in Budapest in 1914, Tabori emigrated to London in 1939, his family was deported to Auschwitz during the war, and he came to the United States in 1943. Known for his writings and plays on the Holocaust—*Cannibals* (1968), *Jubiläum (1983), Peepshow* (1984), and more recently *Mein Kampf* (1987)—he eventually moved back to Europe where he has been a visiting director in Berlin, Munich, Vienna, and Krakow. *Pinkville* was originally written in English and first performed in an American theatre for American spectators. To that extent it may qualify as an "American" play rather than "European" although, at the present time, only the German version is available in print.

As the title suggests, Tabori's play concerns the My Lai and Son My massacres. "Pinkville" was at that time a common slang term used by GIs to refer to My Lai. In fact, much of Tabori's text uses actual quotes from the testimony of Americans involved in the Son My and My Lai trials. Tabori, like Szyszkowitz and others, presents innocent young Americans whom Nazi-like sergeants transform into killing machines. He openly indicts the entire U.S. military for the My Lai/Son My atrocity. Likely as a result, when it opened in New York in 1971 it shocked and offended many in the audience and received negative reviews. *Newsweek* expressed a conservative aesthetic perspective and complained that "bad art is like DDT; it hurts and sickens those it aims to serve."[3] Clive Barnes at the *New York Times* deemed it fitting to observe that "this is not Nazi Germany, or Soviet Russia, for in those circumstances Mr. Tabori could never have produced his play, which is a most savage indictment of American militarism."[4] Even more moderate reviewers felt that Tabori was overstating the facts and was therefore not as convincing as he might have been,[5] that his "heart is in the right place . . . (but) his sinuses seem to be stuffed up with clichés."[6] On the other hand, even critics who generally agreed that *Pinkville* "appears largely to beat a dead dramatic horse" (one may wonder to what "dead horse" the critic was referring, since the Vietnam War was certainly not yet dead in 1971) conceded nevertheless that "the staging is fresh, new and alive"[7] and that it represented "an exciting advance in staging concept."[8] In short, *Pinkville* was formally engaging, perhaps, but thematically and ideologically misguided.

Less the message of *Pinkville*, it would thus seem, but rather the staging of the My Lai slaughter impressed the positive reviewers. They applauded director Martin Fried, who used the ripping up of Raggedy Ann dolls to symbolize the massacre of children.[9] They extolled Wolfgang Roth's "excellent set—complete with fences, rope ladders, bunk beds located at various angles and atmospheric lighting."[10] The play was also praised by Arthur Sainer in the *Village Voice* for its musical score and choreography by Anna Sokolow, who produced a "kind of formal dance piece." The overall acting was obviously strong, especially in the roles played by Michael Douglas and Raoul Julia, contributing to a generally high level of performance. The *Village Voice* dissented from the generally negative consensus, suggesting that the very quality of the performance detracted from its political message. Arthur Sainer concluded that "the movements are too good" and that the play was "too perfect," needing "open rough edges" instead of being "trapped by beautifully smooth enclosures."[11]

My Lai/Son My was an exemplary case of what Tabori considers to be the ultimate demonization of civilians in war. The theme of demonization first appeared in his earlier play *Cannibals*.[12] His experience as a victim of state-directed racial persecution provided Tabori with firsthand knowledge and motivation to be a writer. *Cannibals* exposes the dehumanization of inmates in Auschwitz: Jews, communists, homosexuals, and gypsies. First performed in 1968, *Cannibals* starts with two Auschwitz survivors reminiscing about the war. Their memories form a play-within-a-play that takes place in the extermination camp where, to survive, they eat one of their cell mates. At the end, one of the inmates dreams of an Asian child running through a rice paddy, its flesh burning. This brief allusion to Vietnam and its civilian victims becomes a central theme in *Pinkville*. Oddly enough the dreamer in *Cannibals* is actually comforted by his dream of communion.[13] It shows him that he is not alone to have violated a most basic taboo: cannibalization. In his words: "I was happy because I realized that everybody is a murderer, not only me, everybody, d'you hear?" (Tabori 1982, 264). Indeed, for Tabori, "everybody," even a victim of atrocity, can become the victimizer in the fatal process of dehumanization. Tabori, like poet Erich Fried, is also deeply concerned that images and facts of mass murder not be historicized into oblivion. This leads him to the problem of how to compare the atrocities in Vietnam with Auschwitz without trivializing the unspeakable magnitude of the latter. In part, Tabori rightly suggests, this terrible problem must be grappled with by audiences as much as by playwrights. This is to say that theatre audiences who have witnessed his *Jubiläum* are to "recollect" images of burning in *Pinkville*. *Jubiläum* was first performed in 1983, to commemorate the fiftieth anniversary of Hitler's ascent to power.[14] Here, the image of burning corpses recurs with a vengeance, not only as "Jews in Buchenwald" but as "Reds in Majdenek" and "cripples" in various KZs, etc. (Tabori 1983, 117). While My Lai is no longer explicitly mentioned, its uncanny presence is "felt" through the imagery by the audience who knows Tabori, as are the explicit references to the possibility of the recurrence of atrocities against the foreign, racially "other" workforce today in West Germany (134).

Tabori's special blend of a tragic view of the Vietnam War and smooth theatrical form is transmitted in a cabaret style. In the German version, the sergeant in the role of MC tells the audience—in neo-Brechtian verses— what they will see:

> Honourable audience! We are playing and showing
> The great historical performance of murder
> Company Charlie returns from the war
> With a shooting quota of four hundred hits
> We are singing, we are dancing, telling stories
> We want to throw light on the nature of this war
> and prove with God's gracious will:
> The art is eternal—the art to kill.
> In eight easy lessons, by which you will see
> How one commits a perfect massacre. (Tabori 55)

The "rehearsal" text opens without this totalizing voice. More in the tradition of American drama, it begins abruptly with a character, Native American Consequently Joe, scrubbing the floor.

The play in both versions is divided into seven episodes or lessons, progressing from the recruitment of future GIs in America and culminating in the My Lai massacre. The first few lessons, similar to Terry's *Viet*

Rock and to the opening half of Kubrick's *Full Metal Jacket* (1987), focus on the brutality of U.S. Army sergeants and their systematic demoralization and dehumanization of the recruits. The story centers on the transformation of Jerry, a religious youth drafted into the war. He reaches his breaking point when the sergeant takes his Bible from him and rips it to shreds. Jerry and his companions—Jock, Pothead, an African American named Honeychild, and the aforementioned Native American, Consequently Joe—are all portrayed as diversified but well-intentioned human beings who are gradually transformed into killers by distinctly Nazi-like sergeants. All Tabori's military in positions of real authority are white males who subscribe to the belief that "Every Dead body, that is not White, is a Vietcong" (Tabori 95).

At this point occurs a significant difference between the German and American versions. In the German, all the grunts are dehumanized at the same time and take an equal part in the slaughter of the Vietnamese. In the case of Consequently Joe this demonization is somewhat surprising because, as a Native American, he has long been aware of the white man's violence against other races, in films and on television:

> and he [his father] never let me go to the movies. Consequently I never saw a movie until Gary Cooper was dead. . . . And the first time we tuned in . . . there they was, the goddamn Indians, getting the shit beaten outa them by John Wayne and Barbara Stanwyck or something like that. (Tabori 81)

Yet, in this German version, Consequently Joe is credited with the highest body count among all the GIs: ninety-eight or ninety-nine corpses. On the other hand, in the American version, he is wounded and dies *before* the massacre takes place and is generally portrayed as very friendly with the Vietnamese, especially the children. In other words, the German text shows much more brutally that the ideology of the white male establishment erases all traditional racial or ethnic differences, uniting all the GIs in the fight against the "yellow" enemy. The allusion to political consensus in Hitler's Germany must have been obvious to the German audience. Additional references explicitly evoke the annihilation of the Jews by Nazi hands. This sheds ironic light on Clive Barnes's slap on Tabori's wrist in the *New York Times* that "this is not Nazi Germany." Tabori was not so sure either about current West Germany *or* even about the United States.

In the American version of *Pinkville*, the grunts have more distinct characters and there is room for dissent and reprieve. The Jock, a drug pusher from the 'hood, refuses to shoot innocent women and children. He sabotages the massacre and shoots himself in his leg—a way of getting out of the war. When he is addressing Americans, Tabori suggests that there is always a chance for protest and resistance, although at a price. Logically, then, the Jock story is missing from the grimmer German version where the victimizing "us" are uniformly set against the victimized "them." And how do the "them" look in the play? Since half of the action takes place in Vietnam, one could expect to have a number of Vietnamese characters on stage. However, the only Vietnamese that one sees are helpless women and children. Tabori is one of the few American Vietnam playwrights (to the extent that he can be called "American") who does not show Vietnamese guilty of treacherous brutality. Representing them only as helpless women and children (and no men whatsoever), he emphasizes their victim status. They are totally at the mercy of the GIs who kill, torture, and rape them at will. A young woman tries to run away but is caught and killed. But women who do not run away in order to demonstrate that they are friendly are also slaughtered. It is a "damned if you do and damned if you don't" double bind. Tabori's Vietnamese, reasonable and peaceful people, must expect no mercy from the irrational might of the U.S. Army. This binary reductionism, understandable in the context of Tabori's frustration with the lack of effective *political* protest against the war, does not necessarily make effective political *theatre*. This, too, is a serious generic double bind of Vietnam Protest Theatre.

Pinkville's crazed GIs learn that the Vietnamese, and by extension anyone outside the military "us," must be eliminated because they do not belong to the human race. Tabori implies that prejudices, which are always latent in American society, reach their explosion point during the war. Again, the United States, at least in My Lai, is rather closer to Nazi Germany for Tabori than for the *New York Times*. The soldiers in *Pinkville* have no more feelings of human solidarity than they did at My Lai. The narrow perspective from which they see and judge the "other" leads them to deny human qualities to all those whom they view as "different": enemies, other races, women. That excluding prejudice obviously harms those who suffer from it. But it also dehumanizes those who are prejudiced since they must condemn and discard, in their own nature, features that they censure as features of the "other": the right to be different, to assert independence, to question authority, to appear intuitive, irrational, and mysterious—in short, qualities stereotypically equated with "femininity."

The evil spawned by war, in Tabori's play, must be linked to a general sickness affecting all of American society and not only the sick American GIs. At the beginning of *Pinkville*, the mother of Jerry the Naz' (Nazarene? Nazi?—a wild choice) first formulates her accusation: "I gave you a good boy, and you turned him into a murderer." However, one then learns that Jerry was always a bit off. He spent time in a mental institution because of megalomania and, like Jesus of Nazareth, thought he was God. Later he becomes one of the most brutal killers at My Lai, like the worst of Nazis. Consequently, when the mother repeats her accusing words at the end of the play, one is prepared to see Jerry as an allegory of the whole United States, a nation that is also suffering from lethal delusions of grandeur. The war in Vietnam, viewed from that perspective, is not an anomaly, as so many would have the world believe, but an entirely natural product of the specifically American "sickness" that the French, who are equally willing to risk using disease as metaphor, called the American "cancer."

But this is not all Tabori has to say. Recall that the dehumanized Consequently Joe learned about the white man's violence against his race by watching films and television shows. Is his readiness to kill the Vietnamese influenced by these visual images of the inevitable supremacy of White America? Tabori seems to believe it. Throughout the play, he stresses the role of television in the aggressive promotion of cultural hegemony of the (white) United States. Television creates the image of enemies who can and must then be destroyed.[15] The "other" in that sense, as in the play's lead song, is indeed a "Television Baby." It is television that, for Tabori, carries out the "program"—in every sense—of the white establishment and publicizes the racial nature of the war in Vietnam.

Dialogues between the recruits show that all of them—black, white, Amerindian—hold television and popular films as their basic reference points. It is through mediatized images that they have any knowledge of history and tradition. Indeed, Tabori implies it is television that "recruits" Americans into history and for war. As we have seen, in *Facing West: The Metaphysics of Indian Hating and Empire Building*, Richard Drinnon argued that

> The massacres at My Lai and all the forgotten My Khes in Vietnam had a basic continuity with . . . all the Wounded Knees, Sand Creeks, and Bad Axes. The linkage of atrocities over time and space reveals underlying themes and fundamental patterns of the national history that lawmakers, generals, and so many of their compatriots were eager to forget.[16]

What has happened at My Lai, then, becomes a continuation of a mythical ritual deeply ingrained in the American mind, but at the time of Vietnam it was revived and reinforced by the media. Viewed in that light, *Pinkville* is also a critique of television and mediatized images in general. For this reason, too, Tabori reacts against the concept and reality of Vietnam as the "television war." For television propagates myths that serve the goals of imperialism and colonization. He also points to the numbing effects of mediatized images that no longer function as referents to reality but are spectacles to be consumed in and for themselves. In that spectacularized world, war is not waged on the battlefield but permeates all levels of the spectator's society, overlapping the cultural with the political economic.

Spectacularization, implies Tabori, charges still photographs as well as motion pictures with debilitating effect. In one of *Pinkville's* scenes the sergeant shows off to young recruits the photograph of a woman taken right before she was shot by U.S. troops. Tabori refers here to Ron Haeberle, one of the army photographers who won awards for his photos of My Lai villagers just before they were executed. Criticized for watching passively the scenes of horror in order to photograph them, Haeberle gave his extraordinary account of "the situation behind one of his most famous photographs, the image of a group of terrified women protectively huddling over their children. 'Guys were about to shoot these people,' he recalled. 'I yelled, "Hold it," and I shot my pictures. As I walked away, I heard the M16s open up and from the corner of my eye I saw bodies falling but I did not turn to look.'"[17] Tabori's sergeant offers comparable comments about his pictures: "'Klick' I don't look, I have learned to look without seeing. I look at them as if they were frozen hens in the Supermarket" (Tabori 78).

In the spirit of documentary theatre, much of Tabori's text uses actual quotes from testimonies of Americans involved in My Lai and other "incidents." However, the massacre is not *shown*, as it is in some of the Vietnam plays with photographs and media images, but is evoked with stylized theatrical means that include the aforementioned tearing apart Raggedy Ann dolls to represent the massacre of children. While Tabori uses written and verbal documents, there is no record of pictures or slides as part of his performances. Which may explain why, while the content of *Pinkville* was sharply criticized for its anti-American bias, the staging was not.

The highly theatrical nature of *Pinkville*, supported by an impressive staging and music, did indeed risk distracting the audience from a closer attention to its political message. The use of new forms may have been dictated by the subversive content of the Vietnam Protest Plays, and it certainly enhanced their theatrical effectiveness, but it may also have diminished, when it stressed theatricality too much, theatre's peculiar ability to offer a live/d experience and to create a new feel for other real events. Of course, whether our perception that all reality is in some meaningful way "staged" makes us *more* or rather *less* willing and able to intervene in history remains an open question. We cannot know how many spectators actually left *Pinkville* as antiwar activists,[18] but there is no doubt that Tabori wanted his spectators to leave with at least the memory that they had witnessed real protest, not a mere protest play.

2. FUCK NAM (KUPFERBERG)

Tabori's dramatic strategy testifies at once to an awareness of the perils inherent in excessive theatricality and also to an inability to avoid all of them. Some of the most innovative protest playwrights, from Megan Terry on, seemed rather to believe that the display of attractive staging would better hold audience interest in their play's message. Judging by the reception of their work, it seems that they were not wrong, perhaps because most spectators do need to switch often from the "story," especially a "tragic" story, to the "entertaining" show on the stage. Highly theatrical forms, and other features that distract from the ostensibly more "serious" themes of a play, can invite spectators to remove themselves from the evoked reality, and such a relief is particularly needed when that reality is depressing and disturbing. And sometimes perhaps—in theory at least—political messages can be slipped into the audience's minds while their synapses have been momentarily opened, so to speak, by "pure" entertainment, laughter, sexual desire, and other "distractions." In other cases, however, the distracting features may be indeed too distracting by their appeal or, conversely, by their scandalous nature, as may have been the case for The Performance Group's notoriously "lewd" *Dionysus in '69*. As a rule, however, Vietnam Protest Plays eschewed such low perfor- mance distraction, limiting obscenities and raw sex at most to a few short scenes, verbal allusions, or images. But in one important play, a low form of relief was promoted systematically and brutally, with the result that its potential audiences paid little attention to its other staging strategies and, perhaps, to its message. I refer to Tuli Kupferberg's *Fuck Nam* (1967).[19]

Fuck Nam was never produced in the United States but enjoyed perfor- mances in London, Sweden, and West Germany.[20] Like *Viet Rock*, it may appear disjointed and fragmented, but unlike *Viet Rock* it displays a biting, irreverent spirit, combining images of sexual outrage with images of death in Vietnam.[21] The title is obviously designed to shock the public, as was the British poster that coupled an American flag with a spurting penis. The same erotico-political shock effect is sought within the play in scenes that show American soldiers who masturbate while watching dying children and women in the bombed village of Phoc Nam[22] or who rape and sodomize Vietnamese women in a village café. Cannibalism is also de- picted. Sodomization scenes in particular suggest that *everybody* in Viet- nam was getting "fucked up the ass." Such tactics may have succeeded in shocking some spectators, but they also undermined the aesthetic value of the play and hence, more important, discouraged wider audiences. As P.W.B. noted in a review in 1969, anticipating the oblivion into which *Fuck Nam* was quick to sink:

> As a comment on Vietnam, "Fucknam" makes its point, and the final cannibal- istic scene well emphasizes the blindness of the Americans in prolonging the war, but as a piece of writing it is lacking. This piece is shock tactics, not writing, and the author belongs to the half of the underground which will fade away fast.[23]

The association between sexual violence and death is explained by Kupferberg as an attempt to connect the "sexual frustration of the U.S. and the aggression of the U.S. Marines in Vietnam" (interview). The same connection, one notes, also occurs in Grant Duay's *Fruit Salad*, where Cherry and Banana die while locked in homosexual embrace, and in David Rabe's *Streamers*, where homosexuality leads to death. As such, of course, the link between sex (Eros) and death (Thanatos) is hardly original; it extends to the sources of Western tradition[24] and in mainstream theatre as far back as *Oedipus Rex*. (More specifically, we are uncomfortably close as well to the highly debatable equation of fascism with repressed gay sexuality.) But Kupferberg gives a particularly crude twist to the canon, intending even less to shock the audience than to stun it. To maximize this effect, he polarizes the action of his play between two locales that stand respectively for sex and death: a brothel where the GIs indulge in their sexual excesses, and the battlefields in the "country" where they kill.[25] One may recall an antiwar slogan of the time, a particularly vicious version of "orientalism": "Join the Army. Go to interesting places. Meet [read: fuck literally] interesting people. Kill [read: fuck metaphorically] them."

A different, if more expected, type of polarization divides the characters into two groups contrasted as veritable Angels and Devils: the Vietnamese—bar girls, Napalm Sue, the Vietcong, the café owner—and the Americans—sergeants, a colonel, his wife and his daughter, GIs, and a newspaper cameraman. There is no doubt as to where Kupferberg's sympathies and antipathies lie, and this very obviousness is part of both the interest and the problem of *Fuck Nam*. His Americans are probably more uniformly sadistic (with one problematic exception) than the Americans in any other protest play. Their "perversion" is supposed to reflect the "depravity" of the entire U.S. establishment, if not political unconscious, led by President Lyndon B. de Sade. In that sense, one could argue, GIs have always already been contaminated—even "tragically" predestined—by The System, and their perversion (like Jerry the Naz's megalomania) only required the catalyst of the Vietnam War to reach its full development, its most sadistic symptoms. Paradoxically, then, the violent but sick Kupferberg GIs *also* qualify as victims of the war (fucked, figuratively), engaging in their abhorrent behavior (including lethal fucking, literally) as by-product or cause of their own "tragedy."

Within this general sense of outrage, one special point is particularly problematic: the strong element of homophobia that appears to be in evidence throughout the play (though it is symptomatically unclear whether Kupferberg is *reflecting* or rather *reinforcing* this potentially deadly stereotype). At least as it is written, the play does tend to demonize sodomy as the primary trope for the evils of the Vietnam War—a clearly provocative tack that is or ought to be unacceptable for many.

More generally, but perhaps less offensively, Kupferberg's portrayal of the GIs displays all the signs of a bestiality marked by a lack of restraint, moral or social, in the satisfaction of the basest appetites. The main (not to say only) interests of the soldiers are alcohol, whores, and drugs—all viewed as means to relieve existential boredom. Even their drunken dreams do not rise above low-culture clichés, as in the stumbling Private Nero's phantasms: "I wanta get me a Rockette. I wanna fuck me a Rockette!" (Kupferberg 15). On a daily basis, when relatively sober, their interaction with the Vietnamese is shot through with racist prejudices; the tavern waiter is always a "Fuckn gook creep" (Kupferberg 15). They are brutal and cruel toward the local women/whores whom they force to perform a variety of sexual acts against their will. The "cowboy versus Indian" theme, treated historically in other protest plays, is updated here in a crude sado-sexual form and brought on the stage: the GIs "ride" Vietnamese girls and compel them to cry "ride'em, Cowboy! Ride'em!" while they sodomize them despite their desperate pleading: "No, No, not in the ass!" (Kupferberg 20).

All these forms of violence and domination are attributed to *white* soldiers. *Black* soldiers, it would seem, form an exception proving the rule. They appear to be more sympathetic toward the Vietnamese, and neither kill nor abuse them, presumably out of racial solidarity. On the other hand, they too are shown to be bestial and brutal in other respects. In a racial brawl between the GIs, black soldiers overpower white soldiers and seek to demonstrate their superiority by sodomizing *them*. "Two black soldiers are fucking white soldiers up the ass & two white soldiers are blowing two black soldiers" (Kupferberg 23). On either side of the white/black divide sexual cruelty and "perversions" are thus linked to racism in the overall condemnation of war "sickness." Enigmatically, in this specific area, Kupferberg appears to *deny* that American GIs taken as a group could ever be viewed as potential victims. They may be misled by their leaders, or contaminated by a general mental sickness, but they are as willing to participate in racial violence as the Nazis were in Germany, as the following—remarkably high-brow—doggerel makes clear:

> Trained to Live for the Führer's goals
> Trained to deal with Jews and Poles
> Men who fight like Jürgen Stroop
> Courage take from the SS Troop. (Kupferberg 29)

U.S. war reporters are just as bloodthirsty as the rest of the Americans. *Fuck Nam* restages the notorious scene which, recorded by Morely Safer in 1965, showed marine troops using cigarette lighters to burn down the huts of villagers. Its outrageous spectacularization is magnified in the play when a reporter asks the soldiers to wait while he adjusts the camera. It is also he who supplies a lighter in order to create a better visual effect. In another scene, the picture of burning Thich Quang Duc is projected overhead with a statement specifying how much money the journalist won for submitting that winning "World Press Photo 1963." The entire media network is here accused of abetting a quintessentially sadistic, anally fixated war. The preoccupation with this particular target no doubt explains why Kupferberg wanted the slides to be projected on top of the set, not on a screen, and why they should follow each other at a rapid pace—"channel surfing," as we call it today. The feeling of fragmentation and disintegration that is created by that practice is intended to counteract the "magic" of spectacularization created by pictures on a screen, well centered, fixed and perfectly reproduced. In contrast, images projected on the backstage set, or above it, force the spectator to look hard and focus to make sense out of them and hence register their antiwar message.

Part of Kupferberg's message, let me repeat, is that the Vietnamese "other" is a *total* victim. Without any shared guilt, "it" is subjugated, exploited, and martyrized by the Americans. True, in one scene, Kupferberg sardonically alludes to the economic growth that the war was supposed to bring to Vietnam. However, he hastens to point out, the economic growth exclusively benefits the black market, the prostitution, and the traffic of drugs needed to keep the GIs happy.[26] The economy as well as the occupation force the Vietnamese to cater to the U.S. soldiers, to satisfy their appetite for women, drugs, and American products.[27] In return they are themselves "commodified"—raped, brutalized, slaughtered. As such "others," the Vietnamese are meant to inspire compassion and sympathy based on a perhaps universal (albeit very deeply repressed or suppressed) feeling for justice and aversion to the degradation of fellow humans. But this is not a sympathy that Kuperberg can assume *necessarily* leads to deeper understanding or lasting solidarity. Precisely as his excessive "others," the Vietnamese remain essentially alien in the play. In any case, for Kupferberg, their incomprehensible submission could only be ended by a radical, anarchistic upheaval of the entire social system which forces "others" both to be treated—*and* to behave—*as if* they really are inferior.

Fuck Nam's theatrical form—notably an extensive use of stylized dance movements[28] and the remarkable strategies that made it possible to represent obscene acts on the stage—testified to a good deal of innovation. But it was its content that manifested the most striking originality. For, in 1967, the extent of atrocities carried out by the U.S. troops stationed in Vietnam was still largely unknown to the general public. Exposing drug addiction, prostitution, sadistic killings, and racial conflicts, as well as the bombing and burning of Vietnamese peasants, Kupferberg was largely ahead of the general protest movement. He might have been inspired by the similarity between the victimization of the Vietnamese and the victimization of American people of color that was already brought to the fore by the civil rights movement, which immediately preceded the antiwar movement. In his more daring scenes, he was no doubt also inspired by the avant-garde staging of the sixties. Whatever the reason, *Fuck Nam* remains the first American play at the time that not only showed totally harmless Vietnamese "others" but also presented the Americans as savages who systematically victimized the Vietnamese.[29] The more "mainstream" *Viet Rock*, barely a year earlier, had displayed a good deal of indulgence toward American soldiers and portrayed the Vietnamese as ruthless killers.

The historical interest of *Fuck Nam* goes, however, beyond its formal innovations and its political prescience. It lies mainly in its uncanny vision of the postmodern archetypal "other" in whom coalesce all particular "others": "Blacks," "Indians," "Orientals," and "Women" are treated as debased erotic objects. All of them, and hence the archetypal "Other," are victimized in their flesh and in their soul: killed, raped, sodomized, tortured, and always humiliated. To be an "other" for Kupferberg is to be taken as an inferior and passively to accept it—in life, in death, and, obsessively and submissively, in sex. In sum, a truly inappropriate/d other is felt *everywhere* in Kupferberg's sub-missive way of staging Vietnam Protest Theatre—everywhere, that is, in its *absence*.

AMERICAN I-WITNESSES (RABE, BALK)

> The nation has in the first instance nothing to do
> with questions of national borders, forms of govern-
> ment, or so-called nationality. The concept refers to a
> specific form of male community, one that is
> "yearned for" for many a long year, that rises from
> the "call of the blood." Like sexual characteristics, its
> essential features are incapable of being "learned" or
> "forgotten." The nation is a community of soldiers.
>   —Klaus Theweleit

> The man depicted as the active center of warfare is
> an irresistible charmer hunting for sensations. His
> actions take place amid dying masses of humanity,
> between imperialist powers warring over colonial
> sources of raw materials or world market domina-
> tion; but he remains an absolutely private indi-
> vidual. Though he claims repeatedly to represent the
> "whole," the "nation," he best fulfills that function
> as an isolated, self-interested individual, a man
> searching for the flow of desire. —Klaus Theweleit

1. RABE

Two plays to be examined in the context of "the other" are more conventional, in several senses, than *Fuck Nam* or *Pinkville*; they were also more
successful and had a greater influence on later Vietnam Veteran Theatre.
Though not initially conceived as a sequence, they are often treated by

critics as the first parts of a trilogy, the last part having been published several years later.[1] They offer testimony by a writer who grappled with the problem of Vietnam three times over the crucial years 1969-1975. These plays are David Rabe's *The Basic Training of Pavlo Hummel* (1968), *Sticks and Bones* (1969), and *Streamers* (1975).[2] *Streamers* does not deserve much attention here since it was produced after the end of the Vietnam War and is quite traditional in its form. Rabe's testimony in the first two plays, however, offers a very telling vision of the war because he served in Vietnam as a medic in 1966-1967.[3] It is also significant that Rabe is the only playwright whose plays about Vietnam won several awards and public fame.[4] Rabe's plays must then be surveyed with a special scrutiny of those features of content and form that may account for their positive reception by critics and audiences alike.

When *The Basic Training of Pavlo Hummel* and *Sticks and Bones* were first staged, Rabe was barely thirty years old, but the protest movement in the United States was already at its height. One might expect that, reflecting the general mood, Rabe's plays would express strong opposition to the war, supported by memories of firsthand experiences in Vietnam. Yet, surprisingly, in a 1973 introduction Rabe explicitly claims that his initial intention was *not* to create political, antiwar theatre:

> Finally, in my estimation, an "anti-war" play is one that expects, by the very fabric of its executed conception, to have political effect. I anticipated no such consequences from my plays, nor did I conceive them in the hope that they would have such consequences. I have written them to diagnose, as best I can, certain phenomena that went on in and around me. It seems presumptuous and pointless to call them "anti-war" plays. (Rabe 1973, xxv)

By and large his plays were not *received* as militant manifestations of protest, either. One critic even reached the ironic conclusion that, in *The Basic Training of Pavlo Hummel*, "the enemy is not the Viet Cong or pro-war America. Antiwar America is just as responsible [for the tragedy of the war]."[5] The question arises: Did the content of the play really warrant this judgment? Or was this reception an anticipation of Rabe's later claim (disingenuous or genuine) not to seek a political goal?

The Basic Training of Pavlo Hummel takes place in the United States and in Vietnam. At the onset a grenade kills Pavlo in a Vietnam café: a startling image of war violence in an "everyday" public setting (it could happen here). The audience is first invited to assume that a concealed Vietcong must have been responsible for the assassination, since the grenade is "thrown by a hand that merely flashes between the curtains" (Rabe 1973, 9). But the same scene, repeated at the end of the play, reveals that the killer was another American, moved by jealousy: "Sgt. Wall, there in the corner, beginning to move, is pulling the pin on a grenade" (Rabe 1973, 106). The enemy and the violence have moved from the outside to the inside of the

American camp. In short: The enemy is "us."

The bulk of the play takes place between these twin scenes. Pavlo is resurrected by the ghost of a black soldier, Ardell, and shown his past life in the army. The first act reenacts his basic training in the United States; the second shifts the locale to Vietnam and Pavlo's experiences as a medic. In both locales the focus remains on the Americans, providing Rabe with an opportunity to show them, from the inside perspective of the "us," either as victims of the war or as ruthless aggressors, or as both. Rabe's "us" does not constitute a homogeneous group of American soldiers. They all wear the same uniform, but they do not all represent a same uniform type. The basic distinction is made between the blacks and the whites, for *The Basic Training of Pavlo Hummel* was one of the first major Vietnam Protest Plays where African Americans play complex roles. The second lead character, Ardell, is black, as are three other individualized soldiers: Sergeant Tower, GI Parham, and Jones. Are they more criticized in the play than the whites? Or perhaps victimized by the whites or denied human dignity? Are they reduced, among and by Americans, to the status of the "other"? While no clear answers to these questions can be found in the play, it is striking that, contrary to the common liberal stereotype of victimized blacks, both Ardell and Tower hold positions of power, which surely connotes a racial equality. But there is nothing really "progressive" here—the same theme is used in the right-wing film *The Green Berets*.

More ambiguous is the association of all four blacks with death. Ardell's appearance on the stage is directly called for by Pavlo's death: "The bodies are strewn about. The radio plays. And a black soldier, Ardell, now appears, his uniform strangely unreal with black ribbons and medals" (Rabe 1973, 9). It is as a messenger of the dead, a guide somewhat like Virgil, that he will lead Pavlo through the rest of the play. Sergeant Tower is also a guide on a trip to death as he makes sure that a well-trained Pavlo is sent to Vietnam where he must die. Meanwhile Pavlo is seriously wounded when he rescues Parham from the Vietcong: the black soldier this time is the cause of near death. As for Jones, his connection to Pavlo's death is more circuitous but nevertheless telling when added to the others. He helps Pavlo get the prostitute, Yen, over whom he will later lose his life. Then, in *Sticks and Bones*, the black Sgt. Major who brings David home also will play the role of an emissary of death.[6] And in *Streamers*, the crazy "nigger" Carlyle stabs white recruits Billy and Rooney, killing them before they even reach Vietnam. Obviously black color in Rabe's plays is a/the signifier of death. But does it have further connotations or an ideological impact? Rabe could be taking to an extreme the traditional Western association of black with death (and mourning); or he could express, consciously or unconsciously, an undercurrent of racial prejudice that projects onto blacks the "dark" threat of violence and death that is attributed to all "others" sooner or later.

On several occasions, Rabe draws a clear parallel between African

Americans and Vietnamese, both viewed as racially "other." In *The Basic Training of Pavlo Hummel*, the black Jones says to a Vietnamese prostitute: "You got lips as fat as mine, you know that, Ho?" (Rabe 1973, 79). In *Sticks and Bones*, David's mother discloses a deep-seated racial fear of all that look nonwhite: "The human face was not meant to be that way. A nose is a thinness—you know that. And lips that are not thin are ugly, and it is we who disappear. . . . It is our triumph, our whiteness" (Rabe 1973, 208). Elsewhere Rabe undermines that black/yellow parallel. The complicity of all nonwhites as solidarity figures of the "other" is shattered by Jones's rejection of the prostitute as a human being:

> "That ain't no dead person," I say, "that ain't no dead Ho jus' 'cause she layin' so still. I saw her walk in here." . . . They got no nature these women. . . . Shit, Ho, you insides rotten. You Vietnamese, ain't you? Vietnamese same—same V.D. (Rabe 1973, 80)

Clearly an adequate understanding of Rabe's attitude toward African Americans requires at this point a closer look at his treatment of the Vietnamese "other."

The Vietnamese have a comparatively small role in the trilogy, which corresponds to the choice of America as the dominant geographical locale of the plays. *The Basic Training of Pavlo Hummel* is the only one where half of the action takes place in Vietnam, and it does involve the inclusion of several Vietnamese characters. But only two are identified as real individuals—the prostitute Yen and the Madame of the brothel; the others are anonymous fighting figures. In *Sticks and Bones*, which deals with the return of a veteran to his family, all the action occurs in the American home of Ozzie and Harriet, and the sole Vietnamese character appears in the form of a dreamlike ghost of a girl with whom David had an affair in Vietnam. *Streamers* is set exclusively in the United States before the recruits are sent to Vietnam; there are no Vietnamese in it at all.

The most memorable Vietnamese in the trilogy is the prostitute Yen in *Pavlo Hummel*. Her first words are "creezy, creezy," followed by echoes of French occupation: "Paablo boocoup love. Sleep me all time" (Rabe 1973, 8). Rabe portrays her as a dumb animal: she can hardly speak, and her only function is to provide sex.[7] Her stupidity and sexuality are emblematic of the way Americans in Rabe's plays are accustomed to viewing all Vietnamese: inherently stupid, they all can be bought with American dollars; the women are prostitutes and the men their pimps. Furthermore, even in their sexual capacity they are inadequate, as a corporal tells his men:

> Them slopes; man they're the stupidest bunch a people anybody ever saw. It don't matter what you do to 'em or what you say, man they just look at you. They're some kind of goddamn phenomenon, man. Can of bug spray buy you all the ass you can handle in some places. Insect repellent, man. You ready for

that? You give 'em can of bug spray, you can lay their fourteen-year-old daughter. Not that any of 'em screw worth a shit. (Rabe 1973, 41)

Typical for the play, this offensive passage is not set against any counterimage or speech. Hence it is unclear whether Rabe is *reflecting* racist patterns of thought and language or actually *buying into them*. As shall be seen, in connection with *Sticks and Bones*, any appraisal of Rabe's tendency toward misogyny, male chauvinism, and censure of miscegenation must be seen in the full light of his otherwise effective and arguably salutary deconstruction of the middle-class nuclear family and U.S. imperialism. Nonetheless, a basic problem of gender in cultural studies raises its head. How progressive can a class deconstruction be, if it remains antiwomen at root and hence (in this sense, and in Rabe's case) "antiother" at root?

However, to return to Rabe's first play, the Vietnamese must not be underestimated. While they may appear dumb, there is a more threatening side to them—a "dark" side evoked by Yen's fatal function as Pavlo's nemesis. That threat is latent in an overall potential as enemies, whether male fighters, children, women, or old people. A symbolic story is told about an old man and a little girl who try to blow up an American platoon with dynamite tied to their bodies—the primary object of the GI's sexual desire. This brutal articulation of sex and death is also evoked when two Vietcong slaughter Parham in a particularly suggestive and torturous way.[8] The same Vietcong then turn on Pavlo when he tries to rescue the body of Parham. They are cold-blooded and determined fighters, lethally dangerous. That concrete image certainly clashes with the overall image of Vietnamese stupidity and sexuality, but it is not much more positive. It suggests that the "other" can turn at any time from victim into aggressor. Whether, in this case, the horrifying results of the Vietnamese aggression qualify as true "atrocities," as could be claimed for the slow killing of Parham, or merely have to be taken as an understandable, even acceptable, outcome of self-defense, depends ultimately (questions of director's discretion aside) on Rabe's positive or negative characterization of the enemies, who force the Vietnamese to fight, i.e., the American soldiers.

Which takes us back to the U.S. Army and, more specifically, to the white soldiers who, after all, are more typical than the blacks. And to Pavlo Hummel who best embodies the white majority. Now, in the most objective sense, Pavlo is a victim of the war. His death at the onset of the play is expected to generate a compassion normally reserved for victimized positive characters. But that impression doesn't last. As his past is unveiled, Pavlo is programmed to lose the sympathy of the audience; he is exposed as a pathological liar and a thief. He also shows he is mean and stupid: instead of going back home, he stays in Vietnam to satisfy a base thirst for revenge—to kill more "gooks."[9] On the other hand, he is pathetically, even appealingly clumsy: he shoots himself in the head when he tries to shoot a suspect Vietnamese farmer. In that episode, he is the victim not of war but of his own overzealous drive to kill. Similarly, his actual death is not caused by the war so much as by his own impatient character; he refuses to wait till Yen has finished her business with another client. Besides, it is not reciprocal lovemaking that he wants from her but crude sexual violence: "I'm gonna take her in behind those curtains and I'm gonna fuck her right side up and then maybe I'm gonna turn her over, get her in her asshole" (Rabe 1973, 105). His killer, Sgt. Wall, is no better than Pavlo, no less a displaced homophobe; he attacks him with a switchblade, then throws the fatal grenade.

As embodied in Pavlo and Wall, the white American males are not any more positive than the Vietcong. They do oscillate, as do the Vietnamese, between the roles of aggressor and victim, but their victimization is mainly self-inflicted rather than a curse of the war, let alone imperialism. One could be tempted to conclude that stereotypes of the "other," distributed among all the characters in Rabe's plays, are thus somewhat diluted. It would seem that everybody, whatever his/her race, is assigned a potentially violent and bestial dark "other" inside. Rabe's vision of Vietnam would resemble in that version the Hegelian "night in which all cows are black." Yet a telling observation by Ardell, the black messenger of death and truth, puts this bleak conclusion back into question. Trying to explain Pavlo's dark "other," Ardell pointedly relates it only to race, deciding that, at least inside, the white Pavlo must be black:

> Sometimes I look at you, I don't know what I think I'm seein', but it sooo simple. You black on the inside. In there where you live, you that awful hurtin' black so you can't see yourself no way. Not up or down or in or out. (Rabe 1973, 46)

Must one then conclude that, somewhere in Rabe's mind, the animalistic, violent, threatening "other," viewed as a human being degraded, is somehow (unconsciously) linked with black (or yellow) skin color? And does he suggest that white Americans, when they commit atrocities, are acting like blacks? It is difficult to settle these questions, partly because surprisingly few really shocking atrocities are evoked in *Pavlo Hummel*. The killing of Parham may be appalling, but it is an expected fare in a war, especially on the part of an allegedly "primitive" and "savage" enemy. More shocking is Pavlo's crazed murder of a farmer, about which the audience hears only in a mediating dialogue between Pavlo and Ardell. But Pavlo's memory lacks precision and good faith, and it is Ardell who must provide a more complete, if twice removed, version of the crime.[10] All the other forms of atrocity are also conveyed secondhand and lack visual detail that might betray an underlying, unexamined racial prejudice.

Aside from Ardell who has a comparatively neutral role, there are no truly positive characters in Rabe's first play, no heroes. Everybody is corrupted by the war, including the American sergeant who turns the protagonist into a victim—a victim who is also a victimizer. In that sense, it is the war itself which has the part of the villain; it is the evil that generates both degradation and atrocities. The play creates a space where everything is, in Yen's words, made "creezy" by war; in fact, as Pavlo's brother Mickey says, in relation to the normal world, "Vietnam don't even exist" (Rabe 1973, 66). But, one might argue, paraphrasing Voltaire, if Vietnam didn't exist, it would have been necessary (for Rabe) to invent it. Mickey's vision is bleak, but it calls for revolt or revolution rather than for passive acceptance. If, under the sway of war, all parties are similarly guilty, then it is the war that is the enemy that must be brought to an end. Beyond its discrete contradictory suggestions, the play's overall message is to protest war, but not necessarily Vietnam.

In his next play, *Sticks and Bones* (1969), Rabe turns from Vietnam to the "normal" American world: a middle-class family with two children, a house in the suburbs, a car. He proceeds to show how the irruption of Vietnam shatters that world totally when David, the elder son of Ozzie and Harriet (also of TV fame), returns blind from the war and is driven to suicide by his scarred past and scarring parents. David is definitely "somebody sick" (Rabe 1973, 120), yet another victim of the war. He is afflicted with the same sickness as the GIs in Rabe's earlier play. But there are important differences between the two plays. First, the locale is no longer the battlefield in Vietnam but a "peaceful" United States where the germs of war lie dormant. Second, the responsibility for causing the sickness is shifted from the agents of war, the military or the government officials, to the "average American citizen." On the most obvious level of the plot, David's parents are merely guilty of seeing and treating him as if he were an "other"—an incomprehensible, upsetting, and dangerous "other." But they soon reveal, within their inner selves, an equally disturbing dark "otherness" that spreads around them and distorts their vision. Because they are sick themselves, they project their sickness, first on the fragile David, then on all other potential "others."

A case in point is the only Vietnamese "character," the silent ghost of Zung who haunts David because he has left her behind. From his perspective, shared by the audience, she has a dignity and a capacity to love that raise her way above the one-dimensional whore Yen in *The Basic Training of Pavlo Hummel*. An ethereal figure, she appears as "A girl to weigh no more than dust" (Rabe 1973, 144). But David's father, Ozzie, can only see her as a yellow whore: "Some yellow ass. You put in your prick and humped your ass. You screwed some yellow fucking whore!" (Rabe 1973, 144). For Ozzie, Zung not only stands for the racial "other" but also, *as* woman, she epitomizes the diseased and threatening female "other," contaminated with "dirty, filthy diseases. They got 'em. Those girls. Infection. From the blood of their parents into the very fluids of their bodies" (Rabe 1973, 148). One might wonder whether David's "otherness" is a disease he caught in Vietnam. This overdetermined hatred—part racial, part sexual—manifests a deeper, and no doubt sicker, hatred directed against all women who threaten men with the "otherness" of their bodies. It fits disturbingly well Klaus Theweleit's analysis of *fascist* "male fantasies."[11] In general, it is remarkable how much Rabe's play anticipates—implicitly by showing, though not explicitly by arguing—many of Theweleit's much later insights (1977). It is not clear if Rabe himself grasped the dialectic between the particular and the universal, "us" and "them."

At any rate Theweleit's context clarifies why, when Ozzie tries to expel Zung from his home, he lashes out not at her color, or alienness, but at her *animal darkness*, the mysterious and frightening female body, rejected in quasi-biblical terms: "You are garbage and filth. You are darkness. I cast you down. Deceit. Animal. Dirty Animal" (Rabe 1973, 217). Ozzie projects his sickness with so much power and authority that he contaminates even David who, while still bound by love to the memory of Zung, acknowledges the threat of her diseased female flesh: "She is garbage and filth and I must get her back if I wish to live. Sickness" (Rabe 1973, 177). But Ozzie's fear of the female body goes much farther, as a reader of Theweleit will already suspect. Ozzie is not only frightened by women because their animality threatens male control, taints the blood, and transmits diseases; he is also terrified by their reproductive animal function, their will to bring new life into his world. Figurehead of a patriarchal America, he cannot admit it overtly, but he deeply resents having children, the "poison" carried in his wife's womb: "HARRIET! YOU—YOU! your internal organs—your internal female organs—they've got some sort of poison in them" (Rabe 1973, 174). The real Ozzie, Rabe may be hinting (anticipating Oliver Stone's 1994 *Natural Born Killers*), is as much of an unconscious child-hater and child-killer as the American soldiers in Vietnam who murdered the unborn child of a lynched woman:

> all bone and pain, uncontoured and ugly but for the peculiar melon-swelling in her middle which is her pregnancy, which they do not see . . . the rifle jammed exactly and deeply up into her, with a bullet fired directly into the child living there. (Rabe 1973, 161)

Now, one could well argue that this dramatic but very disturbed image is likely fictional, certainly mediated by a narrative on stage, and perhaps represents only a—more or less "ironic"?—projection of Ozzie's sickness. But comparable images of mutilated pregnant women turned up frequently in Vietnam War narratives, partly because they reflected reality but partly also because, according to Susan Jeffords at least, they visually combined the contrasted biological functions of the two genders: men driven to kill, women to reproduce.[12] Following Jeffords further, and translating contrast into conflict, one could link Zung's disincarnation to man's obsessive fear of *live* prostitutes whose sexuality (which is overpowering) risks entrapping men in what some feel to be an alien, repulsive, and quintessentially "other" act of biological reproduction. A life-giving Zung had to be left in Vietnam; she can only be accepted when she becomes a ghost.[13] However coarse such an "irony" may be, it is certainly true that war, aggression, and violence are, in Rabe's play, exclusively male activities, carried out by both father and son as a form of inherited function—and hence, a big problem indeed, outside conscious control and accountability.

Harriet berates Ozzie: "You thought you knew what was right, all those years, teaching him sports and fighting. Do you understand what I am trying to say?" (Rabe 1973, 133). For Rabe, the same male sickness that fuels racial prejudice, the fear of the female body, and a resentment of children, also leads, for biological or cultural reasons, to an urge to commit aggressive and violent acts, culminating in war atrocities. Because *Sticks and Bones* is set in America, Rabe's development of his "argument" cannot be shown directly on the stage in the form of unmediated scenes of the Vietnam War. Hence the need for various mediating strategies. David for one, his face scarred under his sunglasses, is a frightening figure who bears witness to the violence of war; however, it is not clear how he got his wounds. A much stronger and more repellent scene is described by David as he tells about the murder of the pregnant Vietnamese woman, but it is a verbal description. The only visual sign appears when David explains to his parents the meaning of a "flickering of green" on a photographic slide:

> LOOK! They hang in the greenish haze afflicted by insects; a woman and a man, middle aged . . . left to hang as they had been strung on the wire—he with the back of his head blown off. (Rabe, *Sticks and Bones*, 161)

But that sign as such is unclear, barely visible, and needs the support of words to be fully grasped. Besides, it is not stated overtly who bears the responsibility for this atrocity, and Harriet's suspicion of the "other" actually leads her to attribute the killing to the Vietnamese themselves: "It's so awful the things those yellow people do to one another. Yellow people hanging yellow people. Isn't that right?" (Rabe 1973, 163). Of course one assumes that Americans were guilty, or were intended to be found guilty, since David might have invented the scene in order to disturb his family. He warns, "Because I talk of certain things . . . don't think I did them" (Rabe 1973, 162).

The scandalous nature of such scenes, just like the fatal facial mark (blindness) of David, draws as much power from the contrast with the "normalcy" of Ozzie and Harriet as from their direct verbal or visual impact. They are shocking because they contradict and undermine—at least verbally—the plastic (visual) perfection of the home, which is "very modern, with a quality of brightness, green walls, green rug . . . naturalness, yet a sense of space and oddly a sense also that this room, these stairs belong in the gloss of an advertisement" (Rabe 1973, 120).[14] That atrocities are not staged but simply verbalized does not necessarily diminish their horror, neither in *Sticks and Bones* nor in other Vietnam Protest Plays. On the contrary, visualized or verbalized, they are embedded in the memories of theatre characters, if not in the collective memory of all Americans.

It is not coincidental that the domestic vision of David's home comes straight out of one of the most popular TV sitcoms of all time. Rabe's stage is dominated by a television set on which, as in Grant Duay's *Fruit Salad*, all (other) reality is metamorphosed into a spectacle made for a society of consumers. That this image is not particularly original, as one critic noted in 1971, does not necessarily diminish its significance in Rabe's play.[15] For, as *Sticks and Bones* progresses and the momentum of the play builds, the television set falls apart. Its material breakdown corresponds to the psychological breakdown of Ozzie and Harriet's "perfect" world—shattered by David, his memories of the Vietnam War, and their own consequent disintegration. The television first goes on the blink right after the entrance of Zung's ghost, a first breach in the conventional American time and space frame.[16] Until the end of the play, the TV will remain soundless, driving Ozzie to frustration and madness.[17]

This TV theme in *Sticks and Bones* is reminiscent of the 1971 behaviorist experiment about the disruptive, even violent, reaction of families who were deprived of TV for extended periods of time. The audiences of Rabe's play might have realized that, as they were attending the play, they too were missing their favorite TV shows (and this was before programmed VCR recordings). One might also recall the ironic quip by Jean Baudrillard about the same experiment: "You no longer watch TV, TV watches you (live)."[18] In *Sticks and Bones* the silent fixed slides project mere images on the screen, elusive traces of an elapsed reality that has no relation to the present.[19] Supposed sources of stability and understanding, they are as unreliable as may have been Rabe's vision of Vietnam as the "television war."

A reviewer observed at the time in the *Village Voice* that *Sticks and Bones* attacks the traditional American life and seeks to make it responsible for the war:

> Where *Pavlo Hummel* works best as a documentary of military life, "Sticks and Bones" tells us more about why we are in Vietnam. It shows how people like Ozzie and Harriet are the roots of this war.[20]

Yet, the gender issue aside, the guilt of the traditional family is not very tightly linked to the responsibility for the war atrocities in Vietnam. What is "tragic," according to the more or less tacit logic of the play, is rather that young Americans were forced to *witness* these atrocities, even when they did not cause them directly, *and* that they disturbed them to the point that they could not fit back into the warp and woof of American society without seriously destabilizing it.

Rabe himself might have believed that main-street America was responsible for the war and that war was a total tragedy that victimized everybody. But in his plays, because of their excessive focus on American characters, the concrete manifestations of the war are principally denounced only when they shatter *American* society and the lives of *individual* American youth, like Pavlo and David. Whatever does and could happen to the Vietnamese seems incidental in comparison. *Streamers* (1985) carries this self-centered orientation further. It is not by chance, in this much later play, that the mere fear of going to Vietnam makes the "boys" explode into irrational violence. In Rabe's words, "The war—the threat of it—is the one thing they share" (Rabe 1985, 30). The trilogy's final lesson may be summarized, not without irony, as "War is hell, especially at home."

2. BALK

The Dramatization of 365 Days by H. Wesley Balk (1971/72) is the *only* Vietnam Protest Play that, to my knowledge, was explicitly, extensively, and self-consciously based on a previously published prose narrative.[21] Balk was looking for a text suitable, in his words, for a "theater which uses literature not written for the stage and presents it, abridged but not rewritten, in theatrical form" (Balk 5). The challenge was to transform a literary text, meant to be read, into a staged performance that would place "less stress on the playwright's contribution of situation, dialogue, and characterization, emphasizing instead the performing talents [that] actors and directors can bring to other literary forms" (Balk 5). Balk chose Ronald Glasser's *365 Days* because "it sounded powerful and relevant and seemed to make an important statement about the war" (Balk 4). There remains to see exactly what "powerful" "statement" was made in Balk's own *365 Days*.

The original story is semiautobiographical, recounting Glasser's experience in Japan as a physician treating American soldiers wounded in Vietnam. Discarding the usual protest theatre locales—Vietnam and America—Balk's play takes place in the confined setting of an army hospital in Japan: an enclosed and already quasi-theatrical space. For, in a hospital, it is customary to call the operating room, as if it were a battlefield, a "theatre"—in part safe, in part horrific, like a M.A.S.H. operating tent.[22] Balk's spin-off play focuses on only one small group of U.S. military: those who are too seriously wounded to be adequately treated in Vietnam or to be shipped back home. All the main characters, therefore, are "real victims" of the war, and, not surprisingly, all of them are Americans. There are no Vietnamese on this stage, whether friends or foes; they are evoked only teichoscopically, through the mediation of stories told by the wounded soldiers or in written reports read aloud by doctors. As noted earlier (in the case of Rabe), such mediated representations of the "other" are always somewhat ambivalent, no matter what the intentions of the playwright, director, or actors may be. On the one hand, the horror of war is itself mediated and thus risks becoming acceptable, manageable. On the other hand, the same horror finds a certain home of its own, no matter how mediated: the uncanny, everyday "home" of the consciousness and sub-consciousness (and perhaps conscience) of the Americans.

To be more precise, in Balk's *The Dramatization of 365 Days*, the properly *written* accounts (read aloud, of course) deal less with the war than with the wounds inflicted on the Americans. Almost no references are made in this medium to the Vietnamese "other." However, the *oral* accounts of the patients offer personal evocations of life and action in Vietnam, though again only from an American point of view. These oral descriptions of horror are quite gruesome, partly because of a quasi-medical attention to specific details. Balk wanted to convey on stage the impact of these verbally evoked atrocities, looking beyond "literature which denies depiction in any realistic sense either on stage or in films" (Balk 6).[23] In order to retain the raw power of direct words, Balk decided to sacrifice the tame illusions of realism and, turning toward the resources (and limits) of theatricality, instructed his cast of ten men and four women to exchange constantly the roles they were playing and the numbered voices assigned to them. That technique—reminiscent of Terry's earlier *Viet Rock* or Weiss's *Vietnam Discourse*—ensured that no individual actor would be identified with any specific character, and hence no individual actor's body would be expected to display its individual wounds. The only exception was made for the guitarist—a kind of Chorus—who was to remain the same through-out the play, providing music and singing songs to underscore, by comparison or contrast, the horror evoked, but not really shown, with the words on the stage.

This interesting strategy was significantly modified during the re-hearsals. As Balk notes, while the men kept freely exchanging their roles at random, the women somehow came always to stand for the enemy, the Vietnamese:

> The role of the women was defined almost more quickly than that of the men, and their aesthetic function proved one of the central metaphors of the piece: they came to represent the passive, feminine role of the Vietnamese, as opposed to the aggressive, masculine role of the American, represented by the men. They also represented weapons, wounds, environmental hazards, and mental anxieties, in short anything that acted upon the men from jungle vines to memories of home. (Balk 12)

This deliberately biased distribution of roles could well be viewed as offensive by women in that it identifies them with the "Asian" enemy and vice versa—as if the same type of prejudice were at work on the stage against the Vietcong as in (the rest of) real life against women. A similar double prejudice was at work in Rabe's vision of Ozzie's racism and sexism. It manifests a certain representation of the "other" that was diagnosed by Said: "The Oriental was linked thus to elements in Western society (delinquents, the insane, women, the poor) having in common an identity best described as lamentably alien" (Said 1978, 207). But that identification betrays an interesting contradiction. For the women/Vietnamese in Balk's play are not shown to be particularly passive, or "feminine," notably in stories that refer to the Vietcong's ruses or ruthlessness: not killing a GI but merely wounding him so as to be also able to kill a medic rushing to his rescue;[24] sneaking into an American camp and killing the men in their sleep;[25] setting up networks of booby traps and grenades. In contrast, the aggressive Americans are portrayed as victims of aggression. Only in two instances are they clear aggressors, and in both cases they attempt to give reasons—which, in the context of the play, are not wholly implausible—to justify and legitimate their actions.[26]

One of these exceptions has far-reaching connotations. The basic story is simple. An old Vietnamese man tries to sell stolen Cokes to the GIs. When they refuse to pay, he spits at them and so irritates them that one "trooper brought the weapon smoothly up into the crook of his arm and emptied the magazine into him" (Balk 66). This killing over a few Cokes (a common signifier for American commercialism) is explained (or rather explained away) in part by the old man's provocative insults and in part by his characterization as a cheat and a thief: "little fucker steals 'em from us and then wants us to pay" (Balk 65). But that explanation doesn't sit well as a convincing justification of murder. It rather serves to illustrate the prejudices of those GIs who feel that they have the right to shoot an ungrateful, disrespectful, and dishonest old Vietnamese. It also illustrates a rampant tendency to view the Vietnamese as permanently disturbing "others": basically amoral, often disgusting, and yet unaccountably threatening despite (or because) of their weakness (for American products). The indication that the old man is to be played by a woman merely adds, as in Rabe's plays, a further dimension of alienness. For, as figures standing for the Vietnamese enemy, or more generally for the "other," women in Balk's version of 365 Days are not only aggressive but also, as in this case, sly and deceitful. It would seem that a deep if unacknowledged suspicion of women emerges here or even a potentially lethal dislike—perhaps disclosing Balk's personal attitude, since there is no similar conflation of women with the Vietcong in Glasser's original text. One is reminded of the Theweleitian problematic broached earlier in Rabe's Sticks and Bones. Who is really the "other" in these Vietnam plays: the Vietcong, all people of color, or all women?

Balk's apparent deep-seated prejudice against women is underscored by his contrasted sympathetic treatment of men. Sympathy for the American soldier as a victim is solicited at the onset of the play as male voices discuss the veterans who will return to the United States:

SPEAKER 12: Would they embarrass their families?

SPEAKER 13: Would they be able to make it at parties with guys who were still whole?

SPEAKER 14: Could they go to the beach and would their scars darken in the sun and offend the girls?

SPEAKER 10: Would they be able to get special cars? Above all, and underlining all their cares, would anybody love them when they got back? (Balk 36)

The veterans are all the more pathetic because they appear to have done nothing wrong to deserve harsh treatment at home. Their main goal in Vietnam was merely to survive one year of the war.[27] With the exception of the men involved in the shooting of the old Vietnamese, Balk's GIs display few of the bestial or racist motivations attributed to them in other protest plays. They are portrayed rather as ignorant youngsters for whom the war serves as a valuable learning experience. Contrary to the message in the last words of *Pinkville*, where war is indicted of changing peaceful youth into mad killers, Balk suggests that war may transform bad adolescents into good men, as in the case of Watson, who

> had been a troublemaker since he was six. He was a bitter imaginative, hate filled kid who had been drafted and somehow had survived basic training without ending up in prison. . . . When I met him he had been up front with his unit for almost five months. He was soft spoken, but marvelously animated and alert. The old abusiveness was gone; even the adolescent arrogance had disappeared. (Balk 52)

Or more generally: "There is, honestly, something very positive about being over here. I can see it in myself and my men. Not the war itself, God knows that's hopeless enough, but what happens to you because of it" (Balk 119). Even the officers are not exposed, as in most Vietnam plays, as agents of evil who must bear the blame for victimizing American GIs; rather, they are seen as human beings deeply concerned for their men. One officer even separates the married GIs from the others because "he didn't want all the married ones killed at once" (Balk 49). Another officer, who lets most of his men be slaughtered rather than accept an order to retreat, is generously excused because he is himself "tragically" caught in The System and therefore is misguided:

> They are not dishonest officers, nor are they particularly shortsighted or brutal; if anything, they are incredibly sincere and dedicated men who unfortunately are locked into the early 1940s. (Balk 98)

He is killed by his own troops in a fragging incident.

The play's medical terminology, adding a documentary dimension to the war's horror (or, more accurately, to one horrific aftermath of the war's general horror), helps to increase sympathy for the wounded American men. And the accent is again on "men." For Balk likes to stress injury to properly male attributes. Thus, the victim of a grenade: "His left leg was already gone, and his right leg was shredded up to his thigh. The blast had seared through the bottoms of his fatigues, burning his penis and scrotum as well as the lower part of his abdomen and anus" (Balk 55). The hospital's "final pathological diagnosis" echoes these literally phallocentric concerns:

SPEAKER 14: A. Traumatic amputation of lower extremities, distal right thumb, distal left index finger.
SPEAKER 10: B. Blast injury of anus and scrotum.
SPEAKER 11: C. Avulsion of testicles.
SPEAKER 12: D. Fragment wounds of abdomen.
SPEAKER 13: E. Laceration of kidney and liver, transection of left ureter. (Balk 56)

And so the voice goes on, focusing in minute detail on different extremities, until the last record of the "External Examination" (Balk 57). All the emasculated victims are identified as *white* males; in fact, photographs of the production show neither black nor Vietnamese actors.

A certain tension can be detected between this evidence of physical suffering of the GIs and the statements about their moral fortitude, between war as a source of tragedy and war as a test and legitimation of masculine initiation. It is here that Balk's *365 Days* becomes problematic as a protest play. For the tension enables young soldiers of the United States to be truly the victims of the war but, despite agonizing deaths around them, to remain at peace with themselves and the world. They cry out for compassion rather than censure. To that extent the play is supportive of the "Americans" involved in Vietnam, even though women (of all nations) appear to be excluded from this sympathy. Balk's ultimate point is not to protest but rather, as he claims, to "offset the sinking feeling that some day, when the whole thing was over, there would be nothing remembered except the confusion and the politics" (Balk 34). A traditional "humanist," Balk wants to make sure that human stories will be remembered and not the politics of the war. The lead song of *365 Days* rejects the right to make judgmental attributions of blame; it discloses an underlying apolitical "confusion," a virtual chaos theory about war:

Not that we're different
We don't think we're unique
But the answers we're questioning
Are those we've heard you speak
We haven't decided you're wrong
For experience has its function. (Balk 140)

That such experience excludes the "other" is irrelevant in Balk's patriotic context.

3. FORMS OF DEHUMANIZATION

Coming from the outside to Vietnam Protest Plays for the first time, one could well assume that virtually any type of staged violence, any type of physical and mental suffering or moral debasement, will serve to illustrate the "atrocity" or "degradation," the "horror" or "tragedy" of the war. A closer look shows, however, that only a relatively small number of clearly distinct scenes or images are actually seen on the stage—returning frequently though with varying degrees of emphasis. These recurring themes, cast in quasi-archetypal figures, fall within two fundamental (and contrasted) categories: violence done by American military to the Vietnamese civilian population (in addition to Vietcong soldiers), and—especially in American plays—suffering inflicted by the war on the American soldiers.[28] In either case, even in European plays, the distinction between "us" and "them" is relatively clear. No doubt such a fundamental binary opposition could also be interpreted as a manifestation of a more basic structure, hidden logic, and ideological problem: that is, when violence comes to destroy not only the enemy, whether military or civilian, but also, ostensibly, the very spirit of one's most cherished values (here freedom, responsibility, and dignity), then the distinction between "us" and "them" becomes a casualty as well.

The most usual form of degradation, first registered and indicted in America by Terry in *Viet Rock*, is simultaneously mental and moral. A result of army discipline, it turns raw recruits from (supposedly) independent human beings into compliant conformists, molded by group pressure and bellicose American ideology, and now ready and willing to execute the orders of their superiors. These young soldiers are not totally mindless, nor totally devoid of scruples perhaps; nonetheless they participate in indiscriminate killing without questioning its reasons. A later and harsher variant of degradation, visible perhaps most clearly in Tabori's *Pinkville*, involves a nearly total loss of judgment and ethical values. Dulled by the experience of war, GIs (the name itself is dehumanizing, deriving as it does from "Government Issue") are shown to be transformed into mindless killing androids, mass products of a technological society that has no interest in moral issues. (If there is an answer to the perennial question of whether killers are "born naturally" or "made," Vietnam Protest Theatre cannot be expected to have it.) Dealing death sometimes becomes for GIs "second nature," and, as in the case of Rabe's play *The Basic Training of Pavlo Hummel*, they stand ready to kill white fellow Americans almost as "naturally" as if they were Vietnamese enemies or racial "others." Some GIs are direct victims of that general debasement, and those who survive, like David in *Sticks and Bones*, find it understandably difficult, if not impossible, to adjust after the war to a civilian society that expects them to think and behave (*again*, or is it for the *first time*?) like "normal" human beings. The underlying problem—in both mild and harsh variants—is dehumanization: indiscriminate techno-killing reveals the absence of any conventional sense of responsible action, any usual sense of guilt or accountability.

A rather different type of dehumanization is indicted in plays that focus on the bestiality of the American fighting man. *Fuck Nam*, which offers the crudest image of GIs behaving like animals, remained unstaged in the United States. But other plays that were staged also refer, be it obliquely, to sexual excesses, alcoholism, drug addictions, bestiality, and sadism. The Hell of war they expose breaks down the moral and/or legal constraints that rule civilized human beings. "Free" only to follow their basest drives and passions, the American GIs, but also some Vietnamese friends and foes, become enslaved by their blind instincts, relinquishing rational thought and appeals to reason. Their virtually unlimited potential brutality submits only to superior power in this "total war," and the loss of their own human conscience leads them to deny human conscience "naturally" to others, treating them only as weaker or stronger animals, to be used or feared, often simply killed.

This abject loss of human solidarity is included as yet another form of degradation that is not necessarily associated with the extremes of bestiality. In the army (the plays imply), GIs do not merely learn but actually come to *embody* the idea that the enemy, and by extension anyone outside the military "us," must be treated as if they did not belong to the human race. By a further extension of this logic, some plays (notably Rabe's *Sticks and Bones*) situate the origin of that exclusion in prejudices that exist in American society *before* actual combat (and hence also *after* it), but it is obviously the war that triggers their explosion. Thus, the absence of human solidarity is primarily manifested by combatants on location in Vietnam. It results from the distorted perspective from which so many playwrights (not merely staged characters) judge the "other." Involved here is an a priori denial of even the possibility of any shared qualities between white GIs, who are staged as basically the same, and their "others"—whether these be nameless combatant foes, other races, or, most especially, all women. It should go without saying that this twisted perspective harms most directly those affected by violence that follows logically on these prejudices. (It is no accident that a military code euphemism for killing is "termination with extreme prejudice.") But this perspective also dehumanizes those who are prejudiced since they must condemn and discard (in their own "nature") those human traits that they censure as "other," even (more radically) the *possibility* of genuine otherness. What is killed is the human right, even duty, to be *inappropriate/d*, in Trinh T. Minh-ha's sense.

The mis/representation of horror, degradation, and guilt by individual playwrights—differentiated by gender, national origins, or political ideology—might have shown substantially different perspectives on specific types of the "other." Yet, on the basic issues, there turn out to be surprisingly few variations in approach. One reason may be that in many cases the "other" always already combines several features of precisely some fundamental "otherness" that American and European males appear to fear and to reject. An exemplary "other" figure, a Vietnamese prostitute, is denied humanity not only because she is a woman and an enemy but also because she belongs to a different race and culture, has a different color, speaks a different language, and serves the men as if she were a machine, while always remaining "mysterious" and "inscrutable." Yet the Vietnamese prostitute appears as the "other" only in the plays written by men. Neither she nor other women treated as the "other" have a significant role in the plays by three American women: Terry, Garson, and Adrienne Kennedy—comparatively and problematically—are indifferent to the gender issue.

The European playwrights are not necessarily less sensitive than the Americans to the "otherness" of race and color. But they are more sensitive to class. Great Britain and France were colonial powers in Africa and Asia (as was Germany, much more briefly, in Africa until World War I), and their national history and culture gave them at least some familiarity, no matter how skewed, with the political struggles and psychology of what they thought of as the "Orient." The United States, a relative newcomer to the "Orient," had little knowledge or understanding of African or African-American history, let alone Asia in general or Vietnam. To this extent it stands to reason that Europeans tend more than Americans to view the Vietnam War in terms of historical and, to a lesser extent, socioeconomic processes.

What emerges in most of the plays about the Vietnam War is the awareness of a new imperial (but not so much economic) power at this preliminary stage of the New World Order: the United States.[29] The American plays about Vietnam are cruder about it (ideologically as well as aesthetically) than the European ones. But then they are generally coarser in structure and texture. They indulge in overt sexuality and they reduce the actual or potential enemy to women, to gays, to blacks, to Asians—so that all figures of the "other" tend to coalesce into a single character. But even this archetypal character is represented only when being misrepresented (at the moment of being killed or maimed, for example). Hence it ends by never being represented at all. Instead, American plays prefer to refer to experiences with which their audiences can easily identify and which have a stable place in their history: the Indian Wars as seen in *Viet Rock*, *Fuck Nam*, *Pinkville*, etc., or the histories of African Americans and even women, as seen in Rabe's trilogy. In most of these American plays, then, the social categories of race overdetermine the conception of the "other" and contribute to the definition of the "enemy"—a most uncanny other and enemy, however, who may turn out to have been "us" Americans, "us" Europeans all along. But the overall problematic of this overdetermined "other," racial and male or not, is also basic to the European plays, and it is this shared problematic that I have attempted to grasp here.

The abject horror of war, of *this* war in any event, extends in Vietnam Protest Theatre beyond individual suffering and death, beyond national tragedy, though these are painfully and traumatically involved. This horror resides in the "tragic"—because "staged"—reduction of humans to the level of "things" manipulated by powers that may seem to be "above" them, and thus beyond their control, but which we also recognize deep inside us and must continually struggle to understand and so also, perhaps, as inappropriate/d others, to change.

RE-ACTING TO THE TELEVISION WAR

Television Baby
Television Baby
By the grace of Dr. Spock
When the mothers weren't fuckers
and rock was just rock
What's on Channel seven?
Them teeth all look alike
Here comes Heigh Ho Silver
And the dopey grin on Ike
Television Baby
Switch to Channel Two
Fifty murders daily
And Captain Kangaroo
The war was in Korea
With Commies under beds
And Huac's gone to Heaven
Better dead than red
Television Baby
Grooving in the tubes
fifty murders daily
And Dagmar had the boobs
The whole world your arena
When DiMaggio had his mitt on
And grass was something greener
And pot was something to sit on
Television Baby
Drooling on the Dreck
Hopalong Cassidy
And Howdie Doodie's back
Television Baby
Let's watch Channel Five

Uncle Sam is calling
Will you stay alive?
Heroes born and made oh
Hello and goodbye
Young soldiers never fade oh
They just die.

—George Tabori

The most innovative formal devices of Vietnam Protest Theatre involved the use of media images, that is, mainly photographs and television films—in addition to popular music, as in Tabori's "Television Baby" song in *Pinkville* (1971). Photographs and films are, of course, two quite different media. A televised film shows what Susan Sontag calls "a stream of underselected images, each of which cancels its predecessor," whereas "each still photograph is a privileged moment, turned into a slim object that one can keep and look at again."[1] Nonetheless, I shall partially conflate the two types of images here, referring to both simply as "media images" because the distinction in Vietnam Protest Theatre itself is fluid, as it was for the public at large. Still photographs of the war appeared not only in the printed news but on television, though on TV they were commonly integrated with filmed war reporting. These combined media images were incorporated as visual stage features in the protest theatre and/or foregrounded and integrated *as* plot. In other words, they were not only used *in* theatre but also provided an informing narrative principle for the theatre *as* theatre, a recurring theme that reflects the theatre's ambiguous relationship to mass media, especially television. Needless to say, the function of this overall strategic approach, both formal and topical, was not identical in all Vietnam plays, and the differences are worth noting.

A major strategy emerges historically out of a prior German tradition that started with Brecht and Piscator, using various documents, mainly photographs and films, to reinforce the political message of the play with "real documentary evidence," as events represented on the stage are backed up by "scientific" evidence from the "real world." We have seen that this documentary device reappears in Peter Weiss's *Vietnam Discourse*, Rolf Hochhuth's *Soldiers*, or Daniel Berrigan's *The Trial of the Catonsville Nine*. But there are significant differences. The theatre experiments of the twenties operated with a relatively indiscriminate selection of documents, often chosen more for their novel appeal as technological images than for their specific content. And there was a certain faith that all such images were true. In contrast, the later playwrights of the "documentary theatre" and the Vietnam Protest Theatre were more evaluative, drawing a stronger distinction between what they consider to be "good" evidence and "bad"—often meaning politically correct, but sometimes based on an epistemological standard. Weiss believed, for example, that the general public's knowledge of events is colored by documents created and provided by the dominant social group, and that the purpose of documentary theatre is to rectify that one-sided perspective with alternative "real" documents that offer an effective oppositional vision. Plays by Weiss, Hochhuth, and Berrigan were also supposed to reveal concealed "real" facts about the Vietnam War that can be found in recorded speeches, photographs, newspapers, and other documents. These facts were presented as having at least as high a truth value as any media information, and *their* validity as evidence was rarely questioned by the playwright. To this problematic extent, documents and images used by the protest plays relied on much the same naive trust in the objectivity of modern techniques of reporting as did the coverage of the war in the electronic media of the establishment. But, then, the purpose of the Vietnam Protest Theatre was not to be objective in any *absolute* sense. It sought sooner to present an intentionally confrontational one-sided view, compensating for the one-sided view of the more hegemonic media in order to create a counter-public sphere.

Whether this strategy was fully successful is not decidable, dependent as it is on specific audience response. Just as television images have been said both to have supported and undermined the Vietnam War, so even the most scandalous documents used by protest playwrights no doubt both substantiated the horror of the war and somehow contributed to its anaesthetic spectacularization.[2] In that sense the documentary strategy might have come up against a peril noted by many critics, including Sontag when she argues that:

> [The] aestheticizing tendency of photography is such that the medium which conveys distress ends by neutralizing it. Cameras miniaturize experience, transform history into spectacle. As much as they create sympathy, photographs cut sympathy, distance the emotions. (Sontag 109)

Sontag (whose *On Photography* might have been titled *Against Photography*) actually asserts that even relatively innocent nonprofessional photographs always produce a form of domination.[3] This critique of all media images is surely exaggerated. The point here is that many protest playwrights shared that distrust of the media and, parallel to the first strategy which borrowed documents from these media, they pursued another strategy that linked the censure of the media with the censure of the war. That strategy, essentially thematic in nature, can best be grasped in four plays that illustrate it most systematically.

1. GUARE, VAN ITALLIE, DUAY, GRAY

One of the earliest plays confronting television is John Guare's *Muzeeka* (1967).[4] Like *Sticks and Bones*, *Muzeeka* combines the indictment of war with a satire of suburban North American life and its banal entrapments. Jack Argue lives in a Connecticut suburb of New York City and works at the production of Muzeeka (Muzak), the mind-numbing but seductive blend of synthesized, co-opted music piped into elevators and offices. "Despite" degrees from Yale, Harvard, and Princeton, he is drafted and sent to Vietnam, where he encounters the relationship between war and television.

Guare suggests the existence of "contracts" not only between reporters and the media but also between both and the military. As character Number Two explains ("before Baudrillard," so to speak): "My whole unit was under exclusive contract to NBC. I'm only allowed to fight for NBC. If they see me tomorrow—CBS—they can strip me of all my rank. Cut my payments off back home. They can send me to a unit. Christ, an independent unit. An educational network unit. I'm not fighting for no Channel Thirteen" (Guare 72). Furthermore, the entertainment shows blend the reality of war with its televisual images. The GIs become actors playing at war for the networks, while the death, battles, and other events are mapped onto the schedule of evening shows.

> My old unit wasn't wiped out till the end of *Batman* and the *Ed Sullivan Show.* They must've sat in the black watching for us, watching the television till the show ended and we turned it off. I never knew whether they killed us 'cause we were the enemy or because we turned off Ed Sullivan. (Guare 73)

In 1967 Argue finds that television has the same numbing effect in Vietnam as Muzeeka had in the United States. He is not worried about feeling any guilt when he returns home because "the newspapers and *TV Guide* and my Muzeeka will stick their hands in my ears and massage my brain and convince me I didn't do anything wrong" (Guare 77). He echoes Marshall McLuhan's dictum (also 1967!) that the medium is the message and the massage.[5] Fittingly, Argue's death is staged as in a low-budget television production, with some ketchup spilled on his shirt.

Guare is taking the notion of "television war" quite literally, carrying it out to its *reductio ad absurdum.* His play conflates the real war with a war between the networks, each vying for exclusive contracts (as in the underworld "contract" to murder). And not only the GIs are numbed by television shows but also American civilians who watch the same coverage of Vietnam. It is somewhat surprising that Guare's stage directions do not explicitly provide for the use of TV screens or film projections, even though the content of the play surely encourages directors to do so. But perhaps such visual "reinforcements" of the text appeared to Guare to be too "theatrical." The problem may be that *Muzeeka* already tries to embrace too many media at once or even that theatre is the wrong genre to make his point. Having pushed it so far toward the confrontation with the concept of a "TV war," it is as if it cannot both *represent* such a war and still remain *theatre*. This *in nuce* is a basic problem of "staging the television war"—wittingly or unwittingly illustrated by Guare.

This context is also pertinent to appreciate (Belgian-born, Harvard-educated) Jean-Claude van Itallie's remarkable *TV* (1966), actually written a year earlier than Guare's *Muzeeka*.[6] Although not focused directly on the Vietnam War, *TV* alludes to it as a "television war," and its stress on the televisual aspect of warfare—already in 1966—is in many ways prescient for what was to become the almost standard characterization of "Vietnam." As the title indicates, his subject matter is television, but with a vengeance. The entire stage is the re/creation of the "set" of a major network studio, with the three main characters—Hal, Susan, and George—as news anchors. The play is challenging for several reasons, not least because some of the actors (though, significantly, not the three anchors) must play multiple parts. Thus, Ronnie Gilbert (in the premier production in the Pocket Theatre) played nothing less than the following roles: Helen Fargis, the president's wife, a UGP researcher, a member of the rock and roll group, a peace marcher, Liy Heaven, the headache sufferer in a TV commercial, an evangelist choir member, and Mother in *My Favorite Teenager* (van Itallie 57). And so on—for four other actors as well. Subject positions in this proto-postmodern play are very fluid, very "schizoid" indeed, and yet they are seen as quite well anchored in specific historical and technocultural events.

Appropriately, *TV* begins with a motto by Marshall McLuhan: "He was numb. He had adapted to his extension of himself and had become a closed system" (van Itallie 57). On the back of *TV*'s stage is a large TV screen on which "actual" television footage (reminiscent, today, of *Saturday Night Live*'s "The News") will be projected sometimes with the sound up, sometimes on mute. During this televised pastiche of documents, five actors not only react to the television news but also (unlike in *Saturday Night Live*) actually re/enact it. Conceptually, these actors *are* TV: they are "dressed in shades of gray. . . . Their faces are made up with thin horizontal black lines to suggest the way they might appear to a viewer" (van Itallie 64). Within this scheme, three basic levels of action are taking place simultaneously: (1) the interaction between Hal, Susan, and George which concerns their private (more or less sexual) relationships; sometimes they comment on scenes reenacted by the five actors, but never on the "real" news items projected onto the back screen; (2) the five actors who act out scenes derived from what is projected on the screen; and (3) televised news—in part actual—projected on the back screen. It is particularly through the technocultural interplay between two levels of acting and TV that references are made to Vietnam. It is here in *TV* that the audience can see and hear quite literally perhaps the most striking example of "re-acting to the television war."

While a slide is projected of "Vietnamese mourners," an actor playing the second news announcer steps forward and addresses the audience:

> U.S. spokesman in Saigon said that families would be given shelter and compensation. Our planes are under strict orders not to return to base with any bombs. The United States regrets that a friendly village was hit. The native toll was estimated at sixty. (van Itallie 73)

Then another slide of mourners, and the news announcer's deadpan voice about the death toll:

> This was high, explained spokesman, in answer to questions, because of the type of bomb dropped. These are known as Lazy Dogs. Each Lazy Dog bomb contains ten thousand slivers of razor-sharp steel. (van Itallie 74)

Next come yet another slide of Vietnamese mourners, a cigarette commercial, and the beginning of the television series *The Endless Frontier*. This title links (as do the plays of Terry, Benedetto, and others) the conquest of the "Wild" West to Vietnam—Vietnam becoming just another frontier ("East" following "West") to be "won." Other later "newsworthy" items include a particularly hypocritical speech by President Johnson; images of peace protesters; more commercials and sitcoms; and the central interview of a Vietnam vet, Ron Campbell, by a female talk show host, Carol (van Itallie 108-11). Ron Campbell has decided, unbeknownst to Carol, not to accept a Silver Star for valor because, as he now explains bluntly: "We're committing mass murder." He adds, in the face of Carol's growing exasperation (she wanted a war hero, not a protester): "We're trying to take over a people that don't want to be taken over by anybody." Carol is reduced to repeating "I see, I see," but (ironically) it is increasingly evident that she (like Hal, Susan, and George, indeed the entire American public) precisely *doesn't* see. This blindness, disguised as televisual insight, leads straight into Ron Campbell's most explosive statement—this was 1966 after all: "I was there for a year and a half and every day I saw things that would make you sick. Heads broken, babies smashed against walls" (van Itallie 110). Such remarks, not to say images, were not yet available on living room TV sets. Only then Carol pulls Campbell's plug, abruptly ending the show, without analysis. What follows in *TV* is the TV show *White Cliffs of Dover*, in which a British couple discuss their personal relationship, specifically an apparent turn for the better as a result of experiencing "the war"— World War I or II, that is. War may be Hell, but (as for Balk) it can change people for the better—perhaps the people on TV, van Itallie ironically suggests, if not the audience of his *TV*.

None of these TV shows and news reports in *TV* is treated in any special way nor singled out for particular attention. The audience subjected to staged channel-surfing probably is to assume that van Itallie points to the leveling (but "democratizing") impact of television: its power to "numb"—just as in McLuhan's thesis. War, commercials, politicians' speeches, sitcoms, interviews, actual news footage—all have the same virtual effect. As Archie Bunker used to say in those days: "What's the difference?" Which also means, at least for van Itallie, *no* difference at all, *no* effect at all—except a massively ideological indoctrination, which is strong medicine. The weakness of *TV*, as an example of Vietnam Protest Theatre, is "Baudrillardian": i.e., that the war—in the form of anything resembling a *specific lived* event—is *wholly* absorbed into its mass mediatization, spectacularization, televisualization. Along with every other event.

Grant Duay's *Fruit Salad*, published in 1968, relies on stage devices (much more than Guare though less than van Itallie) to connect its scenes to lived war experiences by the means of reproduced media images.[7] However, in its focus on television, it favors images borrowed from commercials rather than images found in the coverage of the war. Like some filmmakers (George A. Romero and Ridley Scott), Duay actually did write TV commercials before writing *Fruit Salad*, switching to live theatre in order to deal more directly with the war.[8] The play is set in the jungles of Vietnam. Throughout its single act, a screen placed above the stage shows the film of a girl making a fruit salad: "The film is photographed in saccharine colors giving effect of TV commercial" (Duay 121). The three GIs in the play—Banana, Melon, and Cherry[9]—are caught and killed in an ambush. Highlights of that scene are punctuated by the film projected above.

The play never explains who is responsible for the deaths of the three GIs, though perhaps television might be. A note of uncertainty prevails: perhaps some other U.S. troops, not recognizing them, had made a fatal miscalculation? The overhead projector only hints at an answer when, after the slaughter, the image appears in a black-and-white army training film of the soldiers eating their namesakes: Banana eating a banana, etc. (Duay 137) One may infer that the soldiers/cannibals consume themselves (or at least their fruit namesakes) in the form of images, but also that their images are consumed on the television by the American viewing public represented by the pretty plastic girl. The antiwar message is conveyed with these words: "We're cut off! You're skinned! I'm peeled! Melon's chopped up! We're all mixed and ready to eat!" (Duay 135) The sacrifice of the GIs to the war appears all the more ironic because they are—and always already have been—alienated and transformed into spectacularized commercial sight and sound bites.

The inclusion of the black-and-white training tape has a message of its own. Basically, as in traditional documentary theatre, the tape operates as a document: a direct, if also quintessentially reproducible, image of truth, black and white like a newspaper. But, by contrast, it also serves to highlight the *glossy* colors of commercials and the spectacular representation of the war in the media.[10] Reflected in the "colorful" television fruit images, Banana, Melon, and Cherry are replaced by a brand new Banana, Cherry, and Melon: as soldiers they, too, are reproducible, and their deaths are consumed by the American television viewers every night. Such is the purely mechanical aspect of mechanized war in Duay's play. But, anonymously evoked in the black-and-white tape, the three GIs as victims are re/embodied in the three live actors on the stage, which adds an ironic "human" element to "inhuman" war.

This staging of the soldiers' deaths as a personal "tragedy" matched a change that was taking place in the official reporting of American casualties. Instead of quoting anonymous numbers, as was done at the beginning of the war, the media introduced a more personalized approach: "In later years of the war, however, they began apologizing in various ways for the coldness of the numbers. At times they would use still photographs of wounded soldiers instead of the flags."[11] (Already during the war was anticipated the Vietnam Memorial consisting simply of reinscribed names of the American dead.) One might recall that the official Nazi term for the victims of its genocidal policies was *cipher* (*Zifer*)—which means not only "zeros" or "nullities" but also "signs." Duay echoes, and perhaps mocks, the effort to camouflage the tragedy of all soldiers caught in the war by turning it into a personal "tragedy" of individual Americans.[12] As has often been remarked, Western art often functions to reduce complex historical and social problems to individual tragedies. In that context, Duay's play logically makes no explicit reference to the reason any GI might be in Vietnam. Only the television screen above the stage suggests a deciphering of the larger responsibility of American society. The televised images, set at a distance from the staged reality, and thereby clearly exposed as an artificial medium, provide a key cipher for the political message of the play: they point directly to the official and public cynicism of the "television war."

But the most telling criticism of that "television war" was offered only a decade later, in Amlin Gray's *How I Got That Story* (1979).[13] Following the playwright's announcement, "We are a spectacle to you. A land in turmoil" (Gray 108), the play gave up the pretense of showing an unmediated vision of the war, as it might indeed be seen by the military, and switched to the perspective of a reporter who can only cover the *images* of war. Writing four years after the final withdrawal of American troops from Vietnam in 1975, Gray could afford to present a truly retrospective dramatization of what has become public history. It is all the more significant that, in contrast to most other plays written at the time, *How I Got That Story* still focuses on the war in Vietnam rather than switching its attention to war veterans coming home.

How I Got That Story has two main topics. Like many earlier protest plays, it tells the story of violence that took place in Vietnam during the war. At the same time, however, it also tells the story of the quasi-Debordian "spectacularization" of the war: its transformation, through the reporting media, into images so radically severed from their ties to reality that they may be taken for reality themselves. Gray uses two

devices to convey this technocultural problematic. First, his main protagonist, the focal point on the stage, is not a U.S. soldier involved in the real
Vietnam War but a *reporter* who observes and records that war: an incarna-
tion of a media professional rather than a specific single individual. The
principal focus is thus not on fighting but on reporting and reproducing
the reports. The second device concerns the other main character: a
protean "Historical Event." In the performance I saw, the Event was acted
out in different scenes by six different actors, which stressed the artificial
and theatrical nature of the representation of all historical events.[14] These
two devices help to demonstrate how reality is transformed into biased
media images by two distinct processes: first, through the *words* of the
reporter who distorts the events far beyond the inevitable distortion that is
entailed by any verbal narrative; and, second, through the *vision* of the
same reporter who, among all the possible chaotic events, systematically
selects, and indeed is trained to perceive, those events which appear to
him to be promising material for marketable "Events" or spectacles.[15]
When, upon meeting Mme Ing (who likely stands for the much hated Mme
Nu), he remarks, "I've seen you on the cover of *Time* magazine" (Gray 86),
the reporter reveals that his knowledge of current affairs is in fact a
product of media images.[16] Gray's point is that the war reported on the TV,
as well as in radio and press dispatches, is always separated from reality
by a double screen of reporting that is always already based on previous
reporting.

This type of theatrical *mise-en-abyme* is further reinforced by staging
features that spotlight the role of media in shaping the meaning of the
reported events. As in *Fruit Salad*, and for similarly parodic reasons, Gray
uses photographic projections that evoke a TV commentary: "To facilitate
the Event's transformations, masked breaks should be provided on the
back wall. Slides announcing the titles of the scenes, etc., appear on the
back wall, as do photographs of the Event, as described" (Gray 78). The
distinctive spin—if not outright distortion—put on reality by reporters is
further exposed in several more specific scenes scattered throughout the
story.

The plot of the play provides the framework for this fairly systematic
exposure of media and a logical, albeit ironic and thus rather
undecidable, conclusion. In its most general outline, *How I Got That Story*
follows the reporter, a sympathetic character, who changes from a naive
witness, a supposedly objective collector of "neutral" images, into a
Vietcong sympathizer, and finally—symbolizing perhaps a further potential shift in the perceptions of the American public—to a victim
himself of the American media system. From the beginning, however,
doubt is cast on the reliability of his "objective" reporting. In the first
episode, the director of "TransPanGlobal" instructs the reporter *not* to
tell everything he sees; rather, he is to follow the directives of a tacit
(perhaps explicit) censorship:

KINGSLEY: My meaning was, you don't allow some pietistic preconception to subvert your objectivity. You write what you see.
REPORTER: That's very nicely said, Bob. I'll subscribe to that.
KINGSLEY: On the other hand, you don't write everything you see. (Gray 83)

This censorship demands a self-imposed, internalized control of emotions: natural human reactions to pathetic or horrifying scenes risk sending political messages that may be found subversive. Vietnamese girls in a bar, for example, could be viewed by the audience as overly attractive and sympathetic. So the reporter reflects: "The girls look very young. They're pretty. No, that's not objective. Stick to what's objective" (Gray 89). A more dramatic version of that self-censorship takes place when the reporter, like many U.S. reporters in 1963, witnesses the self-immolation of Thich Quang Duc:

> Oh my god. He's burning. People up and down the street are watching. I am too. I'm watching. (Quickly) I'm not watching. I'm not here! I'm a reporter! I'm recording this! (He writes) "The monk was sitting in the center of a column of fire. From time to time a light wind blew the flames away from his face. His face was twisted with the pain." The pain, my god—! (To himself) No! You're not here. You're just recording this. You look at it, you take the pencil, and you write it down. (The Bonze topples sideways) My god. (He forces his pencil to his pad and writes. Tape fades up: a low repeating chant in an Asian-sounding language) "Charred black . . . black circle on the pavement . . . wisps of orange fabric drifted down the street. (Gray 85)

Obviously, Gray's fictional reporter, caught in the media system, doesn't yet feel as guilty as Michael Herr who (though unacknowledged) may have provided Gray with some of the grim recollections of his own stint as a Vietnam reporter:

> There's no way around it, if you photographed a dead marine with a poncho over his face and got something for it, you were some kind of parasite. But what were you if you pulled the poncho back first to make a better shot, and did that in front of his friends? Some other kind of parasite, I suppose. Then what were you if you stood there watching it, making a note to remember it later in case you might want to use it?[17]

The "professional" ambivalence about his relationship to reality eventually affects, however, the reporter's total involvement in Vietnam. Since he cannot report the reality of the war—"as it really is" or as he "actually sees it"—he withdraws from that (im)possible reality, becomes an absent voice.[18] In his words: "I'm someone who's not here—who's here but can't—do anything, except report. . . . I'm alone. It's a condition of the job" (Gray 95). On the stage, of course, he *is* present in the actor's body, and this presence, however ephemeral, suggests an embodied link between the (real) reality of Vietnam and its (conventional) theatre reality. Together, the stage and Vietnam come across with a persuasive facticity.

As an individual, meanwhile, the reporter has his own problems. In contrast to the military, he enjoys an uncomfortable freedom because he does not "have" to go out in the field; his reporting involves a comparatively "free choice" for which he must or could be held responsible:

> GI: You can't want to go. Somebody got to make you go. Some mean old sergeant, damnful captain got to tell you, soldier, grab your gear and get your ass out and hump. You can't want to go.
> REPORTER: I won't get out there if it's not by choice. I have to want to. (Gray 90)[19]

Confused and intimidated by the real GIs, the reporter makes a nuisance of himself and plaintively complains about military stonewalling: "I'm not getting any news! If I'm not getting any news then what in Christ's name am I doing here?" (Gray 94). A piece of shrapnel in his backside solves his dilemma while creating a new one: now he can neither fight nor report nor sit.

The same piece of shrapnel turns him into a "genuine" victim of war, that is, into a potential, though minimal, Public Event for the media. His boss Kingsley is delighted:

> Little guy from Aujourd'hui lost his esophagus last week. Two weeks ago some wop from Benvenuto got his ears blown off. We haven't had an injury in five months. God damn outlets don't believe you're really covering the war unless some blood flows with the ink. . . . We're going to say the shrapnel lodged against your lower vertebrae. That's nothing that a brilliant surgeon, luck and a short convalescence can't cure. (Gray 98)

With more "luck," the reporter could have matched the bragging of a garrulous colleague of his, a crazy one-armed and one-legged photographer who brags about his crippling loss:

> Ooh that was righteous. It was nighttime. I was standing getting pictures of the tracer patterns. BAMMO! from behind! I got an incredible shot of that arm flying off. WHOOSH! Little bit underexposed, but something else, man WHOOSH! (Gray 101)

Exaggeration? Perhaps not. It seems that many photographers in Vietnam had the reputation of being daredevils, returning to pursue the really spectacular photos after numerous brushes with death: "Burrows, Stone and Flynn all died in the war, and Page was seriously injured on several occasions" (Moeller 381). A good image (not to say also a wrong war), like a work of art, deserves all sorts of sacrifices.

Gray comes close here to a "theatre of cruelty" that would be inspired by reality. Or perhaps he is yielding to the temptation of artistic violence, the cruelty both created and depicted in war movies such as *Apocalypse Now* and *Platoon*—a fad of modern art that started with the fascination that the Futurists had for mechanized war. But that may also be a way of looking at life and society, as in Benjamin's analysis of fascism as the aesthetics of politics: "Its [mankind's] self-alienation has reached such a degree that it can experience its own destruction as an aesthetic pleasure of the first order. This is the situation of politics which Fascism is rendering aesthetic. Communism responds by politicizing art."[20] An ironic VC guerrilla tells the reporter: "Your standpoint is aesthetic" (Gray 108).

Eventually the reporter achieves the status of a full-fledged Public Event. This completed transmutation into an Image *follows* his personal change from an "objective" reporter to a Vietcong sympathizer—suggesting perhaps ideological infiltration into the belly of the technocultural beast. He tries to live like a Vietnamese, and becomes—like the Vietnamese—a victim of the war. His dead body lying on the street becomes the latest photographic subject of the now completely limbless crazy photographer. When his camera flashes, the stage goes dark and on the overhead appears the photograph "of the head and shoulders of a body in the same position as the REPORTER's, and dressed identically. The face is that of the EVENT" (Gray 117). The reporter has been dehumanized into a spectacle. The audience are left worrying whether, like the "reporter," they are transformed into events waiting to happen.

In his stage directions, like van Itallie in *TV* and Duay in *Fruit Salad*, Gray calls for the use of black-and-white photographs: "Slides [which] are exaggerated halftone—broken into dots as if for reproduction—and thus suggestive of pictures in a newspaper" (Gray 88). The image of newspapers serves to validate the photograph as a medium of "true" reproduction, but doesn't protect it from apolitical spectacularization. In the version of *How I Got That Story* that I saw in 1989, the slides were not of Vietnam, as the stage directions call for, but showed randomly picked violent scenes from all parts of the world. Queried about that change, the director explained that, staging the play twenty years after Vietnam, the company wanted to draw attention to the United States as a *current* imperial threat, especially in Latin America, and hence any photo of violence served its purpose. I noticed that one of the slides recorded the horror scenes filmed at the liberation of Auschwitz. Asked where the slide came from and what it referred to, neither the director nor the cast could give an answer: it was just an empty image, a spectacular image of tragedy without a reference. At that point any specific project for protest or for political theatre begins to wither, as it does dramatically in van Itallie's *TV*.

The story of the reporter in *How I Got That Story* offers a symbolic process that could be an allegory for the story of Vietnam viewed as a media war. Initially, the media—like the reporter—reduce the Vietnam reality to images. Then, when truth about the war becomes known (in part through theatre protest),[21] the meaning of media's distorted images is destroyed in the public eye, like the reporter's life. Finally, the story of how media manipulated the American people becomes, like the reporter's death, a public Event for yet other media. At the same time, however, the evolution of the reporter also parallels the evolution of the *American public*. At first Americans generally believed in an "objective" version of the war as a political necessity. They eventually discovered a scandalous reality behind the images. Outraged (and nudged perhaps by protest theatre) they became ready to rebel.

Muzeeka, TV, Fruit Salad, and *How I Got That Story* share, in varying degrees, the same critical attitude toward the media: they suspect their representations and involvement in the war, and they use photographs, televised images, and films as documentary evidence of this suspicion. All of these documents are foreign bodies in the theatrical medium, but that very otherness is intended to serve rather than reduce the political impact of the plays. In a comparable situation, Linda Hutcheon notes in *The Politics of Postmodernism* that when photography is mixed with other media, such as advertising and novels, what "the mixing of the text and the image often does is to underline, through the use of direct verbal address to a viewer, the fact that, as a signifying system, pictures too represent both a scene and the look of a viewer, both an object and a subject."[22] Or, as Raymond Bellour suggests, the insertion of photographic stills in a film causes the spectator to reflect, "to think about the film and also the very fact of being in the cinema. In short, the photograph's presence allows me more freely to cathect what I see. It helps me—a little—to close my eyes, although they remain open."[23] The interaction between media to which Hutcheon points may be reversed, and the images may serve to problematize and occasionally clarify the meaning of a theatrical text. The four anti-Vietnam War protest plays discussed here demonstrate how this process can take place.

For example, how does the army training film function in Duay's play, and how do documentary photographs function in Gray's?[24] Obviously, the use of so-called historical documents, whether photos, films, or re-corded speeches, helps to re-create through their representation a (more or less specific) vision of an absent past.[25] In that sense, in *Fruit Salad*, the army training film serves to evoke a "past anterior" to Vietnam. But there is another answer as well, more pertinent for political theatre. Identified by the audience as a "realistic" document, perceived in conjunction with other features on the stage, the film offers a promise, or rather reinforces a preexisting belief, that everything evoked on the stage may belong to the world outside, offstage, and that all signs on the stage, actors included, refer not to fiction but to the same historical events as does the filmic sign. Viewed from that perspective (and whether the audience is aware of it or not—which is itself a huge problem), the pictorial representation of the burning monk anchors *How I Got That Story* in real history. But that answer raises fresh questions. Are photographs really reliable as signs of (outside) reality? Are people correct when they assume that photographs (or films) give a better testimony of the "truth" than a verbal text? Are they really more "objective"? Is it true, as Sontag says, that "the images that have a virtually unlimited authority in a modern society are mainly photographed images" (Sontag 153)? Clearly the answer to all such questions— on stage and elsewhere—is a relative one: "Objective, *compared to what?*" And it is in this space of theatrical relativity that all these plays under consideration operate, more or less effectively.

Is it possible to look at a photographic or filmic image as if it were *not* influenced by interfering subjective factors? To be sure, there are good reasons to accept the prevailing notion that photography or film can "capture" reality better than other representations. Our cultural conventions certainly favor highly iconic signs as the most reliable evidence of the reality to which they refer. But there are many ways of manipulating that convention—in good faith or bad—and most of these ways rely equally on cultural conventions. For example, whereas it may be commonly accepted that a photograph can "capture" reality, it is not similarly expected that it can capture its *meaning*. Even captions, which are almost always at once required, crucial, *and arbitrary*, cannot do that. One can hardly disagree with John Tagg when he argues (following Roland Barthes and others) that:

> What is real is not just the material item but also the discursive system of which the image it bears is part. It is to the reality not of the past, but of present meanings and of changing discursive systems that we must therefore turn our attention. That a photograph can come to stand for evidence, for example, rests not on a natural or existential fact, but on a social, semiotic process.[26]

It is therefore necessary to examine some of the ideological as well as social contexts of documentary images in the protest plays and particularly the origins of these images. In the case of the army training tape, it obviously was made by the U.S. military officials who held power over their military subjects—a power that projected onto the image the fundamental helplessness of the grunts. In *How I Got That Story*, on the other hand, the photos of the burning monk and of helpless Vietnamese were taken not by the army but by civilian reporters. One could claim that they were not actively involved in the war, as the reporter notes in the play, and hence that their documents, though biased in their selection, could be relatively freer of *deliberate* ideological interference. However, the stance of "noninvolvement" is in itself a political choice. Ronald Haeberle was criticized (in Tabori's *Pinkville*, for example) for taking his prize-winning My Lai photographs instead of intervening and trying to prevent the slaughter. And the photographer of the napalmed girl running toward the camera is clearly not doing anything to help her. Hence Sontag: "Taking photographs has set up a chronic voyeuristic relation to the world which levels the meaning of all events. . . . Photographing is essentially an act of non-intervention. . . . The person who intervenes cannot record; the person who records cannot intervene" (Sontag 11-12). This dreamlike inability to move, even to be moved emotionally, is perhaps no better staged than in van Itallie's *TV*.

At stake with photography in general may be a denial of the possibility of human solidarity since, to continue with Sontag, "the camera is a kind of passport that annihilates moral boundaries and social inhibitions, freeing the photographer from any responsibility toward the people photographed" (Sontag 41). One must remember that the reporters in Vietnam were mainly white males,[27] whereas the subjects of images were usually Asians and often women, children, and old people, in short the "other" as a victim.[28] While purporting to "report the news," these photographers no doubt sought also to present exotic subjects, viewed with condescension as that "Other." To quote Tagg again:

> Documentary photography traded on the status of the official document as proof and inscribed relations of power in representation which were structured like those of the earlier practice of photo-documentation: both speaking to those with relative power about those positioned as lacking. (Tagg 12)

How then should the media images be viewed on the stage? Are all photographs to be dismissed (or approved) *tout court*, or should some distinction be made among them? What happens to photographs that are taken from a self-consciously neutral or subversive political perspective, not to make money but to expose wrongdoings? According to Sontag, even they are ineffectual because "the very extent to which a photograph is unforgettable indicates its potential for being depoliticized, for becoming a timeless image" (Sontag 107). A trite reductionist solution would be simply to discount on these grounds the significance of all media images. One should rather look at the context in which each image is placed. The framing device can influence the meaning of a photograph, since as Barthes suggested, "the structure of the photograph is not an isolated structure; it is in communication with at least one other structure; namely the text, title, caption or article."[29] The frame, in Vietnam Protest Theatre, is the *staged* performance during which the images appear. The question then becomes: How does the photographic or televised image relate to the performed text of the play, and how does that in turn affect the meaning both of the image and of the play?

Part of the answer may be found in those protest plays that specifically attempt to restore the initial impact of spectacularized images, that is, to restore the meaning that they may have lost. This goal defines a third strategy in dealing with media. It seeks not to expose the role of media outright, as does the second strategy, but rather to utilize their resources in order to counteract their influence. The selected images are borrowed from television films and well-known photographs and are reproduced in theatre with a revitalized meaning. As an exemplary case, consider the often reproduced image of self-immolation by Thich Quang Duc.[30] However, in order to show how it works within the context of a concrete theatrical performance, it is important to examine in some detail two plays where it occupies a central position. The different treatments it receives offer a sample of formal and thematic theatrical techniques available to Vietnam Protest Theatre. A third play, by Adrienne Kennedy, adapts yet another strategy to recontextualize and demythologize photographs.

2. GRASS, BROOK, KENNEDY

Günter Grass's *Max* (1970) is centered on the mediatized picture of immolation by fire, but with an unusual twist.[31] The planned burning of a dachshund replaces a burning human in an attempt to restore the initial shock value to the image, and thereby to reinfuse the deed with meaning and impact.[32] The entire play, one may claim, deals with the distance required to produce shock, especially the distance between the "real" world, with its pragmatic demand for political commitment, and its more or less distorted representation in memory and in media.

There are four main characters: two teachers who came of age during the Nazi era, Eberhard Starusch and Irmgard Seifer, and two high school seniors, Philipp Scherbaum and Veronika (Vero) Lewand. A parallel is set up between the teachers and their students: Starusch and Seifer both claim to have opposed the Nazis, and Vero and Philipp are protesting the Vietnam War. But the young rebels have little patience with memories of the past. As Vero tells the teachers:

> We're just not interested in what you did when you were seventeen. It's probably true that you did or didn't do something when you were seventeen. Old Hardy more than anybody. Whenever we tell him what's going on in Vietnam, he talks about his days in a teenage gang when the war was on and makes speeches about early anarchism. (Grass 101)

This lack of interest is not without grounds, for the past is quite ambiguous.[33] Seifer discovers a forgotten packet of letters that she had written to Nazi authorities, when she was seventeen (the same age as the young Philipp), to denounce a nearby farmer. She realizes that she had been trying for years to deny the Nazi part of her past, and she struggles with guilt throughout the rest of the play. Starusch too feels guilty because, when he was young, he never did take a direct action that his student, Philipp, now wants to take. The initial German title, *Davor*, appropriately refers to the weight of all that had happened *before*.[34] Obsessed by that "before," in order to dissuade Philipp from burning the dog Max, Starusch shows him old slides of burning bodies, among them the victims of the Allied fire bombing of Dresden. The interplay between the present situation in Germany, the situation in Vietnam, and what happened in Germany's Nazi past anticipates a postmodernist agenda in Jameson's sense: "More interesting, and more problematical, are the ultimate attempts, through this new discourse, to lay siege either to our own present and immediate past or to a more distant history that escapes individual existential memory."[35]

The more immediate question that emerges from *Max*, however, is whether it is better to solve a problem with words or to take direct action. Philipp rejects Starusch's proposal to become editor of a student newspaper where he could deal with "the Vietnam question with complete frankness, and even with pro and con" (Grass 18). "I'd rather do something else," he says, "something relevant that will be a sensation" (Grass 7). He argues that, in the modern world, words ultimately have only a numbing effect on people whereas dramatic images of action can motivate them to act. But Starusch is numb to the outside world, even to atrocities in the Mekong Delta:

> Yes, Scherbaum, I have *read* about it. It's bad. Bad bad. But I must admit that I am more stricken, exposed, and robbed of all sense and security by this aching, this stream of air always aimed at the same nerve, and this throbbing, this localized, regular ache, which isn't actually so bad and is easily deadened by anaesthetic, than by the sum of horrible columns of figures, than by the photographed, immense, and still abstract ache of this world—because it doesn't touch my nerve. (Grass 21)

Starusch's own private pain is too much embedded in German history to be affected by the "tragedy" of "others." To find a way to overcome this psychological anaesthesia, to touch a different nerve, Philipp chooses immolation as a symbolic image of protest against the war and the use of napalm. However, because people have become anaesthetized even against human immolation, too often seen in media images, he wants to burn his dog instead of burning himself. A burning dog—a German dachshund, no less—Philipp believes, will force people to realize that the Americans are burning people in Vietnam.[36] All this is deadly serious and leaves one to wonder why for a German audience a burning dachshund would be more shocking than a burning human—part of Grass's bitter point.

The would-be sensational nature of the project leads to an inevitable failure. To achieve the desired shock effect, Philipp must be assisted by the very media that he despises because they televisually anaesthetize people:[37]

> The press and the TV will be there. We'll make up a leaflet together, right to the point, about the effects of napalm. After they've arrested me or finished me off one way or another, you and your girlfriend can hand it out on the Avenue. (Grass 48)

That prospect does not deter Vero. An extremist in all ways, she welcomes the coverage of a sensational action, in all the newspapers and on television, ensuring the maximum possible exposure.[38] Terrorism, of course, is always dependent on media to publicize its aims. But for Philipp, the anticipated sensationalism and commercialization conflict directly with the genuine feeling of revolt that he wants to stimulate. What will happen if he burns Max? As Starusch predicts: "The reaction of the public? Headlines in the morning paper. . . . And a week later not a soul will be talking about it, because something else will be making headlines" (Grass 70). Persuaded by his teacher that Max's immolation will have no pragmatic effects, Philipp decides to become the newspaper editor and to deal with political issues in its columns.

Grass underscores the potential danger of commercialization throughout his text by inserting lines from American television commercials. His "Oh, I see you wash with Tide" or "Mr. Clean" are to demonstrate that advertisement corrupts everything, including political action. The strong anticommercialism of Grass is obviously tied to his view of media but may originate elsewhere, notably in the more general prejudice of writers and artists who claim to protect a "high culture" against a spreading commercialism. At the time Grass wrote the play, a debate was raging about the commercialization of German television.[39] *Max* may be effective as Vietnam Protest Theatre, but *within* the play the protest against the (corrupt) media is coupled with a certain tribute to that media. This tribute is likely intended to be ironic, but it remains a tribute nonetheless.

A different treatment of the immolation image was offered in 1966 by *US*, produced by Brook's theatre group not only as a response to what was happening in Vietnam but also in an effort to bring some clarity to the barrage of media images that was bombarding the British public every day. Brook noted:

> The problem was—how can current events enter the theatre? Behind this lies the question, why should they enter the theatre? We had rejected certain answers. We did not accept the idea of the theatre as television documentary, nor the theatre as lecture hall, nor the theatre as vehicle for propaganda. . . . We were not interested in Theatre of Fact. (Brook 9)

Yet certain facts had to be acknowledged, or denied, and at any rate used. Reflecting on the early stages of the production of *US*, Brook says that his group consulted media images and stories as well as written historical documents.[40] As a result, while avant-garde in some ways, *US* is also a "typical" documentary play assembled with public statements, pictures, newsreels, films, and historical facts. Recognizable images, shown several times, eventually dominated the performance.

In his production notes for *US*, Albert Hunt tells how one particular figure, "the image of the Buddhist monk who had poured petrol over himself and burnt himself to death as a protest against the war . . . had clearly taken root in Brook's mind as one of the central images of the play" (Hunt 17). The play starts with that image on a "real" slide projected on a screen while the actors enact that immolation on the stage, explaining: "When we burn ourselves, it is the only way we can speak" (Brook 33). Toward the middle of the play, the image is reenacted to evoke the specific self-immolation of Norman Morrison, the American who had that year (1966) burnt himself in front of the Pentagon. Then, in a final twist of the image at the end of *US*, a butterfly is burned, anticipating Grass's idea to burn a dog as a symbol for napalmed human beings. Surprisingly enough, many people were more disturbed by that butterfly scene than by the rest of the play, perhaps because they thought the butterfly was *real*. Is one to believe that, in contrast, everything else was taken to be fictional despite its source in "real" documents? It is likely that the public reacted more vigorously to the (staged) burning of a butterfly than to the (actual) burning of people because the butterfly was here and now, and therefore quite real, and the human victims of fire were in Vietnam and already in a legendary past.

Some of Brook's documentary sources were more obscure. The British public probably did not know the "real life" story of Barry Bondhus, sentenced for damaging U.S. government property and obstructing the draft by "dumping two buckets of human excrement into the files of his local draft board" (Brook 77). Even more obscure was the origin of the theme song, "Zappin' the Cong," which drew on a sequence in a Canadian film about Vietnam and on an article by Nicholas Tomalin in the *Sunday Times*, describing an American officer who called "zapping" the exhilarating action of killing the enemy (Brook 84). Of course, we can "zap" the TV channels, "killing" them for awhile.

To make sure that the public overcame its temptation to treat *US* as just another fiction about Vietnam, but also to counteract—as other playwrights did—the slanted vision of Vietnam offered in the very media Brook was using as sources, he accompanied his re/presentation of newsreels, photos, and documents with pointed comments on their nature and source. Thus, in a long sequence in the middle of the production, he tackles the problem of the role of the "reporter," anticipating Gray's play on the spectacularization of the war. Noting that reporters in Vietnam are "exiled" from their native countries, Brook insists on the strangeness of their perspective, from which all previously learned rationalizations, modes of interpretations, and solipsistic points of view must appear unreal. He

compares the reporters to Pavlovian dogs going insane inside an experimentation cage: "Poor newspapermen in Saigon sit around like those
dogs, with all their conditioned reflexes all screwed up" (Brook 95-96). The
inference to be drawn is that the individual reporters ("eyewitnesses" but
also "I witnesses") are no longer sane human beings; hence, since they
alone as an estate are responsible for collating and disseminating news for
the outside world, the vision of Vietnam shown to the world is itself mad.
For Brook, the reporters are not villains but victims of army bureaucracy
just like anyone sent to Vietnam. *US* doesn't try to conceal how out of
touch the reporters are with the culture of Vietnam. Staying in air-condi-
tioned Western hotel rooms, waiting to be briefed by the military, they are
as removed from Vietnam reality as the average TV viewer at home. "Few
ever leave Saigon, few ever meet the Vietnamese. Vietnam, for them, is this
room. From this room comes 90% of all stories, all articles, all ideas about
the war. When you read about Vietnam in your newspaper the report
probably came from this room, already processed, homogenized, made fit
for human consumption" (Brook 96-97). The problematic status of the
information received and disseminated by the press is also reflected in
another scene, portraying a military press briefing. Based on an actual
newsreel recording, it shows various bureaucratic aberrations. That scene
worked effectively on stage, though perhaps not as well as when it was
viewed in the newsreel document, as Brook freely admitted (Brook 96-97).

For Brook, not all images that the media produce must be always
dismissed, and it is the *use* that is made of them that counts primarily,
provided it is not a commercial use. "You can actually go to Vietnam and
take a few pictures of burned babies and sell your honest doubt to the
Sunday Supplements" (Brook 173-74). The particular choice among images is always difficult. It brings back the basic questions: How effectively
can one use the documents in theatre? Does a multimedia presentation
have its merits?

What emerges from Brook's practice is that there exists a vast information pool from which only a few images have been and must be selected to
be shown in the theatre. There is no need to look hard for surprising
images; some of the most effective are those which have already been
popularized by the media: the figure of the burning monk or that of
Nguyen von Troi, the NLF hero who tried to assassinate McNamara—two
Vietnamese figures that will reappear a year later in Gatti's *V comme
Vietnam*. The risk, as was mentioned before, is that transferred to the stage
these images lose their initial power and become *only* anaesthetic images,
fragments of the world spectacle. Brook says that his intention was to
restore their (supposedly) initial shock value, to evoke the reality and
remove or delimit spectacularization:

> We were all of us saturated by newsreels and reports and television
> programmes. Horrors no longer had any effect on us. But in a theatre, in a

ritualized situation, it might be possible for us to see the horrors in a fresh way. (Brook 16)

But Brook's confidence in the ritual revitalization of images apparently was not total, since he also exploited various other forms of mechanical despectacularization, occasionally borrowing from electronic media. He tried, for example, to emulate the nonlinear presentation of news in newspapers, where competing bits of information reach the reader simultaneously, in contrast to a linear unfolding as in a novel, a movie, or the television news. He tried to force theatre to be what Barthes claimed it essentially was: a symphony of signs competing for attention. (Along similar lines the Federal Theatre Project of the thirties was called "The Living Newspaper.") He wanted to have two huge television screens at the sides of the stage, both displaying newsreels, slides, and photographs. Since there is always a degree of flattery in imitation no matter how critically or paradoxically intended, these innovations aping television received a mixed reaction. Some critics objected to the lack of coherence resulting from the integration of a new(s) medium with traditional forms of theatre.[41] Others criticized the attempt to create a new total medium with heterogeneous genres.[42] And some viewed the play simply as a disaster. Failing to see that a new synthesis was supposed to be achieved, they saw on stage only a reproduction of preexisting material with no new value, message, or theme: "In short, the play tells us nothing that is not already being said day in and day out on news broadcasts, in films, TV and the press."[43] Another critic stated in the British *Sunday Telegraph*:

But it is at least arguable that anyone who has seen monks in flames, legless children, mutilated corpses, charred countryside, through the electronic immediacy of television may find the sight of well-fed actors hobbling and gibbering an impressive illusion rather than an unbearable reality.[44]

Judging by that last opinion, *US* failed, at least for some spectators, as an effective political theatre because it could not match the incomparably greater persuasive power of the media already in place, which it attempted to exploit, to expose, and to replace. For that critic, the ritual magic of theatre did not refresh the vision of horror trivialized by photographic and filmic images; rather, it theatricalized it into aesthetic show.

Adrienne Kennedy's *An Evening with Dead Essex* (1973) is a short one-act play based on a "true story."[45] It tells of Mark "Jimmy" Essex, an African American working-class Vietnam vet who, from "atop Howard Johnson Motor Lodge, New Orleans," shot and killed "three policemen, two hotel guests and a hotel employee" (Kennedy 67). The play has six characters: a director, an assistant director, two actors, one actress, and a projectionist. All the characters, with the notable exception of the projectionist, are African American. The main frame of the play deals with rehearsals of an inserted play about Jimmy Essex. This frame structure is similar to Hochhuth's *Soldiers* except that, in this case, the complete play-within-a-play is never shown to the audience, which sees only a series of disjointed scenes exploring different facets of the life of Essex—"channel-hopping" between them, as it were. Most of this information is taken from newspaper clippings, posters, photographs, and other "real" documents about the otherwise never seen or heard Essex. More important, all these documents—or rather protodocuments—are provided by the white projectionist who remains totally silent. As the man behind the projector (literally, the machine that projects, indeed shoots, mediatized messages into the mediatized world), the projectionist controls not only what can be seen of the dead Essex but the order in which it is seen. On the one hand, then, the projectionist (like a film editor) more or less consciously censures the real according to unknown principles of selection; on the other hand, he allows us to see and hear what otherwise might not be seen or heard at all. For there are almost no other nonmediatized sources of information available about Jimmy Essex and uncounted other African American Vietnam vets. We only have oral history, perhaps, and *An Evening with Dead Essex*. The projectionist stands for the white establishment that controls—typically behind the scenes and offstage—the lives of Americans of color. But the projectionist stands also for the mass media generally which, under the guise of neutrality and objectivity, conceal their various ideological, racial, and class biases in selecting "all the news that's fit to print." The director of the inserted play-within-a-play makes this point explicitly: "Each soldier should talk about how brutally used he felt to fight a darker brother for a country that despises him even more than his Vietnam enemy" (Kennedy 68).

The theatricality of this ingenious, deceptively simple play—its way of staging an otherwise occluded aspect of the television war and contemporary technoculture—enables Kennedy to spotlight deep contradictions between the reality of the black soldier and the white mythology that distorts even as it documents. Newspaper articles cited near the end of the play state that Essex "developed a hatred for whites while serving in the Navy" (Kennedy 77). But the performance reveals that his New Orleans killings, terrible though they are, were not a reaction to his Navy experience, but rather a disillusionment—individual and collective—with the entire hypocritical social system encountered—as yet another "frame"— both before and after the Vietnam War. With songs and prayers taken from African American culture, the play reconstructs the "framed" Essex's identity—or rather one such identity—and his "failure" to "readjust" to a white society that could never "adjust" to him *except* by treating him as a pawn and weapon. The play-within-a-play provides Kennedy and her audience with a critical perspective—or, as Brecht would have said, a "social gestus"—with which to reimagine the life of one man, who also stands for thousands, and is at once a weapon and a victim of "the

American way of life" and hence of the television war.

Perhaps one could conclude by saying that Kennedy asks us to rethink, with Walter Benjamin, the Socratic dictum that "the unexamined life is not worth living." Jimmy Essex was given little, if any, leisure time in his life for philosophic introspection. Rather, *An Evening with the Dead Essex* shows that "only that historian will have the gift of fanning the spark of hope in the past who is firmly convinced that *even the dead* will not be safe from the enemy if he wins. And this enemy has not ceased to be victorious."[46] So it is, then, that Jimmy Essex takes his place among other inappropriate/d others and plays his part in reacting to the television war.

3. TOWARD POSTMODERNISM

The common policy of the plays discussed here is to despectacularize the media images and project, onto the stage, a more "authentic" vision of the war. The interaction between images and live actors was to bring out the urgency of the issues against which the playwrights wanted to protest. It also served to counteract the process of reification whereby the image of the burning monk, and all other mediatized pictures of the war, become inert in public memory. For as Jameson notes, under postmodern conditions, "it is memory itself that has become the degraded repository of images and simulacra, so that the remembered image of the thing now effectively inserts the reified and stereotypical between the subject and reality or the past itself" (Jameson 1991, 123–24). Because of its live nature, theatre could turn representations into a lived experience, with a renewed feeling of immediacy and the urge to act accordingly. It is in this sense that one may understand Hannah Arendt's claim that theatre is the "political art par excellence."[47] Since it cannot be fully reproduced, theatre always restores specificity to historical events, the complex meaning informing the incandescent image: a real human burning himself in protest is not *just* a sensational photograph. When they first appeared, many atrocious images of death did shock and outrage the public, but through constant exposure and overuse, this initial response became dulled, except in theatre with its vivid illusions. Against all odds, it often seems, Vietnam Protest Theatre succeeded in recapturing the lost immediacy of war.

That goal was achieved by the means of three main strategies used to deal with mass media and their images. In the first and most traditional sense, à la Weiss and Hochhuth, these images provided a documentary reinforcement for the message of the protest plays. Images as documents stood as historical evidence of "reality," served to educate the audience, and persuaded it to take political action. By the second strategy, à la Guare, Duay, and Gray, media images became examples (or embodiments) of the impact of media on the reporting of the war. They were discussed in the plays and, in some cases, integrated into the plot. They played their part in the more general indictment that "high culture" and tradition, in this case theatre, direct against "popular" or "low" culture, represented by mediatized images, especially television. The most systematic development of this strategy is found in plays written in the United States where television was more commercialized than in Europe.[48] Finally, by the third strategy, à la Brook, Grass, and Kennedy, the media images were recontextualized on the stage in an attempt to counteract their spectacular reification.

These three functions/strategies, while presented separately for the sake of analytic clarity, are often combined empirically in any given play, sometimes overdetermining a single image. There are many variations in their implementation and results. But one way or another, most of the Vietnam Protest Plays seem to be determined to deal with media images, either in form or content.[49] The ubiquitous projection of photographs and films can be seen as an acknowledgment that theatre, in a society overwhelmed by the slanted messages of the media, cannot deny their influence, and that even the most revolutionary theatrical staging—and its function as a type of *Gesamtkunstwerk*—must integrate mediatized images in order to minimize their effect. At least this seems to have been the paradoxical and ambivalent approach adopted by the Vietnam protest playwrights.

One might be tempted to invoke here the old adage "If you can't beat them, join them." For to join an enemy is often to *become* that enemy, rather than the Trojan horse in its midst. The playwrights often expected that, by integrating television and media images into their staging, they would change them into properly theatrical features, enabling the Vietnam theatre to incorporate their power. However, another aspect of this problem articulates the insertion of media in theatre more directly with the phenomenon of postmodernism.

While postmodernism obviously may be defined in various ways, it appears always somehow to involve a trend toward pastiche, including multimedia representations. According to Jameson, at the root of this trend lies an increasingly pressing need to "defamiliarize" stale art forms:

> "Representation" is both some vague bourgeois conception of reality and also a sign system (in the event Hollywood film), and it must now be defamiliarized not by the intervention of a great or authentic art but by *another* art, by a radically different practice of signs. (Jameson 1991, 123)

In the case of theatre, however, a real defamiliarizing rejuvenation of its iconic representations cannot, by its logic as living performance, come from a different medium, such as cinema, but requires the development of a new theatrical practice germinated by "new" signs. The insertion of mass-produced media images, particularly photos, in the traditional domain of theatre represents such a new practice, especially since photography can be viewed as the art form par excellence of postmodernism.[50]

Mixing photography with theatre almost necessarily expresses an intrusion of postmodernist multimedia into live performance. The critical tension between presentation and mediatized representation is both a cause and effect of postmodernism.[51]

Consciously or not, photographs and televised images on stage not only conflate various media but also undermine and de-auraticize the "high" values of the theatre medium interacting with the "low" culture of television.[52] But there are other manifestations of postmodernism in the protest plays. Most of them eschew linear stories, dismissing the traditional Aristotelian unity of time/action/place. They offer episodic narratives held together by a tenuous thematic thread that links disjointed scenes. This type of fragmented, even "schizoid," narrative has also been identified and analyzed as a product of postmodernism.[53] The very structure of the plays thus exhibits what has been called the "cultural dominant" of postmodernism.[54] My point is to push postmodernism back into the sixties not only, say, to Herr's 1968 novel, *Dispatches*, but earlier, and with more consistency, to the staged war of Vietnam Protest Theatre.

In the same postmodernist spirit, anti–Vietnam War theatre denies a traditional role to the "hero." With the exception of Rabe's *Sticks and Bones* and *The Basic Training of Pavlo Hummel*, none of the plays have a forceful "authoritative" protagonist who, whether successful or not, victim or winner, commands the progression of the plot. Even Adrienne Kennedy's *An Evening with Dead Essex*, allegedly centered on Essex, does not present him as a character on stage. *How I Got That Story* is more problematic since the reporter does hold the center of attention. But he is anonymous, a type rather than an individual, and he stands for the process of *r*eporting, *r*eproducing the news, so that his role is essentially defined by reproducibility, not his uniqueness qua individual. Finally, this play conforms as well as the others to the postmodern movement away from the individual subject.[55]

The postmodern prolepsis of the Vietnam Protest Theatre was surely influenced by the intellectual and social developments of the time, though many of the protest playwrights hardly fit the image of postmodernist thinkers. The Vietnam War was different from any war before it, and therefore it needed new forms to be represented in all its chaotic difference. "This first terrible postmodernist war cannot be told in any of the traditional paradigms of the war novel or movie" (Jameson 1991, 44). And theatre, we may add. As ephemeral as the plays were, as ineffective as their protest may have been, the engaged theatre of this period may also have found in the postmodern spirit the proper paradigm for its protest against the "television war."

ANTIMEDIA: VIETNAMESE THEATRE AS PACIFIC RESISTANCE

No scientific instrument can verify the existential
nature of life in this story.   —Thich Nhat Hanh

[N]ationalism declares the domain of the spiritual
its sovereign territory and refuses to allow the colonial power to intervene in that domain.
                                        —Partha Chatterjee

Few of the recent studies about the Vietnam War, even those dealing explicitly with protest theatre, mention, let alone analyze, protest plays written and produced by the Vietnamese. This omission is unfortunate in light of the exceptionally rich theatrical tradition of Vietnam and its use of theatre as a cultural-political weapon, most recently in struggles against European and American colonialism and imperialism. Part of a large tradition of global protest, but also a unique contribution in its own right, Vietnamese theatre has been resisting assimilation and incorporation by Western audiences, remaining a response on the margins. As put by the Vietnamese filmmaker and theorist Trinh T. Minh-ha in *When the Moon Waxes Red: Representation, Gender and Cultural Politics* (1991):

> The margins, our sites of survival, become our fighting ground and their site for pilgrimage. Thus, while we turn around and reclaim them as our exclusive

territory, they happily approve, for the divisions between margin and center should be preserved, as clearly demarcated as possible, if the two positions are to remain intact in their power relations. Without a certain work of displacement . . . the margins can easily recomfort the center in its goodwill and liberalism; strategies of reversal thereby meet with their own limits.[1]

During the Vietnam War, the National Liberation Front and Vietcong were able to draw on the long history of Vietnamese theatre to develop extensive culture-drama programs which had itinerant groups of performers travel from one hamlet or village to the next, educating the people, spreading the word of communism, and calling for resistance against the South Vietnamese and the United States armies. The performances stressed both visual and verbal messages and could change their thematic content from day to day, adapting it to current events. They constituted an exceptionally flexible and effective type of theatre for a rural, often illiterate or preliterate, and largely pretechnological society. And so they were rightly recognized by the Joint U.S. Public Affairs Office (JUSPAO) as a major medium for spreading enemy propaganda. Of such concern was the impact of North Vietnamese and Vietcong theatre troops that JUSPAO began to imitate them, promoting several theatrical performing groups for the South Vietnamese and the Americans. Among them were the Van Tac Vu Cultural Drama Teams, which engaged in "cultural seed planting" and served "as a uniquely credible means of communication between the government and the people in a rural society where word of mouth and face-to-face discussion remain the major means of communication."[2]

Theatre played an important role on both sides in Vietnam, and any balanced account of the history of that conflict ought to reserve a place for it, including that written by the Vietnamese themselves (difficult though this may be to research, in part because they are rarely preserved). I shall be looking here at a Buddhist play that attempted to negotiate the space between the two main competing ideologies, staging an ostensible neutrality in their interstices, and between margin and center. In the words again of Trinh, "On the one hand, truth is produced, induced, and extended according to the regime in power. On the other, truth lies in between all regimes of power" (Trinh 30). The play in question undertook to find a truth not merely between, even beyond, the ideological positions of North and South Vietnam but also between, and beyond, the positions of East and West, "Third World" and "First," "theatre" and "fact," the "technocultural" and the "primitive."

Thich Nhat Hanh's *The Path of Return Continues the Journey* was published in English translation in 1972, with a foreword by Daniel Berrigan, by the Hoa Binh (Peace) Press in New York City, which was linked to the Jesuit Thomas Merton Life Center.[3] Born in 1926 in Dalat, Nhat Hanh became a novice monk at the age of sixteen. After studying literature and philosophy at Saigon University, he went to Princeton in 1961 to study philosophy of religion and lectured on Buddhism at Columbia two years later. He returned to South Vietnam, where he was already viewed as one of the most popular poets in the early 1960s, and took a leading role, through writing and publishing activities, in various Buddhist social and political movements before he was exiled from his native country. A Zen master, poet, and scholar, he is the author of more than sixty books including scholarly exegeses of Buddhist texts, stories about Vietnam, and his own works for practical meditation.[4] Still exiled, he lives in France, where he writes and does political work for refugees around the world. In the pacifist tradition of Ghandi, he has exerted a direct influence on Thomas Merton and Martin Luther King, Jr., being nominated by the latter for the Nobel Peace Prize. He was a founder of the School of Youth for Social Service (SYSS), serving as Chair of the Vietnam Buddhist Peace Delegation up to the Paris Accords. Like many Buddhists, he opposed *both* North Vietnamese communism *and* the repressive, U.S.-backed South Vietnamese government. In his case he attempted to synthesize European existentialist philosophy with Buddhist pacifism. He outlined his political, literary, philosophical, and religious convictions in a short preface to some of his explicitly political poems, which appeared, in his own translation, in the *New York Review of Books*, 9 June 1966.[5] (Three years earlier to the day, Thich Quang Duc had immolated himself.) This 1966 preface, entitled "A Buddhist Poet in Vietnam," was a major antiwar document of the period, and the subversive nature of his argument made it impossible for Thich Nhat Hanh to return to Vietnam. Nhat Hanh moved to a Buddhist retreat in Paris, where he lived throughout the war, pursuing his writing and other antiwar activities as spokesman for the Vietnamese Buddhist Peace Delegation (VBPD).

A word about the context of Thich Nhat Hanh's pacifism is required. In the West, roughly speaking, there were at the time two main positions on the war, sometimes combined.[6] (1) It was a war between the whole of Vietnam on the one side versus the United States and Saigon on the other (in the South, according to this view, the National Liberation Front [NLF] and its allies were the sole legitimate representatives of the South Vietnamese people). And/or (2) The war, which had a civil war aspect, was basically a result of competition between the great powers for hegemony over Southeast Asia. While Vietnamese Buddhists accepted the partial validity of both positions, they officially added three more. (3) The war was fought between two warring parties, but most of the suffering was that of a defenseless third party: the civilian population, North and South. "We want to be saved from salvation," was a pithy Buddhist slogan that resulted.[7] (4) *Primary* culpability for the war and suffering rested with the United States and Saigon, not with the North Vietnamese, though the Communists bore serious *secondary* responsibility. This prompts the thesis that "on balance, the Buddhist position was closer to that of the NLF than to that of the U.S./Saigon" (Wirmark 11). (5) Within Saigon-controlled territory, the war was mainly an attack against poor, unarmed, defenseless people waged by the United States and its puppet regime. This exceptionally nuanced Buddhist position—particularly its asymmetrical insistence on primary (i.e., U.S.) and secondary (i.e., communist) responsibility—is crucial to understanding what otherwise would seem to be an enigmatic, not to say incoherent, ideological stance on the part of Buddhists, including Thich Nhat Hanh in his play. Note also that the South Vietnamese government had *constitutionally* outlawed "neutralism," "procommunist neutralism," and "communism" equally—all of which were to be dealt with under draconian emergency laws (Wirmark 10). Nhat Hanh's play may seem uncontroversial today in the West; at the time, in the Vietnamese context, it could have been his death sentence. His stance on both neutrality and nonviolence was complex. Simultaneously emphasizing and nuancing his basic position, he wrote:

> No! We are not against revolution and liberation. We are against the other side, the side of the institutions, the side of the oppressors. The violence of the system is much more destructive, much more harmful, although it is well-hidden and not so visible. We call it institutional violence. By calling ourselves nonviolent we are against all violence, but we are first against the *institutional* violence.[8]

We should expect, as a consequence, that Nhat Hanh's play contains a critique also of *theatre* as an institution or medium, especially *Western* theatre. Around this time (1972/73), he outlined basic tactics for Buddhist resistance against the war in a programmatic pamphlet entitled *Love in Action: The Nonviolent Struggle for Peace in Vietnam.*[9] These tactics included the traditional illegal practice of shaving one's head, aid to all deserters and protestors, noncooperation with the Saigon government and U.S. media, and fasting and prayer (collective and individual). Not least were two other tactics of "love in action": the reappropriation of traditional folk poetry for political education, *and* the practice of self-immolation by both lay people (Nhat Chi Mai) and monks (Thich Quang Duc) as a way of awakening and educating the people. It is precisely these last two forms of antimedia resistance that Thich Nhat Hanh's dramatic work sought to articulate.

Briefly, the play is based on a historical event: the self-immolation of a young nun, Sister Mai, and the killing of five young men. Thich Nhat Hanh adds two more figures (also based on fact): Vui, "a young girl student of the School of Youth for Social Service [SYSS], Saigon," and Lui, "a young woman teacher [and] political prisoner just released from jail," who was also part of the SYSS. Both were murdered in April 1964, "during a terrorist raid on the School by a group of unknown persons" (Nhat Hanh 1972, 6). They appear in the shape of talking, visible ghosts.

Thus, *The Path of Return Continues the Journey* is similar to Berrigan's quasi-documentary play, *The Trial of the Catonsville Nine*, in that it is likewise based on a "true story." In fact, a statement by Berrigan entitled ". . . Their Speech is all Forgiveness. . .," frames Hanh's play. It is signed with a facsimile of "Dan Berrigan, S.J."—conveying at once a sense of existential authenticity and familiarity (the reproduced signature and the nickname), but also official sanction or legitimation (The Society of Jesus). This framing is completed by an equally significant but anonymous closing statement on the final page, where, blocked out, an appeal is made for the Vietnamese Buddhist Peace Delegation—with its address in Paris.

So much for the "Franco-American" framing. It is then striking to find that this properly "Vietnamese" text is preceded by yet another framing device: a page-long statement, entitled elliptically (echoed by Berrigan's elliptical title) "Love Enables Us. . . ." It is undersigned with a facsimile hand-written signature, this time "Nhat Hanh" in English script—suggesting that it is written explicitly for the American version. This statement by Nhat Hanh serves two purposes, corresponding to two distinct aspects of his play (part related, part contradictory): first, it provides an anonymous third-person factual reference to the murder of four students/ workers of the SYSS on the bank of the Saigon River in 1967; second, in quoting the author's own enigmatic words, it "guarantees" not only the truth of the murder story (which, however, doesn't really need such a guarantee, since it is supposedly well known and documented, albeit less in the United States than in Vietnam) but also the authenticity of the story of what happened afterwards, posthumously, to the four dead students and the self-immolated nun, Mai, who came (Hermes-like) to guide them in a boat up the river. This second part of the story, the author freely admits, is a lived (read: poetic) rather than scientific (read: historic) truth. Certainly, it is moved not by any conventional Western principle of dramatic conflict but rather by "love" (as is the entire play itself); and it is to lead hermeneutically to ever higher levels of "love," if one is willing to join the author in his imaginary boat and row together with him. Remember, too, that "love" for Vietnamese Buddhist war resisters is not merely an interpersonal or theological principle but also political, illegal even. All these words, images, and thematics of "love" clearly set apart this "play" from the Western Vietnam Protest Theatre, even as this genre approaches to embrace it. It does share with it, however, the mission to tell a greater truth about the war than the mediatized vision produced by the more "exact" technologies of film "truth" on TV.

Let us take up the author on his invitation and, as the play proper begins, join him and his characters on the sampan. They are just getting ready to row with their bare hands. And this rudimentary physical activity, along with other small gestures, is virtually all the action that will take place on the boat and in the play (where stage directions are also at a bare minimum). The text, meanwhile, offers a fragmented version of the death of the characters, as related by them posthumously, and a long poetic debate on the meaning of life, war, and violence. Much of that discussion, lead by the nun Mai, is devoted to philosophical and/or moral consider-ations that preach understanding and forgiveness—even (indeed espe-cially) forgiveness for those who kill "us"—most evidently inspired by Buddhist trust in love and tolerance. To quote a characteristic summation: "Let us hope that our earthly lives, as well as our deaths, have sown the seeds of tolerance and love" (Nhat Hanh 1972, 27).

Clearly such a play cannot fit easily into the canons or forms of traditional Western theatre. Its marginality includes the fact that it has no acts, no scenes, little or no dramatic or conceptual progression of any type. It rather evokes a poem recited by several voices, something that could qualify in the West as a specific "performance" (a dramatic monologue collectively recited), but would be questioned as "theatre." But then any definition of "theatre" as genre or medium is a matter of cultural opinion. To be appreciated fully in its own terms, *The Path of Return Continues the Journey* must be historicized and contextualized within Vietnamese cul-ture, particularly the theatrical form known as Cheo, meaning "boat play."[10]

Cheo has always been performed for and by the people; it is a legiti-mate part of "popular culture," in a way that Western theatre very rarely is. Cheo performers would float in a boat down the river, often singing the text. They would address the spectators along the river's banks, somewhat like performers of the street theatre, and invite them to join the perfor-mance. The text is readily alterable in the light of current events. There are no entrance fees. But Cheo has never been a subsidized State theatre. It was and is an independent form, often serving—as part of this traditional generic norm—to oppose authorities in power, whoever they might be. Formally and politically, Cheo seems to illustrate Augusto Boal's thesis in *Theatre of the Oppressed* (1985), even though it was developed in an entirely different historical context:

> All the truly revolutionary theatrical groups should transfer to the people the means of production in the theatre so that the people may utilize them. Theatre is a weapon, and it is the people who should wield it.[11]

To be sure, the pacifist Nhat Hanh would object to this militant metaphor to describe his mission in *The Path of Return Continues the Journey*.

The river on which Mai's sampan is floating has both a literal-physical and a symbolic-metaphysical meaning. It is literal-physical because it obviously refers to the common generic venue of the Cheo boat plays: the rivers on which performers move from village to village to offer their performance in a land heavily dependent on river travel. One has the distinct impression that *The Path of Return Continues the Journey* was initially intended to be performed on a river boat—the sampan in the story.

But the river also refers metaphysically to the symbolic river mentioned in Nhat Hanh's framing statement:

> Is there a river that separates the two sides, a river which no boat can cross? Is such an absurdly complete separation possible? Please come over to my boat. I will show you that there is a river, but there is no separation. (Nhat Hanh 5)

Here, again, one confronts—in a poetic, quasi-mystical mode—the use of a theme often alluded to in Western protest plays: the real and yet also illusory border between the two Vietnams, South and North, and perhaps between the two armies in conflict, or even between the two continents or two ideologies—a separation that Western (especially European) playwrights sometimes denounce while acknowledging it, but more generally accept and further legitimize (mainly in American plays). For the monk Nhat Hanh, this is a separation that Buddhism is set to dispel. Finally, the river both distinguishes and yet articulates life and death. In an uncanny sense, the voices on the sampan are messages from the fictional dead to the living audience (or reader).

The roots of *The Path of Return Continues the Journey* in the Cheo tradition account for other peculiar features of the play that might otherwise be inexplicable—for instance, the reiterated invocation of the power of Sutras. The main intertextual reference is the *Prajnaparamita Sutra*, first recorded circa 400–600 A.D. Nhat Hanh subsequently published his own commentary on this Sutra in 1992.[12] Alluded to so often in *The Path of Return Continues the Journey,* this Sutra, rather than the play at hand, seems to be the crucial source of wisdom. This cross-referencing likely results as much from the association of the Cheo with religious celebrations as from the playwright's own Buddhist convictions. Now, Sutras such as the *Prajnaparamita* are intended not to be read so much as to be memorized and hence embodied—for the purpose of meditation and practical application—by the seeker of enlightenment or "Bodhisattva" (literally "enlightenment-being"—the Buddhist ideal). The enlightenment in question is not merely personal but also that of others, with the ultimate goal being nothing less than the full enlightenment of Buddha *for everyone.* This explains the character, lines, and role of Sister Lien. Both in the play and in real life, she is a teacher in the SYSS, but she likes to refer whenever possible to the *Prajnaparamita.* According to this Sutra, the concept of Bodhisattva is an overdetermined part of an elaborate sign system that appears to be contradictory but aims at purifying all apparent contradictions and appearances. The Sutra informs us:

> The word "Bodhisattva" is a word for . . . the purity of views, of Delight, of craving, of arrogance, of Adornment, of mental satisfaction, of Light, and of

physical happiness. It is a word for the purity of visual forms, sounds, smells, tastes and touchables.[13]

Two main consequences emerge from this doctrine that would shape the staging of *The Path of Return Continues the Journey*. The first is formal, the second thematic.

Formally, playwright and viewers must cooperate in realizing that what we see and hear concretely on stage (or imagine in the text) must always be grasped, conceptually if not actually, as a part of a process aimed at higher or deeper truths than what is merely visible and audible. The precise location of these truths (ontologically and epistemologically but also theatrically) may seem problematic. Presumably they lie not as much "outside" the performance of text—say, as some "transcendent" wisdom—as a viewer imbued with Western thinking might assume. Nor are these higher truths strictly "immanent," either. Rather, resolutely "marginal" to all such binary categories, they are to be grasped, somehow, as both transcendent and immanent, and yet neither. It is in this sense only that they are "metaphysical." Which is to say that they are part of a single "path" (*tao, do*): a "continuing path of return" in and around the Bodhisattva ideal. And the play becomes a metaphysical sortie against war. Its ideal is represented not only by certain set dialogues and/or monologues (a moot distinction in this conceptual world) in *The Path of Return Continues the Journey*—a partially "religious," partially "theatrical" artifact—but also by its structure as a variation of the generic norm of Cheo.

Important in this context is also the *thematic* point of reiterated references to the *Prajnaparamita Sutra* that turn *The Path of Return Continues the Journey* into a play of pacific resistance. One of the central teachings of the Sutra is that the Bodhisattva, while traveling on his or her path in or toward the so-called Buddha-field (i.e., the realm in which a Buddha teaches and brings sentient beings to spiritual understanding), has no ultimate reason to be fearful of *anything or anyone*. For example, in a section of the Sutra entitled "Five Places Which Inspire Fear" (and we can imagine Vietnam during the war as having at least five such places), one learns that

> a Bodhisattva should not be afraid if he finds himself in a wilderness infested by robbers. For Bodhisattvas take pleasure in the wholesome practice of renouncing all their belongings. A Bodhisattva must cast away even his body, and he must renounce all that is necessary to life. He should react to the danger with the thought [as expressed elsewhere in the Sutra]: "If those beings take away from me everything that is necessary to life, I should feel no ill-will toward them."[14]

The goal of all Nhat Hanh's texts—always willing to defer to the higher authority of the Sutras—was clearly pragmatic: "When I write them I feel

I am trying to speak very simply for the majority of Vietnamese who are peasants and cannot speak for themselves; they do not know or care much about words like communism or democracy but want above all for the war to end so they may survive and not be maimed or killed" (Nhat Hanh 1966, 36). The translation of *The Path of Return Continues the Journey* might be offering a glimpse for English speakers (who likely have not internalized the Sutras) of the mentality of an "inappropriate/d other," which is traversing a path that is always going just beyond Western patterns of political and theatrical understanding. In its inappropriateness from the point of view of Western categories, even if it depends on them, this path strives to remain inappropriated for as long as possible.

Another leitmotif in *The Path of Return Continues the Journey* functioning in dialectical relation to its master Sutra lies in a few humorous dialogues no doubt inspired by the bawdy tradition and stock comic figures of the Cheo. More significant for our purpose is the centrality of the female figure, the wise Mai.[15] That centrality too is provided by the Cheo model, but it also reflects the fact that the theatrical groups in the areas controlled by the Vietcong were composed of women.[16] In the play the sampan, real and metaphysical, is steered by Mai as she tries to reach two other martyred young women. Thus, it is women who serve as anchors for the audience's physical reality or, to change the metaphor, as the polar points between which the males move and interact, in life and in death, in fiction and in reality. Men, by contrast, can sometimes be coaxed to make pro- found statements (especially if they have advanced Buddhist training), but they can also act and talk in rather silly fashion. For example, one of the four male SYSS graduates, Tho, says that one of his "dead" comrades "is a little devil, but a lovable little devil. . . . I don't know whether he really was all that bright or not" (Nhat Hanh 1972, 7). The female-dominated gender hierarchy of this male playwright may have been normal or expected in a Cheo play, but it does acquire a more subversive quality when matched against the patriarchal might of the U.S. forces in Vietnam and against the reduction of Vietnamese women to service jobs, prostitution, or victims of rape—not only in real life but in their representations in the Western Vietnam Protest Plays and the mass media generally. Thich Nhat Hanh's Vietnamese Protest Play thus offers a certain gender, as well as antimedia, resistance to some of *the* most prevalent stereotypes on the American and European protest stage.

In other ways, too, the choice of the Cheo as the paradigmatic theatrical form is already a form of protest, opposition, or resistance. For Cheo, though one of the oldest theatre forms, has rarely been recorded in writing. Performed "for the simple people," it has eluded written appropriation, including that by the Vietnamese elite influenced by and/or educated in foreign cultures. The other traditional form, the Tuong, often performed in the Chinese language, rests on a strong Chinese foundation. The two modern forms, especially the Cai Long, originated as part of the French influence, starting with adaptations of French classics such as Molière or Racine. The Cheo alone could be seen as a "properly Vietnamese" theatrical form, a uniquely national product standing for the Vietnamese people as a whole and against the colonial or modern imperialist powers: France, England, the United States. Simply by adopting the Cheo form, Nhat Hanh formally suggests—by design or not—that the ongoing war against the Americans in Vietnam is articulated to the long history of resistance against all other foreign invaders, none of whom are successful for long.

While it is so much traditionally Vietnamese, *The Path of Return Continues the Journey* is also comparable to the Western protest plays. The most obvious convergence is grounded in the spectacular nature of a single shared image: the scene of self-immolation of a war protester—whether Thich Quang Duc, Nhat Chi Mai, Norman Morrison, or whomever. In theatre, re/producing the kernel of an originary event, a live person is momentarily aflame in protest, before being swallowed up by relentlessly reproduced simulacra.

The dominant mass media made no serious effort to understand the social context and/or motivations behind the act of self-immolation. The fact that it might be a *Buddhist* monk, for instance, was important for TV mainly for its visual effect: the flaming orange of the gown in the interstices of the orange and yellow flames. What was occluded is the religious and political meaning behind both act and image. In *Love in Action* Thich Nhat Hanh took great pains to emphasize that this ultimate act of sacrifice for peace must occur spontaneously, is a wholly individual decision, and must never be ordered by anyone else. The media transforms a sacred rite, with a complex and deep history, into yet another spectacular Western image, seen by Western eyes, for which what is visible is necessarily subjectivized and depoliticized. It is not living theatre but precisely television (among other technologized mass media) which is the most powerful tool in the colonization of the so-called Third World. American television and its images are disseminated throughout the world, in the hegemonic attempt, paraphrasing German filmmaker Wim Wenders, to "colonize the global unconscious." In terms of technoculture, the flow from developed to underdeveloped nations is a one-way street.[17] This is the threat faced by all protest playwrights, but by few more than "Third World" intellectuals like Nhat Hanh; hence his recourse to new—or rather very old—strategies of resistance.

The printed copy of *The Path of Return Continues the Journey* contains six interspersed wood block prints entitled *Visage*. Produced by Vo-Dinh, also the play's translator, these are quasi-abstract re/presentations of the self-immolation of Phan Thi Mai, once a real person and now the lead character in the play. Nhat Hanh centers his play on this immolation, yet this act is said to have occurred in an atmosphere of peaceful and quiet resignation as taught by the Sutras. Death, even the most apparently horrific, is here part of a process of rebirth and reincarnation—which is to be grasped as an act of love and effective resistance against violent death dealt by the "other." An attempt is made not only to connect the action of self-immolation to a larger philosophy of life and death but also to a specific political agenda. Mai's ghost speaks:

> I stood on the balcony and looked at my own body enveloped in flames. Yes, I think I even smiled although my eyes were full of tears. All the people around me were weeping . . . an Army captain arrived and wanted to examine and confiscate my charred body. (Nhat Hanh 1972, 19)

She attempts to wrest back a counterimage of death from an image commodified, warped, and polluted by the Western mass media.

Let us now look at how the "others" are represented in the Vietnamese text. One sees the reverse of many American plays where Americans define the "other" with such vengeance. In Thich Nhat Hanh's play, the people or "strangers" who have killed the Vietnamese social workers, and who are presumably still alive in real life, are not represented. They are only evoked in vague terms, once again a form of teichoscopia or "view from the wall." When the killers are described (and it is left to a director whether or not the death scene is to be reenacted on the stage), their true identity (national and racial) is left seemingly ambiguous: "a group of armed men . . . some wore black clothes, some uniforms. One of them had a raincoat and another a poncho. Some wore military caps and bullet belts. I know who they were." "I know who they were, too. You don't have to say" (Nhat Hanh 1972, 14). The problem, however, is that *we* don't know who the killers are. ("Black uniforms" suggest Vietcong, "ponchos" imply Americans.) Arguably, this ambiguity is intended by the playwright. Perhaps it is we, the Americans, who are responsible, and we cannot see ourselves on stage, except metaphorically. Had the play been performed in South Vietnam in 1972, it would have been the Vietcong who would be implicated. Performed in the North, it would have been the South Vietnamese and the Americans. In the list of characters the 1967 murder of the two women, Vui and Lien, is depicted only as having occurred "during a terrorist raid . . . by a group of unknown persons." This refusal (or inability) to name the killers thus functions as a "structured textual gap" (German *Leerstelle*), which must be filled in, semantically and politically, by the audiences depending on their "choice." This semiotic or hermeneutic notion, this principled refusal to represent—related perhaps to certain Buddhist meditation practices that require making the mind "blank"—distinguishes Nhat Hanh's play from all Western Vietnam Protest Plays, where the enemy (whether Vietnamese or American) is clearly identified and all trace of ambiguity is lost.[18] At one point a character says, "How can I see you if you do not have a body?" (Nhat Hanh 1972, 13). A major challenge.

While the victims in the play do not blame the (American?) soldiers for killing them—soldiers are only carrying out orders—they *are* chided nonetheless for their ignorance, which is culpable. Ignorance, as the Sutras and this play teach, is something that can be corrected. Which makes Americans, when they are explicitly mentioned, all the more guilty in their chauvinistic prejudice and unwillingness to find out what is actually going on in Vietnam:

> The American knew absolutely nothing about Vietnamese history and culture or the truth of the conflict in which he was playing a part. He was certain of only one thing: the V.C. was his enemy. . . . He could hate the V.C. only because he really did not know what the V.C. were. (Nhat Hanh 1972, 24)

Nhat Hanh actually pities the Americans: "Who really kills them? Their own fear and hatred and prejudice" (Nhat Hanh 1972, 25). But we never see *these* Americans on stage, and only one American appears in our mind's eye as readers. Not only is the referent "American" under- or unrepresented, it seems it *cannot* be represented, in this play at least, *except* in an oblique way.

What then becomes the function of "theatre" here and its relation to a very specific war, in a very specific country, at a very specific time? What can be theatre in a systematically underdeveloped country, a country under violent siege every day, a country whose very existence is continually threatening to disappear? Before the war, as one character in the play, the former head of the Performing Arts Committee, puts it, "art was used as a means for rural reconstruction and social development. We used poetry, painting, music and theatre to serve the people" (Nhat Hanh 1972, 11). Nhat Hanh seems to repeat what Gramsci argued in the 1930s when attempting to resist fascism from his prison cell: When "cultural functions predominate," "political language becomes jargon," and "political questions are disguised as cultural ones," and as such they become "insoluble."[19]

All the characters in the abstractly titled *The Path of Return Continues the Journey* remain "dead," even as they are given a "life" on the stage. This irony is pointed out again and again by one of the characters, Hy: "Art is life itself . . . we may say we're dead, but in reality we are still alive" (Nhat Hanh 1972, 11). In the world of art as theatre, they live on as play. And Mai duly responds: "But Hy, how can you say that we no longer have pure bodies? How can I see you if you do not have a body?" (Nhat Hanh 1972, 13).

Perhaps it can be said that, however disembodied this "theatre" may be, its existence (i.e., the collaborative effort of Nhat Hanh and Berrigan) demonstrates that it is possible, during global crisis, to forge a *community* of response and resistance to war across national and linguistic borders and peripheries—an artistic protest more or less independent of other forms of protest and yet in solidarity with them. Which brings us back, at the end of this study, to the fact that the play before us has a foreword by

Berrigan, who had tried to achieve a sort of intellectual resistance community, who desired fervently that theatre would be instrumental in this project, and whose own play, *The Trial of the Catonsville Nine*, had been censured in 1971, even by a generally sympathetic reviewer, for its "superior nobility."[20]

To quote Berrigan again: "The religious resistance in this country cannot help but take into special account, with a special gratitude, the Vietnamese Buddhist movement. Spiritually speaking we are the closest to them" (Nhat Hanh 1972, 3). Thus is forged a metaphysical, if not physical, articulation of peace movements, a virtual transcendence of the Western death machine. Still citing Berrigan, "We Americans cross the great waters with our techniques of death, supersonic instruments of appetite . . . to smell out and destroy the least lurking evidence of life. . . . 'Let it all come down!' is the manic whine of the Machine" (Nhat Hanh 1972, 4). So it is, in this text at least, that Western imperialist aggression is linked to the machines of war and is then resisted, by the imagined moral superiority of a technologically inferior "other," who turns out, however, to be "our" true friend: the friend, that is, not of all Americans, or of humanity at large, but of the embattled peace movement—in all *its* technological weakness and in all *its* moral strength. In other words, unlike television and the television war—with all their moral weakness and victorious technological might.

But there is more. Theatre is everywhere one of the oldest art and/or ritual forms. As such, it often explicitly or implicitly re/enacts modes of "reincarnation" and "rebirth," both by representing such transformation and by attempting to trigger it in members of the audience. At least this seems to be the Jesuit-Buddhist intent of Thich Nhat Hanh and Dan Berrigan, S.J. And it is hardly for the theatre historian, critic, or theorist to decide, perhaps even to know, whether this transformation has occurred in actual audiences.

At one point in *The Path of Return Continues the Journey*, Sister Lien is reported walking and reading the *Prajnaparamita Sutra*. Appearing, she says: "Our country will be destroyed and our people will suffer even more than they already have. The cycle must be completed" (Nhat Hanh 1972, 18). The tone is one of extreme complaisance and peace with the world— a pacific acceptance of (and hence, in this logic, also resistance to) what has happened and what will happen—up to and including being violently raped and murdered. For, as Berrigan reiterates in his introduction, "their speech is all forgiveness of hope and joy." But is it, and can it be effective? One of the most remarkable things about political theatre is its ability simultaneously to provoke and to elude censorship, precisely because its *written* text, which appears fixed and innocuous, can become quite subversive and even transformative when *staged*. Whether that could have occurred with this particular Vietnamese Protest Play—or any other—is a question that cannot be decided—at least not in the main context of "staging the Vietnam War."

NOTES

PREFACE

1. Theodor W. Adorno, *Minima Moralia: Reflections from Damaged Life* [1951], trans. E. F. N. Jephcott (London: Verso, 1987), 143.

2. See Raymond Williams, "Drama in a Dramatized Society" [1974], in his *On Television: Selected Writings*, ed. Alan O'Connor (London: Routledge, 1989), 3-13. Hereafter cited as Williams.

3. Raymond Williams, "Distance" [1982], in Williams 13-21; here 16.

4. "The real consumer becomes a consumer of illusions. The commodity is this factually real illusion, and the spectacle is its general manifestation." Guy Debord, *Society of the Spectacle* [1967] (Detroit: Black and Red, 1983), Thesis 47. Hereafter cited as Debord.

5. There have been extensive studies on different aspects of filmic response to the Vietnam War. I will allude to some of the main works throughout this book, noting already here, however, that much more is available about Hollywood than about foreign films. For a recent survey of Hollywood production, see Antony Easthope, "Realism and Its Subversion: Hollywood and Vietnam," in *Tell Me Lies about Vietnam: Cultural Battles for the Meaning of War*, ed. Alf Louvre and Jeffrey Walsh (Milton Keynes: Open University Press, 1988). Hereafter cited as *Tell Me Lies*. Also in the same anthology, see Jeffery Fenn, "Vietnam: The Dramatic Response," 199-210—though this short essay, too, focuses on American response, and makes no pretense to comprehensiveness. The most comprehensive analysis to date remains *From Hanoi to Hollywood: The Vietnam War in American Film*, ed. Linda Dittmar and Gene Michaud (New Brunswick: Rutgers University Press, 1990). For important analyses of various aspects of the response of American culture and the media to "Vietnam" see the anthology *The Vietnam War and American Culture*, ed. John Carlos Rowe and Rick Berg (New York: Columbia University Press, 1991), including Claudia Springer, "Military Propaganda: Defense Department Films from World War II and Vietnam"; Rick Berg, "Losing Vietnam: Covering the War in an Age of Technology"; John Carlos Rowe, "Eyewitness: Documentary Styles in the American Representation of Vietnam"; Michael Clark, "Remembering Vietnam"; Susan Jeffords, "Tattoos, Scars, Diaries, and Writing Masculinity"; David James, "The Vietnam War and American Music"; and W. D. Ehrhart, "Poetry." This anthology hereafter cited as Rowe and Berg. Finally, for an analysis of how the Vietnam War and its films have fundamentally altered the "viewing formation" of American audiences, see Timothy Corrigan, *A Cinema without Walls: Movies and Culture after Vietnam* (New Brunswick: Rutgers University Press, 1991).

6. With the resulting slant in the orientation of the information since "those involved in making, reporting and editing news accordingly have an incentive to shape it so as to attract audiences and, sometimes, to encourage particular interpretations through its content and form." Murray Edelman, *Constructing the Political Spectacle* (Chicago: University of Chicago Press, 1988), 90.

7. Marshall McLuhan and Quentin Fiore, *The Medium Is the Massage* (New York: Touchstone, 1989), 133.

8. For an extended argument that Korea, not Vietnam, was the first "television war," see Bruce Cumings, *War and Television* (London: Verso, 1992).

9. The knowledge of the Vietnam War in Europe also heavily relied on television coverage, often rebroadcast from American networks.

10. Jean-Marie Serreau, "Ist das Theater noch zeitgemäss?" *Theater Heute* (September 1965): 1. Hereafter cited as Serreau.

11. Michael Herr, *Dispatches* (New York: Avon, 1968), 215. Hereafter cited as Herr.

12. This is not to say that response to film is entirely passive, by any means, but rather that there is almost no possibility for film to respond to audiences at the point of production as theatre can do. For an imaginative account of active film viewing—a zone between objectivity and subjectivity—see Tom Conley, *Film Hieroglyphs: Ruptures in Classical Cinema* (Minneapolis: University of Minnesota Press, 1991).

13. Certainly there have been too few studies of the response of musical culture to the Vietnam War. On popular music and the war, see, e.g., John Storey, "Rockin' Hegemony: West Coast Rock and Amerika's War in Vietnam," in *Tell Me Lies*, 181-98, and James, "The Vietnam War and American Music," in Rowe and Berg, 226-54.

14. Bertolt Brecht, "The Radio as an Apparatus of Communication" [1932], *Brecht on Theater: The Development of an Aesthetic*, trans. and ed. John Willett (New York: Hill and Wang, 1964), 52.

15. Hans Magnus Enzensberger, "Constituents of a Theory of the Media" [1970], in *Video Culture*, trans. Stuart Hood, ed. John Hanhardt (Rochester, N.Y.: Visual Studies Workshop Press, 1986), 98. On Brecht and Enzensberger, see further Siegfried Zielinski, *Audiovisionen: Kino und Fernsehen als Zwischenspiele in der Geschichte* (Reinbek bei Hamburg: Rowohlt, 1989), 209-10.

16. Daniel C. Hallin, *The "Uncensored War": The Media and Vietnam* (Berkeley: University of California Press, 1989), 118. Hereafter cited as Hallin.

17. See, e.g., Peter Braestrup, *Big Story: How the American Press and Television Reported and Interpreted the Crisis of Tet in 1968 in Vietnam and Washington* (New Haven: Yale University Press, 1983). See further the editors' introduction to *Tell Me Lies about Vietnam*, 1-29.

18. Michael J. Arlen, *The Living Room War* (New York: Penguin, 1966), xiv. Hereafter cited as Arlen. For an opposing point of view, see Ben H. Bagdikian, *The Media Monopoly: Words That Succeed and Politics That Fail* (Orlando: Academic Press, 1977); and Jonathan Schell, *The Real War: The Classic Reporting on the Vietnam War* (New York: Pantheon, 1987).

19. On the influence of the American media coverage of the war on the way in which the British government handled reporting during the Falkland Islands crisis, see Robert Harris, *GOTCHA! The Media, the Government, and the Falklands Crisis* (London: Faber and Faber, 1983).

20. On the way that the Reagan administration "excluded the media from the opening phases of the invasion of Granada," see Hallin 4. For more extensive analyses of both American and international media coverage of the Gulf War, see *Triumph of the Image: The Media's War in the Persian Gulf—A Global Perspective*, ed. Hamid Mowlana, George Gerbner, and Herbert I. Schiller (Boulder: Westview Press, 1992).

21. For an interesting analysis of "the fully ideological role that television was and is intended to serve . . . as the herald of the American empire," see Joyce Nelson, *The Perfect Machine: T. V. in the Nuclear Age* (Toronto: Between the Lines, 1987), 120.

22. Fred J. MacDonald, *Television and the Red Menace* (New York: Praeger, 1985). Hereafter cited as MacDonald.

23. Edward S. Herman and Noam Chomsky, *Manufacturing Consent: The Political Economy of the Mass Media* (New York: Pantheon, 1988), 177. Hereafter cited as Herman and Chomsky.

24. "It is a highly significant fact that neither then nor before, was there any detected question of the righteousness of the American cause in Vietnam, or of the necessity to proceed to full-scale 'intervention. ' By that time, of course, only questions of tactics and cost remained open, and further discussion in the main-stream media was largely limited to these narrow issues. While dissent and domestic controversy became a focus of media coverage from 1965 the actual views of the dissidents and resisters were virtually excluded" (Herman and Chomsky 172).

25. "The first [of two factors in the president's power to control foreign affairs] was the ideology of the Cold War: the bi-partisan consensus forged during the Truman and Eisenhower administrations, that had identified foreign policy with 'national security,' and hence removed most foreign policy decisions from the agenda of political debate. . . . The second factor, ironically was professional journalism itself. The assumptions and routines of what is often known as 'objec-tive journalism' made it exceedingly easy for officials to manipulate day-to-day news content. There was little 'editorializing' in the columns of major newspapers at the time of the Tonkin Gulf incident: most of the reporting, in the best tradition of objective journalism, 'just gave the facts'" (Hallin 24).

26. "As a result, the New Journalism of the 1960s, the Hunter-Thompsonesque, drug-inspired, high-wired, stream-of-perhaps-you-could-call-it-consciousness writing, seemed uniquely suited to the war." Susan D. Moeller, *Shooting War: Photography and the American Experience of Combat* (New York; Basic Books, 1989), 327.

27. The first "video war" is already upon us, as depicted in Harun Farocki's film/video about the revolution in Roumania in December 1991, in which he contrasts official CNN coverage of the events with home videos made by Rouma-nian civilians. See *Videograms einer Revolution* (1992). Rock musician Peter Gabriel has attempted to harness this potential of video by collaborating with the Reebok Foundation to donate inexpensive video cameras to various designated "trouble spots" around the world so that citizens might capture human rights abuses on camera. On the other hand, the failure of video footage of the beating of Rodney King in Los Angeles to convince jurors may make such interventions seem epistemologically and politically naive, quite apart from the enormous practical problems involved.

28. "Control of information by itself, however, by no means explains the effective-ness of their efforts. There was, in fact, a great deal of information available which contradicted the official account; it simply wasn't used" (Hallin 20).

29. Michael Parenti, *Inventing Reality: The Politics of the Mass Media* (New York: St. Martin's Press, 1986), 174.

30. "While in the U.S. media rarely strayed from the framework of the state propaganda system, others were unconstrained by these limits: for example, the *Le Monde* correspondents cited, or British photo-journalist Philip Jones Griffiths" (Herman and Chomsky 224).

31. "The U.S. media continued to report the subsequent atrocities, but from the standpoint of the aggressors. One had to turn to the foreign press to find reports from the Zones held by the South Vietnamese enemy" (Herman and Chomsky 195).

32. John A. Walker, *Art in the Age of Mass Media* (London: Pluto Press, 1983), 39.

33. See *Vietnam Images: War and Representation,* ed. Jeffrey Walsh and James Aulich (New York: St. Martin's Press, 1989), esp. Robert Hamilton, "Image and Context: The Production and Reproduction of *The Execution of a VC Suspect* by Eddie Adams," 171-83.

34. Gabriel Kolko, *Anatomy of a War, the United States, and the Modern Historical Experience* (New York: Pantheon, 1985), 309.

35. Jean Baudrillard, *The Evil Demon of Images,* trans. Paul Patton and Paul Foss (Annandale, Australia: Power Institute of Fine Arts, 1984), 19. Hereafter cited as Baudrillard 1984.

36. For a perceptive account of the various levels of mediation—particularly psychological—in the reception of filmic images that could be applied productively also to staged ones, see Kaja Silverman, *The Acoustic Mirror: The Female Voice in Psychoanalysis and Cinema* (Bloomington: Indiana University Press, 1988), esp. chap. 1, "Lost Objects and Mistaken Subjects."

37. See *Selections from the Prison Notebooks of Antonio Gramsci,* ed. and trans. Quintin Hoare and Geoffrey Nowell Smith (New York: International, 1971), 323.

38. See Bertolt Brecht to Jean Renoir, Max Gorelik, and others in March 1937, in his *Letters,* ed. J. Willett and R. Manheim (London: Methuen, 1990), 248-51. Prospective members of the society were to include: Brecht and Eisler in Germany; Auden, Isherwood, and Doone in England; Gorelik and MacLeish in the United States; Moussinac and Renoir in France; Per Knutzon, Nordahl Grieg, Per Lagerkvist, and Per Lindberg in Scandinavia; Eisenstein, Okhlopkov, and Tretiakoff in the USSR; Burian in Prague; and Piscator, living in Paris.

39. Edward W. Said, *Imperialism and Culture* (New York: Knopf, 1993), 289.

40. See Aijaz Ahmad, *In Theory: Classes, Nations, Literatures* (London: Verso, 1992), who takes to task Said's earlier work, among others, for not dealing radically enough with this problem.

41. See *She, the Inappropriate/d Other,* ed. Trinh T. Minh-ha, special issue of *Discourse* 8 (fall-winter 1986/87), and her *Woman, Native, Other: Writing, Postcoloniality, and Feminism* (Bloomington: Indiana University Press, 1989).

42. See David Harvey, *The Condition of Postmodernity: An Enquiry into the Origins of Cultural Change* (Oxford: Blackwell, 1990) and Fredric Jameson, *Postmodernism, or, The Cultural Logic of Late Capitalism* (Durham: Duke University Press, 1991)—neither of whom, however, deals with live theatre.

INTRODUCTION

1. As is evidenced by the controversy surrounding Robert S. McNamara's belated admission that Vietnam was a "wrong war," in his book (co-authored with Brian VanDeMark), *In Retrospect: The Tragedy and Lessons of Vietnam* (New York: Random House, 1995).

2. Part of the legacy of the Vietnam War has been the development by the U.S. military (e.g., Pentagon and National Security Council) of the doctrine known as L.I.C. or L.I.W. (Low-Intensity Conflict or Warfare), which includes the principle that the United States will be at a state of "permanent war" into the foreseeable future. This doctrine emerged out of the defeat of traditional military tactics and strategies in Indochina that were predicated on what is now perceived by the military as the impossible goal of winning war in the Third World outright and definitively. See *Low-Intensity Warfare: Counterinsurgency, Proinsurgency, and Antiterrorism in the Eighties,* ed. Michael T. Klare and Peter Kornbluth (New York: Pantheon, 1988) and Tom Barry, *Low-Intensity Conflict* (Albuquerque: Resource Center, 1986).

3. Jean Baudrillard, *The Evil Demon of Images,* trans. Paul Patton and Paul Foss (Annandale, Australia: Power Institute, 1987), 16-17.

4. For an overview of recent Vietnam War historiography and the main lines of debate about the origins, conduct, and consequences of the war, see Ben Kiernan, "The Vietnam War: Alternative Endings," *American Historical Review* 97, no. 4 (October 1992): 1118-37. See also Stephen Vlastos, "America's 'Enemy': The Absent Presence in Revisionist Vietnam History," in *The Vietnam War and American Culture,* ed. John Carlos Rowe and Rick Berg (New York: Columbia University Press, 1991), 52-74. Hereafter cited as Rowe and Berg.

5. One could argue whether Vietnam was ever a tangible reality since it was fought thirteen thousand miles from the United States and most of the people writing about Vietnam have never been there.

6. Phillip Knightly, *The First Casualty* (New York: Harvest, 1975), 407. Hereafter cited as Knightly.

7. See for example Nora M. Alter, "Changing Directions in Staging War: Beyond *Mann ist Mann*," *Communications*, 70-78; Norioki Ariizumi, "Vietnam War Plays," in *The Traditional and the Anti-Traditional: Studies in Contemporary American Literature*, ed. Kenzaburo Ohashi (Tokyo: American Literature Society of Japan, 1980), 191-200; Robert Asahina, "The Basic Training of American Playwrights," *Theater 9*, no. 2 (1978): 33-34; C. W. E. Bigsby, *A Critical Introduction to Twentieth-Century American Drama*, vol. 3: *Beyond Broadway* [1985] (Cambridge: Cambridge University Press, 1990), esp. part 5, "The Theatre of Commitment," hereafter cited as Bigsby; Samuel J. Bernstein, *The Strands Entwined: A New Direction in American Drama* (Boston: Northeastern University Press, 1980), which includes a chapter on David Rabe's *Sticks and Bones*; N. Bradley Christie, "David Rabe's Theater of War and Remembering," in *Search and Clear: Critical Responses to Selected Literature and Films of the Vietnam War*, ed. William J. Searle (Bowling Green, Oh.: Bowling Green State University Popular Press, 1988), 105-15; Michael L. Counts, *Coming Home: The Soldier's Return in Twentieth-Century American Drama* (New York: Peter Lang, 1988); David J. DeRose, "A Dual Perspective: First-Person Narrative in Vietnam Film and Drama," in *America Rediscovered: Critical Essays on Literature and Film of the Vietnam War*, ed. Owen W. Gilman Jr. and Lorrie Smith (New York: Garland, 1990), 109-19; Weldon B. Durham, "Gone to Flowers: Theatre and Drama of the Vietnam War," in *America Rediscovered*, 332-62; Jeffrey Fenn, "Vietnam: The Dramatic Response," in *Tell Me Lies about Vietnam: Cultural Battles for the Meaning of War*, ed. Alf Louvre and Jeffrey Walsh (Milton Keynes: Open University Press, 1988), 199-210; Catharine Hughes, *Plays, Politics and Polemics* (New York: Drama Book Specialists, 1973); Kate B. Meyers, "Bottles of Violence: Fragments of Vietnam in Emily Mann's *Still Life*," in *America Rediscovered*, 238-55; Michael Paller, "Dispatches from the Front," *Theatre Week*, 21-27 November 1988, 28-33; Don Ringlada, "Doing It Wrong Is Getting It Right: America's Vietnam War Drama," in *Fourteen Landing Zones: Approaches to Vietnam War Literature*, ed. Philip K. Jason (Iowa City: University of Iowa Press, 1991), 67-87; James A. Robinson, "Soldier's Home: Images of Alienation in *Sticks and Bones*," in *Search and Clear: Critical Responses to Selected Literature and Films of the Vietnam War*, 136-46; Rodney Simard, *Postmodern Drama: Contemporary Playwrights in America and Britain* (Lanham, M.D.: University Press of America, 1984), with a chapter on Rabe; and Toby Silverman Zinman, "Search and Destroy: The Drama of the Vietnam War," *Theatre Journal* (March 1990): 5-26. There are at least four unpublished dissertations on Vietnam War drama not including my own (1991): Carole Anne Winner, "A Study of American Dramatic Productions Dealing with the War in Vietnam" (Ph.D. diss., University of Denver, 1975); George Shafer, "Rhetorical Dramaturgy of Anti-Vietnam War Drama" (Ph.D. diss., Kent State University, 1976); Bonnie Culver Bedford, "The Die-Hard Dad: Killing Him in the Coming Home Fiction and Drama of Vietnam" (Ph.D. diss., State University of New York at Binghamton, 1991); and Bradley Jon Wright, "American Theatre about the Vietnam War" (Ph.D. diss., Cornell University, 1993).

8. For example, I will not discuss Brian DiFusco's *Tracers*, which came out of a collaborative project in the 1980s with a Vietnam vet performing group.

9. Because I limit my study to dramas that refer directly to the U.S. intervention in Indochina, I shall not discuss plays that can be read as commenting on Vietnam obliquely via treatment of other wars or of war in general, such as the Theatre Workshop's *Oh What a Lovely War*, Charles Wood's *Dingo*, Jules Pfeiffer's *The White*

House Murder Case, Joseph Heller's *We Bombed in New Haven,* or Boris Vian's *The General's Tea Party.* Nor shall I treat here the numerous topical reworkings or restagings of classics pertaining to war, including Greek tragedies, Shakespeare's histories, or later nineteenth- and twentieth-century plays such as *The Good Soldier Schweik.*

10. For an extensive anthology and analysis of various types of antiwar "street" theatre all around the United States, including that produced by Latino and women's groups, see *Guerrilla Street Theatre,* ed. Henry Lesnick (New York: Bard/ Avon, 1973). Hereafter cited as Lesnick. See also Bigsby 291-365; Edward G. Brown, "The Teatro Campesino's Vietnam Trilogy," *Minority Voices: An Interdisciplinary Journal of Literature and the Arts* 4, no. 1 (spring 1980): 29-38, hereafter cited as Brown; Stefan Brecht, *The Original Theatre of the City of New York from the Mid-Sixties to the Mid-Seventies,* Book 4: *Peter Schumann's Bread and Puppet Theatre* (London: Methuen/Routledge, 1988), esp. 461-598 ("The Vietnam War: Street Agitation during the Sixties)," hereafter cited as S. Brecht; and Wolf Vostell, *"Miss Vietnam" and Texts of Other Happenings* (San Francisco: Nova Broadcast, 1968). Particularly difficult to document and analyze but significant for the most expanded sense of "theatre" (e.g., that of Situationism or neo-Situationism) are the many "events" "staged" by the Yippies: perhaps most notably the attempted "Levitation of the Pentagon" (Washington, D.C., October 1967). In a sense, the entire "March on Washington" was "theatre." There was considerable crossover between demonstrations and guerrilla theatre. For example, SDS RATs typically contained practical information not only about fast-breaking current events but about how to organize more explicitly political interventions. It should also be noted that the Living Theatre, though it rarely addressed the war, was an overall inspiration for much other group work and protest art. Its self-imposed exile to Europe (and its significant influence there, including on the mainstream stage) remains germane both to the Vietnam era and its legacy.

11. The American Playground (anon.), "A Note on Guerrilla Theatre" [1969], in Lesnick, 308-10; here 308.

12. Interestingly the theme of the Chicano Vietnam experience (including a funeral in Texas for a marine who had earned the Medal of Honor) had been taken up earlier in a non–street play: Harvey Einbinder's *Mah Name is Lyndon* (New York: Lady Bird Press, 1968).

13. Michael Brown, "Some Dynamics and Aesthetics in Pageant Players Street Theatre" [summer 1971], in Lesnick 133-51; here 147.

14. See *Hair: The American Tribal Love-Rock Musical* (Boston: Beacon Press, 1966). For an early analysis, see Carole Ann Winter, "A Study of American Dramatic Productions Dealing with the War in Vietnam" (Ph.D. diss., University of Denver, 1975), esp. chap. 1, "The Effect of the Vietnamese War on the Entertainment World," 1-31.

15. See, e.g., David E. James, "The Vietnam War and American Music," in *The Vietnam War and American Culture,* ed. John Carlos Rowe and Rick Berg (New York: Columbia University Press, 1991), 226-54—which passes over *Hair* in silence.

16. See Raymond Bellour, "Psychosis, Neurosis, Perversion," in *A Hitchcock Reader,* ed. Marshall Deutelbaum and Leland Poague (Ames: Iowa State University Press, 1986), 311-31; See also Robert B. Ray, *A Certain Tendency of the Hollywood Cinema, 1930-1980* (Princeton: Princeton University Press, 1985) and Slavoj Žižek, "In His Bold Gaze My Ruin Is Writ Large," in *Everything You Always Wanted to Know about Lacan (But Were Afraid to Ask Hitchcock),* ed. Slavoj Žižek (London: Verso, 1992), 211-72.

17. See *Miss Saigon: A Musical,* by Alain Boublil and Richard Maltby Jr., with music by Claude-Michel Schönberg. It premiered at the Theatre Royal, Drury Lane, in September 1989. According to a note by Mark Steyn on the playbill, the

musical received "the most heartfelt first-night ovation since *My Fair Lady.*" Small surprise that the Vietnam War is hardly mentioned.

18. See Slavoj Žižek, *Tarrying with the Negative: Kant, Hegel and the Critique of Ideology* (Durham: Duke University Press, 1993), esp. chap. 6, "Enjoy Your Nation as Yourself!"

19. In some cases, however, the Europeans were better informed. For example, the My Lai massacre of March 1968 was not officially released to the world press until November 1969, and more coverage—both front-page and in-depth—occurred initially in Europe than in the United States. See Knightly, 390-400; and Edward S. Herman and Noam Chomsky, *Manufacturing Consent: The Political Economy of the Mass Media* (New York: Pantheon, 1988), 195. Hereafter cited as Herman and Chomsky.

20. Symptomatic of the relative ineffectiveness of political theatre as a force in North American society, and of the latter's indifference to it, is that both Bertolt Brecht and Erwin Piscator returned to Europe from exile disappointed and disillusioned with the possibilities of protest theatre. See Maria Ley-Piscator, *The Piscator Experiment: The Political Theatre* (Carbondale: Southern Illinois University Press, 1967); and Christopher D. Innes, *Erwin Piscator's Political Theatre* (Cambridge: Cambridge University Press, 1972). Hereafter cited as Innes 1972.

21. Daniel Berrigan, "To the Actors from the Underground," *Poetry–Drama–Press,* ed. Michael True (Maryknoll: Orbis Books, 1988), 267.

22. Susan D. Moeller, *Shooting War: Photography and the American Experience of Combat* (New York: Basic Books, 1989), 360.

23. For more detailed information on JUSPAO activities and a reprint of some JUSPAO files, see "Vietnam," *Drama Review* 13, no. 4 (summer 1969): 146-53.

24. Martin Esslin, *Theater Heute* (January 1968): 22.

25. See Fredric Jameson, *Postmodernism, or, The Cultural Logic of Late Capitalism* (Durham: Duke University Press, 1991), 1-54. Hereafter cited as Jameson 1991.

26. Part of the difference in treatment of protest plays there may also be attributed to the difference between the reputation, and hence prestige, of individual American and European playwrights. In the United States the protest plays were principally written by young playwrights and performed for off-Broadway audiences by "avant-garde" groups. In Europe, on the other hand, they were written and produced by top theatre people in major theatres: e.g., Armand Gatti and André Benedetto in France; Peter Weiss, Rolf Hochhuth, and Günter Grass in West Germany; Peter Brook and David Hare in England.

27. "When Hochhuth had begun to write there was no talk of bombardments, but the premiere of *Soldiers* will turn the world into a political podium: It has become a Vietnam play." *Theater Heute* (February 1967): 6.

28. *Theater Heute* (May 1967): 39.

29. *Frankfurter Allgemeine Zeitung,* 20 January 1969.

30. I am referring, for example, to the case of Tuli Kupferberg's *Fuck Nam,* which, although written in America, was never performed in the United States, according to its author in a letter to me.

31. Andrew Ross, *No Respect: Intellectuals and Popular Culture* (New York: Routledge, 1989), 183.

32. See, e.g., Elaine Scarry, "Watching and Authorizing the Gulf War," in *Media Spectacles,* ed. Marjorie Gerber, Jann Matlock, and Rebecca L. Walkowitz (New York: Routledge, 1993), 57-73.

33. Guy Debord, *Society of the Spectacle* (Detroit: Black and Red Press, 1983), Thesis 18. "Real beings," a literal rendition of Debord's "étres réels," has here the sense of "part of reality." Debord, *La société du spectacle* (Paris: Champ Libre, 1971), Thesis 18. Hereafter cited from the English as Debord.

34. Max Horkheimer and Theodor W. Adorno, *Dialectic of Enlightenment* [1944]

(New York: Continuum, 1988), 139. Hereafter cited as Horkheimer and Adorno.

35. When I am using the expression "real war," here and hereafter, I am referring to reality in the same sense as proposed by Benjamin: i.e., that behind the mosaic of representations there is an extratextual truth, though we may have no more than heuristic access to it. Thus, I postulate as given that on some level of what we call "reality" a terrible armed conflict took place involving sacrifice, suffering, death, and destruction.

36. Today, to be sure, there has been a powerful resurgence of explicitly political theatre: e.g., plays about AIDS and the homeless, various forms of feminist and women's theatre, Chicano theatre, and so on.

37. See Peter Bürger, *Theory of the Avant-Garde* [1980], trans. Michael Shaw (Minneapolis: University of Minnesota Press, 1984).

38. Mailer's *Why Are We in Vietnam?* was followed within a year by his *The Armies of the Night: History as a Novel, the Novel as History* (1968), in which he re/ created, in third-person voice and quasi-fictional form, his participation in the massive October 1967 antiwar demonstration in Washington, D.C. Halberstam's *The Making of a Quagmire* (1965) was the first remarkably prescient book of reporting by the journalist who had won a Pulitzer Prize for his coverage of the war in 1964. He followed up with another Vietnam novel, *One Very Hot Day* (1968).

39. Several important anthologies began appearing by 1967-68, including *Where Is Vietnam? American Poets Respond* (1967), which includes poems from Read-Ins; *A Poetry Reading against the Vietnam War* (1967), a particularly influential collection; *Artists and Writers Protest against the War in Vietnam: Poems* (1967), which included work by Bly, Creely, Duncan, and James Wright; Donald Gardner's 1967 poem "Litany for the Dead in Vietnam"; *War Poems* (1968), including work by Allen Ginsberg and Gary Snyder; *Twowindows Folio II* (1968), which included Kay Boyle's "Lost Dogs of Phnom Penh"; *Boondock Bards* (1968), with poems by vets reprinted from *Pacific Stars and Stripes,* some critical of the war; *Z: An Anthology of Revolutionary Poetry* (1968), included works by such Americans as Bukowski, Di Prima, Margaret Randall, Julian Beck, and Judith Malina but also by Than Hai and Ho Chi Minh; and *Thunderbolts of Peace and Liberation* (1968), which mixed Vietnamese voices (including monks and nuns) with that of Kupferberg.

40. There exist, of course, relatively abundant studies devoted to Vietnam War films, especially later Hollywood productions but also independent responses, particularly documentaries. About both genre, see *From Hanoi to Hollywood: The Vietnam War in American Film,* ed. Linda Dittmar and Gene Michaud (New Brunswick: Rutgers University Press, 1990). On the problem of documentaries, see chap. 4, "Other Forms: Documenting the Vietnam War," with essays by David E. James, "Documenting the Vietnam War"; Michael Renov, "Imaging the Other: Representations of Vietnam in Sixties Political Documentary"; David Grosser, "'We Aren't on the Wrong Side, We Are the Wrong Side': Peter Davis Targets (American Hearts and Minds)"; and Barry Dornfield, "*Dear America:* Transparency, Authority, and Interpretation in a Vietnam War Documentary." Also see again Rick Berg, "Losing Vietnam: Covering the War in an Age of Technology," and John Carlos Rowe, "Eyewitnesses: Documentary Styles in the American Representations of Vietnam," both in Rowe and Berg.

41. Contrast the complex reflections on this entire problematic by Vietnamese filmmaker Trinh T. Minh-ha in her film *Sur Name Viet Given Name Nam* (1989).

42. *The Anderson Platoon* (Pierre Schoendorffer, France, 1966).

PART 1

1. I would argue that national/ist categories do not ultimately transcend ideological matters of class, gender, sexuality, race, ethnicity, etc., but rather coexist, combine, and sometimes compete with them.

2. Homi K. Bhabha, "Introduction: Narrating the Nation," in *Nation and Narration*, ed. Homi K. Bhabha (New York: Routledge, 1990), 4. Hereafter cited as Bhabha.

3. Michael Geyer, "Historical Fictions of Autonomy and the Europeanization of National History," *Central European History* 22, no. 3/4 (September 1989): 316-42; here 318. Hereafter cited as Geyer.

4. See Walter Benjamin, "Theses on the Philosophy of History" [1940], in his *Illuminations*, ed. Hannah Arendt, trans. Harry Zohn (London: Fontana, 1973), 255-66 and *Das Passagen-Werk*, ed. Rolf Tiedemann, 2 vols. (Frankfurt am Main: Suhrkamp, 1982), 1:570-611.

5. For example, 1968 became known as "the year of official anti-Americanism." Manfred Wekwerth, "Berliner Ensemble 1968," *Theater Heute Jahresheft* (February 1968): 21.

1. PLAYING IMPERIALISM (AMERICA'S WAR)

1. Though the final troop withdrawal was not until 1975, many people hold the view that the protest movement began to decline after the Kent State massacre of May 1970.

2. Thus, e.g., I do not discuss Tom Cole's *Medal of Honor Rag* (1977), Emily Mann's *Still Life* (1979), Stephen Metcalfe's *Strange Snow* (1983), Brian DiFusco's *Tracers*, or Shirley Lauro's *A Piece of My Heart* (1988). For a more comprehensive study of this subject, see Toby Silverman Zinman, "Search and Destroy: The Drama of the Vietnam War," *Theater Journal* (March 1990): 5-26.

3. Megan Terry, *Viet Rock and Other Plays* (New York: Simon and Schuster, 1966). Hereafter cited as Terry.

4. Jerry Tallmer, *New York Post*, 14 November 1966.

5. Martin Gottfried, *Women's Wear Daily*, 14 November 1966.

6. Michael Herr, *Dispatches* (New York: Avon, 1968), 234. Hereafter cited as Herr. Widely taken as a significant precursor of postmodern fragmentation (dislocation of the subject, pastiche), Herr himself was anticipated in this respect by Vietnam Protest *Theatre*—which, however, rarely appears in accounts of the theory and genealogy of the postmodern condition.

7. *Variety*, 30 November 1966.

8. Joseph LeSueur, *Village Voice*, 17 November 1966.

9. Megan Terry, *Viet Rock*, dir. Stavros Doufexis, Städtisches Bühne, Nürnberg-Fürth, 18 April 1968.

10. "Peter Weiss in his *Vietnam Discourse*, . . . does not place human beings on the stage, but carriers of banners . . . however, the revue *Vietrock* shows both sides." Hermann Dannecker, *Lindauer Zeitung*, 23 April 1968.

11. "The whole thing is not presented, as with Peter Weiss, with documentary means but totally with the props of theatre which reach back to agitprop theatre in the manner of Meyerhold." Klaus Colberg, *Hessische Allgemeine Zeitung*, 23 April 1968.

12. "This play is so far removed from the conventional style of theatre that it cannot be grasped, nor staged, in terms of aesthetic categories alone." Walter Fenn, *Nürnberger Nachrichten*, 20 April 1968.

13. Alf Brustellin, *Süddeutsche Zeitung*, 14 April 1968.

14. See the photograph of the slogan and the transcript of the performance "Song of the Mighty B-52" by the People's Street Theatre, New York, Students for a Democratic Society, in *Guerrilla Street Theatre*, ed. Henry Lesnick (New York: Bard/Avon, 1973), 82-86. Hereafter cited as Lesnick.

15. A similar scene recurs both in Ron Kovic's novel *Born on the Fourth of July* and Oliver Stone's 1989 film: both contain war games that the hero as a child plays in the woods with his friends.

16. The fear of being called "feminine" or "homosexual" shadowed U.S. Marines into Vietnam, where they reacted strongly to the fact that Vietnamese would often hold hands and touch each other in public. "The custom proved to the GIs that South Vietnamese men were homosexuals, and this diagnosis explained why the Vietnamese were incompetent warriors, raising the question about why Americans had to die in defense of perverts." Loren Baritz, *Backfire: A History of How American Culture Led Us into Vietnam and Made Us Fight the Way We Did* (New York: Ballantine, 1985), 7. Hereafter cited as Baritz. Of course, given the nature of male bonding in warfare, this "diagnosis" might have also been a sign, at a deeper level of repression, that the Vietnamese might be precisely *more* competent warriors than Americans.

17. For a detailed examination of the male-oriented sexual language in the boot camp scene of *Full Metal Jacket*, see Susan White, "Male Bonding, Hollywood Orientalism, and the Repression of the Feminine in Kubrick's *Full Metal Jacket*," *Arizona Quarterly* 44, no. 3 (1988): 120-44.

18. "Vietnam representation is thus more than a comment on a particular war: it is an emblem for the presentation of dominant cultural ideology in contemporary society." Susan Jeffords, *The Remasculinization of America: Gender and the Vietnam War* (Bloomington: Indiana University Press, 1989), 5.

19. For the thesis that "the war machine" operates outside all forms of political sovereignty, which it can also potentially smash, see Gilles Deleuze and Félix Guattari, *Nomadology: The War Machine*, trans. Brian Massumi (New York: Semiotext[e], 1986).

20. Derek Walcott and Gary M. Friedman, "Heavenly Peace," unpublished play, second draft, *circa* 1973. The manuscript, "based on poems by Daniel Berrigan, S.J.," was sent to Berrigan and is presently in the Berrigan Collection, Karl A. Kroch Library, Cornell University. Hereafter cited as Walcott and Friedman.

21. "Everyone in Vietnam called dangerous areas Indian country. Paraphrasing a bit of Americana, some GIs painted on their flak jackets THE ONLY GOOD GOOK IS A DEAD ONE. They called their Vietnamese scouts who defected from the Communists Kit Carsons" (Baritz 37).

22. Historical (Kit Carson) and fictional heroes (John Wayne) are one and the same in this context. "It is astonishing how often American GIs in Vietnam approvingly referred to John Wayne, not as a movie star, but as a model and a standard. . . . These nineteen-year-old Americans, brought up on World War II movies and westerns, walking through the jungle, armed to the teeth, searching for an invisible enemy who knew the wilderness better than they did, could hardly miss these connections" (Baritz 37). The first major box-office release about Vietnam, *Green Berets* (1968), featured John Wayne as both director and star.

23. John Hellmann, *American Myth and the Legacy of Vietnam* (New York: Columbia University Press, 1986), 15. Hereafter cited as Hellmann.

24. "Vietnam was bound up in those expectations of returning to the landscape of American myth. Thus the enduring trauma of Vietnam has been the disruption of the American story. The war was a lost crusade, the costs of which were obscenely high" (Hellmann 221).

25. Perhaps it is worth noting in this context that whereas Americans refer to "horizons" as something one can go *beyond*—as in the image or myth of the West as a "new horizon"—in European discourse, from Kant to Husserl and beyond, "horizon" points to a *limit* that one cannot normally transgress.

26. Kopit's intention was to "explore what happens when a social and political power imposes itself on a lesser power and creates a mythology to justify it, as we did with the Indians, as we have tried to do in Vietnam" (from "Arthur Kopit," in *Contemporary Authors*, vols. 81-84 [Detroit: Gale Research, 1979], 304). It is also interesting that Johnson's wife, Lady Bird, was distinguishing herself at that time

by attempting to beautify America, in part through limiting the use of billboards on highways and in part through a media blitz designed to eliminate trash—a veritable war against littering. The most effective TV advertisement of this campaign was the image of an old Native American on horseback looking at discarded trash along a highway, a single tear running down his cheek.

27. According to Baritz's sharp formula, this solipsistic thinking that everyone is like Americans and therefore should strive for the same values was at the root of many problems. For "the advantage of imposing the imperial American self on the rest of humanity is that it serves as a justification of ignorance" (Baritz 17).

28. John Wayne uses a similar "argument" in *Green Berets*.

29. With the exception of the mother as noted earlier. The German production did not strictly adhere to this division: the strong statement "This war is worms" (which could have come from the Thirty Years' War) was spoken by a soldier instead of a woman, and it might also have occurred in a production of a number of European plays, not least in *Mother Courage*.

30. Barbara Garson, *MacBird*, dir. Roy Levine, Village Gate Theater, New York, 19 January 1967. Published as *MacBird* (New York: Grove Press, 1966). Hereafter cited as Garson.

31. James Davis, *Daily News*, 23 February 1967.

32. See John Berger, *Ways of Seeing* [1972] (London: BBC, 1977).

33. Of course, it would be interesting to know on which political side the various reviewers were, though in a sense this question is irrelevant, since they all, along with Garson, were likely part of the same problematic of self-critical patriotism.

34. Dwight MacDonald, *New York Review of Books*, as cited on the dust jacket of *MacBird*. My emphasis.

35. Robert Brustein, *New York Times*, as cited on the dust jacket of *MacBird*.

36. Richard P. Cooke, *Wall Street Journal*, 24 February 1967. Of the other newspapers that contained reviews—*Christian Science Monitor, Newark Evening News, New York Post, New York Times, Washington Post,* and *World Journal Tribune*—not one made any reference to the war in Vietnam.

37. "*MacBird* grew from a slip of the tongue when Barbara Garson, speaking at an antiwar rally in Berkeley, California, in August 1965, quite accidently referred to the First Lady of the United States as Lady MacBird Johnson. Since it was just a few weeks after the Watts insurrection and the Berkeley troop-train demonstrations, the opening lines of the play suggested themselves immediately: 'When shall we three meet again / In riot, strike, or stopping the train.' She decided to write a fifteen-minute skit or playlet based on *Macbeth* to be performed at the October 15-16 International Days of Protest." Garson, ix.

38. *MacBird* premiered in London on 1 November 1967 at the Theatre Royal, directed by Joan Littlewood. All subsequent performances were shown at a "club theater." It premiered in Germany on 15 March 1968 at the Württembürgische Staatstheater Stuttgart, directed by Peter Palitzsch.

39. The Lord Chamberlain forbade the performance of the play: "[It] represents the head of state of a friendly nation in an unfavorable light." *Frankfurter Allgemeine Zeitung*, 4 November 1967.

40. "Faerber urges the administrative and theatre advisory board to recommend to the theatre director to remove the play on April 5." *Stuttgarter Nachrichten*, 21 March 1968.

41. From program of *MacBird* (Frankfurt/Main: S. Fischer, 1968).

42. *Theater Heute* (April 1968): 8.

43. Daniel Berrigan, *The Trial of the Catonsville Nine*, Good Shepherd Faith Church, New York, 10 February 1971 (Boston: Beacon Press, 1979). Hereafter cited as Berrigan.

44. Arthur Sainer, *Village Voice*, 11 February 1971.

45. In the play Philip Berrigan remarks: "We have already made it clear / our dissent runs counter / to more than the war / which is but one instance / of American power in the world / Latin America is another instance / So is the Near East" (Berrigan 30).

46. Edith Oliver, *Time*, February 1971.

2. PERIPHERAL CONTESTATIONS (BRITAIN AND AUSTRIA)

1. Botho Strauß, "Vietnam und die Bühne," *Theater Heute Jahresheft* (1968): 40.

2. Peter Brook, *US* (London: Calder and Boyars, 1968). Hereafter cited as Brook.

3. "The actors step forward with the paper that Vietnam was wrapped in . . . it is streaked with paint from his body . . . an 'action painting.' They rip it in half" (Brook 58).

4. Peter Brook, *Nouvel Observateur*, 1 February 1967.

5. "Marine: I'd never think of shouting 'Gung Ho' or 'Geronimo' anymore" (Brook 66). The expression "Gung Ho" was used by U.S. Marines first in World War II in Asia and later in the Korean War. Ironically, the phrase derives from a Chinese expression meaning "work together," "cooperate." Geronimo, of course, was the last of the great Indian warriors to be captured by U.S. government forces.

6. In his *GI Diary*, written during training camp and while on tour in Vietnam from 1965 to 1967, David Parks exposes the racism he encountered as a black upper-middle-class soldier in Vietnam. He also reflects on the dilemma faced by black service men: "Frankly I'm mixed up. The Stateside news bugs me. On the one hand you have Stokely Carmichael saying Negroes shouldn't be fighting for this country. On the other hand some Negro leaders think just the opposite" (Parks 106). Not only Stokely Carmichael but Martin Luther King Jr., Malcolm X, and Huey Newton all denounced the role of African Americans in the war. For more information see *Vietnam and Black America: An Anthology of Protest and Resistance*, ed. C. Taylor (Garden City, N.Y.: Anchor, 1973). In addition, many African American musicians such as Marvin Gaye, John Lee Hooker, and Jimi Hendrix voiced their protest through their music, as did Jamaicans including Jimmy Cliff. See Mary Ellison, "Black Music and the Vietnam War," in *Vietnam Images*, ed. Jeffrey Walsh and James Aulich (New York: St. Martin's Press, 1989), 57-68.

7. In Britain a play must first obtain a license from the Lord Chamberlain before it can be performed.

8. Still clear in the memory of British subjects was the recent conflict in the Near East and loss of the Suez canal.

9. See Russell A. Berman, *Modern Culture and Critical Theory* (Madison: University of Wisconsin Press, 1989), 210-22.

10. Benedict Anderson, *Imagined Communities* (London: Verso, 1991), 6. See further Partha Chatterjee, *The Nation and Its Fragments: Colonial and Postcolonial Histories* (Princeton: Princeton University Press, 1993).

11. Gerald Szyszkowitz, *Commander Carrigan* (1968), rights with Merlin Verlag, Hamburg. Hereafter cited as Szyszkowitz 1968. It premiered at the Baden-Baden Theater der Stadt on 6 December 1968. Rewritten in 1990, it was then published in revised form in Szyszkowitz, *Theater Stücke* (Vienna: Neuer Breitschopf Verlag, 1991). Hereafter cited as Szyszkowitz 1991.

12. Gerald Szyszkowitz, program notes, *Commander Carrigan*, Baden-Baden, 1968, 2.

13. He explores this theme of repression and brutality in relation to World War II in his 1991 play *Friedemann Puntagim oder Die Kunst des Vergessens* (1991), in Szyszkowitz 1991.

14. This notion is also suggested in the poetry of BBC broadcaster and dissident communist Erich Fried, a former Austrian living in London, whose collections of poetry include *Und Vietnam und: Einundzwanzig Gedichte* (Berlin [FRG]: Verlag

Klaus Wagenbach, 1966). Hereafter cited as Fried.

15. A similar aimlessness characterizes the ex–cold war spy played by Eddie Constantine in Jean-Luc Godard's *Germany Year 90 Nine Zero* (1991).

16. In Fried's poem, "Pastor R. in Hamburg" (published in 1966), the same point is made about German-American relations: "But how long / can I still say 'Friends' / 'Friends you have erred / in Vietnam and Santo Domingo'" (Fried 13).

17. See Fredric Jameson, *The Geopolitical Aesthetic: Cinema and Space in the World System* (Bloomington: Indiana University Press and London: BFI, 1992).

18. Fredric Jameson, *Signatures of the Visible* (New York: Routledge, 1992), 26-27.

3. "DOCUMENTING" PRESENT AND PAST (GERMANY)

1. On Benjamin's notion of "dialectical image" in this sense, see his *Das Passagen-Werk* [1927-1940], ed. Rolf Tiedemann, 2 vols. (Frankfurt am Main: Suhrkamp, 1983), 1:570-611.

2. Rolf Hochhuth, *Soldiers: An Obituary for Geneva* [1967], trans. Robert David MacDonald (New York: Grove Press, 1968). Hereafter cited as Hochhuth. Hochhuth returns to the Vietnam topic in his 1987 *Judith*, in which a returning Vietnam vet decides to assassinate the U.S. president. Interestingly, of all Hochhuth's plays, *Soldiers* appears to be the only one not to have been reissued, attesting perhaps to its power still to disturb.

3. Siegfried Melchinger, "Hochhuths Neue Provokation: Luftkrieg ist Verbrechen," *Theater Heute* (February 1967): 6.

4. From the theater program of *Die Soldaten* ("PUBLIK: Materialien zur Zeit," ed. Theater der Freien Volksbühne), January 1967.

5. *Soldiers* premiered in North America on 1 May 1968 at the Billy Rose Theater, New York City.

6. Clive Barnes, *New York Times*, 2 May 1968.

7. Leo Mishkin, *Morning Telegraph*, 3 May 1968.

8. Erich Fried, *Und Vietnam und: Einundzwanzig Gedichte* (Berlin [FRG]: Verlag Klaus Wagenbach, 1966), 7 and 55.

9. For detailed coverage of this debate, see *The Storm over the Deputy: Essays and Articles about Hochhuth's Explosive Drama*, ed. Eric Bentley (New York: Grove Press, 1964).

10. Actually, the American Civil War, ending in 1864, had anticipated modern war in significant respects, not only the extensive death of civilians but also the quasi-mechanized warfare and the use of photography and electric communications.

11. "There were three exemplary events: the first was Auschwitz, the second Hiroshima, the third Cambodia. What happened in Cambodia was a scale model, a schema, a caricature of what's happening on a world-wide scale. The military class is turning into an internal secret-police. Moreover, it's logical. In the strategy of deterrence, military institutions, no longer fighting among themselves, tend to fight only civilian societies." Paul Virilio and Sylvère Lotringer, *Pure War*, trans. Mark Polizzoti (New York: Semiotext[e], 1983), 92. Hereafter cited as Virilio and Lotringer.

12. See, e.g., *Der "Führerstaat": Mythos und Realität; Studien zur Struktur und Politik des Dritten Reiches*, ed. Gerhard Hirschfeld and Lothar Kettenacker, introduction by Wolfgang J. Mommsen (Stuttgart: Klett-Cotta, 1981), esp. the essay by Tim Mason, "Intention and Explanation: A Current Controversy about the Interpretation of National Socialism," 21-41.

13. This debate among professional historians about the links between business and the Nazis was represented in North America by the "structuralist" (i.e., Marxist) account by David Abraham, on the one hand, and by his chief antagonist, Henry Ashby Turner, on the other. Both summarized the earlier debates going

back into the 1950s in different ways, and drew different consequences. See David Abraham, *The Collapse of the Weimar Republic: Political Economy and Crisis* (Princeton: Princeton University Press, 1981), and Henry Ashby Turner, *German Big Business and the Rise of Hitler* (New York: Oxford University Press, 1985). Abraham's book was badly flawed by its philological imprecision (even when the revised edition was republished in 1985 with Holmes and Meier), though its basic argument was not necessarily destroyed by this negligence.

14. On *Deutschland im Herbst* in its historical context, see Thomas Elsaesser, *New German Cinema: A History* (New Brunswick: Rutgers University Press, 1989), esp. 260-68, and Anton Kaes, *From Hitler to Heimat: The Return of History as Film* (Cambridge: MIT Press, 1989), esp. 25-28 and 79-80.

15. Sinkel, a lesser-known member of New German Cinema, went on to use this part of *Deutschland im Herbst* to make his eight-hour epic *Väter und Söhne* (Fathers and Sons), which was shown on German television only in 1986, though it had gone into production in 1979. Films by R. W. Fassbinder in Germany and by Pier Paolo Pasolini in Italy also contributed much to this perception of a fascist continuum in Europe from pre- to postwar society.

16. See Christopher Innes, *Modern German Drama: A Study in Form* (Cambridge: Cambridge University Press, 1979), 172-76. Hereafter cited as Innes 1979.

17. The connection between war and economy has been recently made more problematic by Virilio, who argues that "the situation is no longer very clear between the civil and the military because of the total involvement of the economy in war—already beginning in peacetime" (Virilio and Lotringer 10).

18. "With his political-moral questions, Hochhuth is tied with every fiber to the Hitler period and the situation of World War II. Only with scraps of insinuations does he succeed in relating to questions of today—Vietnam." Henning Rischbieter, "Realität, Poesie, Politik," *Theater Heute* (November 1967): 16.

19. Hochhuth, *Guerillas: Tragödie in 5 Akten* [1970] (Reinbek bei Hamburg: Rowohlt, 1973), 20.

20. First performed at the Städtische Bühne, Frankfurt am Main, 20 May 1968. Peter Weiss, *Two Plays*, trans. Lee Baxandall (New York: Atheneum, 1970). Hereafter cited as Weiss.

21. Michel Foucault, "History of Systems of Thought" [1970/71], in his *Language, Counter-Memory, Practice: Selected Essays and Interviews*, ed. Donald F. Bouchard, trans. Donald F. Bouchard and Sherry Simon (Ithaca: Cornell University Press, 1977), 200.

22. In Marx's famous words, for example, "Men make their own history, but they do not make it just as they please. They do not make it under circumstances chosen by themselves, but under circumstances directly found, given and transmitted from a past. The tradition of all dead generations weighs like a nightmare on the brain of the living." Karl Marx, *The Eighteenth Brumaire of Louis Bonaparte* [1852], in the *Marx-Engels Reader*, 2d ed., ed. Robert C. Tucker (New York: W. W. Norton, 1978), 595.

23. "In the nineteenth century, Britain used its navy, to keep law and order, in the world. . . . In this century it is we, who are ready and willing to assume the burden of leadership" (Weiss 165).

24. See Paul Virilio, *War and Cinema: The Logistics of Perception* [1984], trans. Patrick Camiller (London: Verso, 1989). Hereafter cited as Virilio 1989.

25. The German reads: "Kampfflugzeuge / Raketen Bomben / Napalm und Gas / Panzer Automobile / Fernsehgeräte / auf deren Bildschirmen ihr / uns zeigt bei Tag / und bei Nacht / Generäle und Stars / brennende Dörfer / Leichenhaufen / Ruinen und Schrott." Weiss, *Vietnam Diskurs*, in his *Stücke* (Frankfurt am Main: Suhrkamp, 1977), 2/1:258.

26. On theatre policies in Germany under U.S. and Allied occupation after

World War II, see Wigand Lange, *Theater in Deutschland nach 1945: Zur Theaterpolitik der amerikanischen Besatzungsbehörden* (Frankfurt am Main: Peter D. Lang, 1980).

27. "Still in the last year, the organizers of 'Experimenta' renounced *US*, Peter Brook's Vietnam revue, out of consideration for the American 'colony' in Frankfurt. But now nobody thinks anymore about being silent about Vietnam in order to spare American feelings." Hans Daiber, "Nachsitzen unter Polizeischutz," *Handelsblatt*, 22 March 1968.

28. These adjectives are drawn from a number of reviews and can be found in the following articles among others: Joachim Kaiser, "Vietnam oder: Die Bühne als politische Anstalt," *Süddeutsche Zeitung*, 22 March 1968, 71; Max Christian Feiler, "Einparteienstück als Geschichtsunterricht," *Münchner Merkur*, 8 July 1968; Günther Rühle, "Der lange Feldzug des Peter Weiss," *Frankfurter Allgemeine*, 22 March 1968, 70.

29. Gerd Fischer, "Dreistundenlang ostasiatische Geschichte," *Neue Ruhrzeitung*, 22 March 1968.

30. Max Christian Feiler, "Einparteienstück als Geschichtsunterricht," *Münchner Merkur*, 8 July 1968.

31. See Jane Shattuc, "*Contra* Brecht: R. W. Fassbinder and Pop Culture in the Sixties," *Cinema Journal* 33, no. 1 (fall 1993): 35-54.

32. Siegfried Melchinger, "Theater und Revolte: 2. Antithesen," *Theater Heute Jahreshefte* (1968): 34-35.

33. Hermann Dannecker, "Der 'Viet Nam Diskurs' von Peter Weiss," *Lindauer Zeitung*, 22 March 1968.

34. Jean-Marie Serreau, "Ist das Theater noch Zeitgemäss?" *Theater Heute* (September 1965): 1.

35. Some critics were not as sanguine. Thus, in a 1968 review, Urs Jenny noted: "Even television, which of late has been making some efforts, remains apparently ineffectual; also only those who are already interested, or so it seems, watch Vietnam broadcasts on the screen. Why then should the theatre, in its marginal position, be able to change anything in that situation? Of course, it can do nothing, but it suffers, silently or out loud, feeling its impotence, feeling that even a performance of *Vietnam Discourse* turns out to be an act of self-confirmation for actors and a friendly audience, and nothing more." See Urs Jenny, "Ja, die bösen Amerikaner," *Süddeutsche Zeitung*, 8 July 1968, 12.

36. Weiss, unpaginated program notes for *Vietnam Diskurs,* as performed in 1968 in Frankfurt am Main. Hereafter cited as Weiss 1968.

37. The use of fiction rather than documentary can allow for substantially greater freedom of expression—without necessarily sacrificing political effectiveness. In the case of European and American intervention in Vietnam, a case for political fiction was made as early as 1955 in Graham Greene's *The Quiet American,* which exposes the deep commitment of U.S. "advisors" in Vietnam. It begins with the disclaimer, "This is a story and not a piece of History," but of course it was also a piece of history. Greene, *The Quiet American* (Harmondsworth: Penguin, 1955), 5. One of the mottoes of the novel is taken from Byron: "This is the patent age of new inventions / For killing bodies, and for saving souls, / All propagated with the best intentions" (7). Similarly Pontecorvo's 1966 film *The Battle of Algiers* begins by asserting that it "contains not one foot of documentary," but of course it was also a kind of documentary. And so on.

38. Münchner Kammerspiele, 5 July 1968.

39. See Charlotte Nennecke, "Revolution seit über 200 Jahren," *Süddeutsche Zeitung*, 2 July 1968.

40. Hans Bertram Bock, "Ohne Duselei," *Abend Zeitung*, 24 June 1968, 12.

41. Urs Jenny, "Ja, die bösen Amerikaner," *Süddeutsche Zeitung*, 8 July 1968, 12.

42. Louis Althusser, "The 'Piccolo Teatro': Bertolazzi and Brecht: Notes on a

Materialist Theatre" [1962], in his *For Marx,* trans. Ben Brewster (New York: Vintage Books, 1979), 151.

43. Berliner Schaubühne im Hallescher Ufer, 15 January 1969.

44. "At the end of the Berlin premiere, Neuss announced that the police chief indeed had informed [him] that the collection of money by the theatre 'does not need a permit,' but could not be permitted, because of an expected 'disturbance.'" *Süddeutsche Zeitung,* 16 January 1969.

45. This was not the only East German attempt to "document" not only Vietnam but also its own contribution to the recent German past. Over an eleven-year period, from 1966 to 1977, the East German film collective H & S (led by Walter Heynowski and Gerhard Scheumann) made over a dozen films about the Vietnam War from various angles. Some of these films, particularly those involving the responsibility of interviewed U.S. pilots for the devastation of Vietnam and its civilian population, can be read as tacit critiques of any government in which one is trained "just to follow orders," including not least of all the GDR. See *Dokument und Kunst: Eine Werkstatt. Ein Thema. Elf Jahre. Dreizehn Filme. Vietnam bei H & S* (Berlin [GDR]: Akademie der Künste der Deutschen Demokratischen Republik, 1977).

46. For a basic account in English of Piscator, see Chrisopher D. Innes, *Erwin Piscator's Political Theatre* (Cambridge: Cambridge University Press, 1972).

47. See William J. Mitchell, *The Reconfigured Eye: Visual Truth in the Post-Photographic Era* (Cambridge: MIT Press, 1992). Hereafter cited as Mitchell. Mitchell, dean of the School of Architecture at MIT, analyzes how digital image manipulation and synthesis has broken down any remaining confidence in the veracity of photographic evidence and documentation, and he discusses the technosocial consequences of this epistemological breakdown.

48. Siegfried Kracauer, *Theory of Film: The Redemption of Physical Reality* (London: Oxford University Press, 1960), 46.

49. Walter Gropius as quoted in Erwin Piscator, *The Political Theatre,* trans. and ed. Hugh Rorrison (London: Eyre Methuen, 1980), 183. Hereafter cited as Piscator.

50. Max Horkheimer and Theodor W. Adorno, *Dialectic of Enlightenment* [1944], trans. John Cumming (New York: Continuum, 1988), 125.

51. Jean Baudrillard, *Simulations,* trans. Paul Foss, Paul Patton, and Philip Beitchman (New York: Semiotext[e], 1983), 141.

52. Herbert Marcuse, "Some Social Implications of Modern Technology" [1941], in *The Essential Frankfurt School Reader,* ed. Andrew Arato and Eike Gebhardt (New York: Continuum, 1990), 138-82; here 143.

53. See further Innes 1979, 206-13.

54. "But this is not science, this is theater, and the only thing that gives one courage is that between the reality of which the stage by its very nature can only reproduce a modest reflection, between history and ourselves, we can place the actor" (Hochhuth 127).

4. FROM COLONIALISM TO CYBERWAR (FRANCE)

1. André Benedetto, *Napalm* (Paris: P. J. Oswald, 1968), hereafter cited as Benedetto 1968; Armand Gatti, *V comme Vietnam* (Paris: Seuil, 1967), hereafter cited as Gatti. Neither play has been translated into English.

2. According to a review, *Napalm* is Benedetto's *Guernica.* Jaques Dupuy, *Provençal,* 7 February 1967.

3. While the Americans might not have represented the Vietnamese in theatre or films simply because they did not care about them, the French often seem to have believed that they already knew the Vietnamese through association during the colonial past.

4. Benedetto refers to McNamara as either Mac Namara or Namara.

5. Gatti seems to have had higher expectations than Benedetto about the intellectual level of his spectators; his play displays a sophisticated vocabulary and a more intricate syntax.

6. "The Secretary's apparent numbers fetish seemed to amuse some people, while it made others want to chew the carpet. He simply believed that problems that could be quantified should be." Leon Baritz, *Backfire: A History of How American Culture Led Us into Vietnam and Made Us Fight the Way We Did* (New York: Ballantine Books, 1985), 104. Hereafter cited as Baritz.

7. Paul Virilio and Sylvère Lotringer, *Pure War*, trans. Mark Polizotti (New York: Semiotext[e], 1983), 63. Hereafter cited as Virilio and Lotringer.

8. Virilio and Lotringer, 83. For a fuller development of this thesis, see Virilio, *War and Cinema: The Logistics of Perception* [1984], trans. Patrick Camiller (London: Verso, 1989).

9. This scheme continues in Benedetto's later Vietnam play, *Chant funèbre pour un soldat américain,* in which one soldier (Uncle Sam) is confronted by *two* Vietnamese farmers.

10. The first French trading station was opened in the Red River Delta in 1680, establishing a French presence; however, the French conquest did not become an ongoing process until the rule of Emperor Ming Mang (1820–1841). The French fought several successful battles resulting in the occupation of Da Nang (1847), Saigon (1859), and Hanoi (1873) and the treaties of Hue (1883–1884) which established a French protectorate over Tonkin and Annam. After World War II, the French returned and retained power until their final defeat at Dien Bien Phu in 1954.

11. Ho Chi Minh studied for some time in Paris and was a member of the French Communist Party. As an illustration of what came to be viewed as the "traditional" colonial relationship, see Marguerite Duras's semiautobiographical novel, *Barrage contre le Pacifique,* relating her childhood in Indochina. Two popular songs in France before World War II were titled "Ma Tonkinoise" and "En pousse-pousse"! Most recently, in 1992, three French movies were released which depicted Vietnam as a French colony: *Dien Bien Phu, The Lover,* and *Indochine* (the 1993 Oscar for Best Foreign Film).

12. The V in Gatti's title refers to Vietnam but also evokes the memory of V for Victory, which Churchill popularized during World War II with two fingers lifted in a V shape with its further allusion, via Morse code, to Beethoven's Fifth Symphony. The play's title thus can be understood as an announcement of Victory for Vietnam.

13. In March 1953, the SFIO officially withdrew support for the war, though many members did not toe the line. Many socialists had protested against it much earlier, but without much success. For a detailed account of the French attitude toward the war, the decline in popular support, the fluctuations among leftists, see Jacques Dalloz, *La guerre d'Indochine, 1945–1954* (Paris: Seuil Points Histoire, 1987), 158-228. Hereafter cited as Dalloz.

14. It is possible that they intended to express a French irritation with the policies of the U.S. government, which in 1950, promised to assist France's war effort in Vietnam, but then, drawn into the war in Korea, reduced its financial help while slowly gaining influence in Saigon at the price of friction with the French authorities. Gatti and Benedetto probably were aware of these international expectations and disappointments (Dalloz 180, 196–98).

15. This is indicated by the director speaking directly to the audience: "Actors will follow each other. And, since after each performance they will ask you to tell them your dreams, you might as well get ready to make a good impression on them. You are well aware that they will use the dreams that you tell them to add new scenes to their repertory" (Gatti 98).

16. It is unfortunate that practically no plays written at the time by Vietnamese

playwrights about the war are available in translation, so it is harder to compare and contrast their vision with that of the French. One exception is Nhat Hanh, *The Path of Return Continues the Journey* (New York: Hoa Binh Press, 1972).

17. See Norman Bryson, *Looking at the Overlooked* (Cambridge: Harvard University Press, 1990), 30.

18. Roland Barthes, *Mythologies,* trans. Annette Lavers (New York: Hill and Wang, 1983), 116-21.

19. In Hochhuth's play *The Soldiers,* the ambiguous power of the free press is also alluded to: "American: And above all, the fact we don't win is all the fault of the press. Russian: The press? Ours is never giving trouble." Rolf Hochhuth, *Soldiers: An Obituary for Geneva* [1967], trans. Robert David MacDonald (New York: Grove Press, 1968), 51.

20. Gatti himself was by profession a journalist, a foreign correspondent. In a sense, he too had "defected" with his play.

21. The same idea is expressed by Quadrature: "Vietnam images are affected with gigantism. Theo: An image, after all, is but an image. Quadrature: But it must not be viewed as such, but for what it presupposes [in its rationality]" (Gatti 102).

22. Joyce Nelson, *The Perfect Machine: T.V. in the Nuclear Age* (Toronto: Between the Lines, 1987), 25.

23. André Benedetto, in *Le Provençal,* 23 February 1967.

24. Ibid.

25. *Le Dauphiné,* 3 February 1967.

26. Henri LePine, *Marseillaise,* 8 February 1967.

27. For a detailed treatment of this question see Richard Drinnon's *Facing West: The Metaphysics of Indian Hating and Empire Building* (New York: Schocken Books, 1980, 1990). Thus, "the massacres at My Lai and all the forgotten My Khes in Vietnam had a basic continuity with those of Moros on Jolo and of Filipinos on Samar at the turn of the century, and of Native Americans on the mainland earlier—all the Wounded Knees, Sand Creeks, and Bad Axes. The linkage of atrocities over time and space reveals underlying themes and fundamental patterns of the national history that lawmakers, generals, and so many of their compatriots were eager to forget" (457).

28. Johnson is even ready to annex Vietnam: "This country is the 51st state of the Union, yes or no? The U.S. border follows the 17th parallel, yes or no?" (Benedetto 128).

29. Fourteen officers were charged with the My Lai massacre, but only Lieutenant William L. Calley was convicted.

30. Benedetto's second play is a one-act piece with very little dialogue. There are only three central characters: a male and a female Vietnamese and an American GI, Sam. The GI wears a huge papier mâché head draped with an American flag, thus offering a dehumanized, symbolic, synecdochic representation of the United States (Uncle Sam). He is in the process of dying throughout the play, while trying to evoke the pity of the Vietnamese. The Soldier implores "Have pity!"—to which the Vietnamese respond by listing all the crimes of the Americans: "Those who exterminated the Indians. Those who enslaved the Blacks. Those who dropped the atomic bomb on Hiroshima and Nagasaki" (Benedetto 1972, 21). At the end Sam elicits their pity: "Poor little child" (35).

31. Neither Puerto Rico, nor the Philippines, nor the Pacific Islands, though occupied by the United States, were viewed then, especially in France, as traditional colonies. In the case of the Philippines, the perception is somewhat different. For example, Kidlat Tahimik's bittersweet film *Perfumed Nightmare* (1977) forges clear links between the various waves of imperialist colonization, economic exploitation, and cultural rape of his native country.

32. Olivier Todd, *Nouvel Observateur,* 1 February 1967.

33. See again, in just this context, the film *Loin du Vietnam*.

34. Whether Benedetto intended to imply here that a better TV coverage of the Algerian War might have helped bring it to an earlier end is a matter for speculation. As a rule, he (and many other French) viewed television as a typically American cultural product and, *as such*, to be distrusted. On the other hand, as was noted, Benedetto relied on the TV coverage of the Vietnam War to get his information, as did almost everyone else.

35. For a perceptive account of the reception of the Algerian War, see *La guerre d'Algérie et les Français*, ed. Jean-Pierre Rioux (Paris: Fayard, 1990). Hereafter cited as *La guerre d'Algérie*.

36. In his brilliant documentary film *Le jolie Mai* (1962), Chris. Marker captures the broad spectrum of French reaction to this crucial historical movement.

37. Jean-Paul Sartre, *The Condemned of Altona* [1960], trans. Sylvia and George Leeson (New York: Vintage Books, 1963), vii.

38. "Yet in 1972, ten years after the fighting ended, the French public suddenly realized that it had been deceived about what was happening during the war, and a hunger became apparent in France for facts that should have been provided at the time. An illustrated weekly magazine devoted entirely to the history of the war sold 4,000,000 copies per issue. Books describing the fighting became national best-sellers. Parisians queued to see a long documentary film, *La guerre d'Algérie*, that included newsreel footage—long suppressed by the censor at the time—of French soldiers shooting down an Algerian peasant for no apparent reason." Phillip Knightly, *The First Casualty: From the Crimea to Vietnam: The War Correspondent as Hero, Propagandist, and Myth Maker* (New York: Harcourt Brace Jovanovich, 1975), 358.

39. Thus Henri Alleg, in *La Question*, exposed French tortures already in 1958, and soon *Paris Match* printed images of war atrocities that were not allowed to appear on French television. For a further discussion of that censure, especially after the peace treaty, see *La guerre d'Algérie*, 553-603.

40. The government censorship of films that exposed the French military past has had a long history: Stanley Kubrick's *Paths of Glory* (1957), a sharp critique of the French Army in World War I, was forbidden in France till the late sixties, and Marcel Ophüls's *Le chagrin et la pitié* (1971), a harsh exposé of the French collaboration with the Nazis, originally produced for television, was widely denounced and withdrawn from that medium.

41. The Algerian debate continues in France. See Thomas Ferenczi, "Les troubles de la mémoire," *Le Monde*, 26 August 1990.

42. Heinrich Vormweg, "Die Maschine versagt," *Süddeutsche Zeitung*, 21 November 1968.

43. See Edward W. Said, *Orientalism* (New York: Vintage Books, 1978), for a relevant discussion of French and British imperial rule.

44. Rita Maran, *Torture: The Role of Ideology in the French-Algerian War* (New York: Praeger, 1989), 51.

45. Iain Chambers, *Migrancy, Culture, Identity* (New York and London: Routledge, 1994), 62.

PART 2

1. Since the Holocaust, the problematic of the representation of evil or "tragedy" in drama and other aesthetic forms has come increasingly to the forefront. See Friedrich Dürrenmatt's "No more tragedy after WWII" and Adorno's "No more poetry after Auschwitz." More generally on the problem of tragedy in the twentieth century, see George Steiner's seminal study, *The Death of Tragedy* (New York: Hill and Wang, 1961).

2. Annette Insdorf poses the following question in the introduction to her book

on Holocaust film: "Filmmakers and film critics confronting the Holocaust face a basic task—finding an appropriate language for that which is mute or defies visualization. How do we lead a camera or pen to penetrate history and create art, as opposed to merely recording events? What are the formal as well as moral responsibilities if we are to understand and communicate the complexities of the Holocaust through its filmic representations?" Annette Insdorf, *Indelible Shadows: Film and the Holocaust* (New York: Cambridge University Press, 1989), xv.

3. See Edmund Burke, *A Philosophical Enquiry into the Origin of Our Ideas of the Sublime and Beautiful* [1757], ed. James T. Boulton (Notre Dame: University of Notre Dame Press, 1968), 39.

4. Claude Lanzman's *Shoah* has a unique impact as a testimony of the Holocaust precisely because it filmed a present-day reality "aurally," without trying to re-create a past tragedy "visually"—though of course it really did both in its own terms.

5. Earlier films about Vietnam, such as *Apocalypse Now*, still resort to highly stylized abstraction to show the war, whereas more recent examples such as *Platoon, Full Metal Jacket*, and *Casualties of War* focus on pure violence and atrocities.

6. Michael Taussig, *Mimesis and Alterity* (New York: Routledge, 1993), 24, 31.

7. For a relevant discussion of the relation between aesthetics and anaesthesia, see Susan Buck-Morss, "Aesthetics and Anaesthetics: Walter Benjamin's Artwork Essay Reconsidered," *October* 62 (fall 1992): 3-41.

8. The now defunct Grand Guignol in Paris specialized, and excelled, in the convincing staging of horrifying scenes where blood was flowing from gaping wounds, and brutal murders and tortures seemed to be committed on the stage. See Mel Gordon, *The Grand Guignol Theatre of Fear and Terror* (New York: Amok Press, 1988).

9. See Heinar Kipphardt's *In the Case of Oppenheimer*, Richard Schneider's *Prozess Richard Waverly*, or Peter Weiss's *The Investigation*.

5. PERFORMATIVE SUB-MISSIONS

1. Peter Brook, *US* (London: Calder and Boyars, 1968). Hereafter cited as Brook.

2. *Pinkville* premiered 17 March 1971 at the American Place Theater, New York. It had been unofficially presented the previous summer at the Berkshire Theatre Fest. The text has never been published in English, nor has a record of the script been kept in the archives at the Performing Arts Library at Lincoln Center. This is surprising since the Center does have all other plays by Tabori. Michael Douglas won an award for his performance; Raoul Julia also starred. Interestingly enough, the text is readily available in German, and I have referred to both the German edition (George Tabori, *Spiele*, ed. Peter von Becker [Cologne: Prometh Verlag, 1984]) and the unpublished English language rehearsal text (translated by Peter Hirsche). There are considerable variations between the two texts. The German version hereafter cited as Tabori.

3. Jack Kroll, "Bellow of Rage," *Newsweek*, 29 March 1971.

4. Clive Barnes, "*Pinkville* Rages at War's Brutality," *New York Times*, 18 March 1971.

5. "Some of what has been set down in 'Pinkville' is honestly out of recent history and there are scenes which make any Yankee wince. It's a pity that Tabori had to overstate his case." Edward Sothern Hipp, "'Pinkville' Revisited," *Evening News*, 18 March 1971.

6. George Oppenheimer, "Casualties are in the Audience," *Newsday*, 18 March 1971.

7. Sege, *Variety*, 7 April 1971.

8. Marilyn Stasio, *Cue*, 20 March 1971.

9. "All of this is sharply, inventively staged by Martin Fried, down to the business of tearing Raggedy Ann dolls to shreds as though they were Mylai [sic] children. It is constantly buoyed by a jabbing musical score." *New York Times*, 21 March 1971.

10. Sege, *Variety*, 7 April 1971.

11. Arthur Sainer, "'It Was No Big Deal' Revisited," *Village Voice*, 18 March 1971.

12. For a translation, see Tabori, *The Cannibals* [1968], in *The Theatre of the Holocaust: Four Plays*, ed. Robert Skloot (Madison: University of Wisconsin Press, 1982). Hereafter cited as Tabori 1982. Its American premiere was on 3 November 1968 in New York City.

13. Note that Tabori's articulation of communion and cannibalism is not mere poetic license; it has considerable anthropological depth. See *From Communion to Cannibalism: An Anthology of Metaphors of Incorporation*, ed. Maggie Kilgour (Princeton: Princeton University Press, 1990).

14. See Tabori, *Jubiläum* [1983], in his *Spiele*, 107-41. Hereafter cited as Tabori 1983.

15. Dwight MacDonald's *Television and the Red Menace* (New York: Praeger, 1985) examines how network television helped bolster the cold war by creating and reinforcing images of the communist enemy.

16. Richard Drinnon, *Facing West: The Metaphysics of Indian Hating and Empire Building* (New York: Schocken Books, 1980, 1990), 457.

17. As cited in Susan D. Moeller, *Shooting the War: Photography and the American Experience of Vietnam* (New York: Basic Books, 1989), 377.

18. "We have all read, and been shocked by, these very eventualities in the newspapers. We know them as real. Merely illustrating them in the theater, with no new information added, does not bring them closer. It takes them farther away, turns them back into make-believe again. That is no help." *New York Times*, 21 March 1971.

19. *Fuck Nam* was performed at the Open Space Theatre in London on 31 December 1969. To my knowledge, and Kupferberg's, it was never performed in the United States. Like *Pinkville*, the play is not available in print, and very few libraries have typescript copies (one exception is the extensive Vietnam Collection at the Kroch Library, Cornell University). The edition I am using is a copy sent to me by the author: Tuli Kupferberg, *Fuck Nam* (New York: Birth Press, 1967). Hereafter cited as Kupferberg. A German translation exists in *Radikales Theater*, vol. 1, ed. Ute Nyssen, trans. Jürgen Bansemere (Cologne: Kiepenheuer and Witsch, 1969). All information concerning Kupferberg will be drawn from a personal interview on 10 August 1990. Hereafter cited as interview.

20. "The Americans were sensitive to so many obscenities. The play was not performed in the United States; once it was performed in Sweden. On the coming Monday, citizens of the BRD and 50 critics, will see it for the first time in Wuppertal." *Der Spiegel*, 26 January 1970, 5, 123.

21. "The illustrations are to be projected onto the set & cover all of stage rear & are projected on top of the action (on top of the set, *not* on a screen) at automatically timed intervals (divide total time of play by number of slides & have automatic timer take over). Colored illustrations may also be used. The ones included in the script are by way of examples. They can be changed as new ones are found in current newspapers & mags. They are to be biased, however, toward the ironic" (Kupferberg 6). Kupferberg was interested in using "media as a takeoff point for poetry and theatre." A book of his "News Poems" is illustrated by media photographs.

22. The play on the word "Phoc" / "Fuck" was inspired by the fact that many Vietnamese villages included "Phoc" in their name (interview).

23. P. W. B., *The Stage and Television Today*, 9 January 1969.

24. It has been amply explored by Sigmund Freud, Wilhelm Reich, Herbert Marcuse, and Georges Bataille, among others.

25. Kupferberg's play is exclusively set in Vietnam, i.e., the "Orient." With his obsessive stress on violent sexuality, he may be alluding to a stereotype identified by Said: "Once again, the association is clearly made between the Orient and the freedom of licentious sex." Edward W. Said, *Orientalism* (New York: Vintage Books, 1978), 190.

26. This is one of the few early plays that makes any reference to either prostitution or drug use by Americans in Vietnam. Ironically, the extent to which this was a problem became fully a part of the American psyche only when it was confirmed by vets themselves.

27. Today, as Vietnam considers opening its doors once again to Western tourists, there is understandable concern that doing so will turn the country into another "pleasure playground"—like Thailand for Western men in the 1990s. See Don Luce, "Back to Vietnam," *The Nation*, 28 February 1994, 257.

28. Kupferberg was also a member in the sixties of the underground rock group The Fugs (*aka* Fucks). Their performances often included pantomimed skits. In one show and song, "Kill for Peace" (also an antiwar slogan), Kupferberg played a crazed marine who tries to feed chocolate to a dead Vietnamese child; enraged by his lack of success, he proceeds to smear it like excrement all over the baby's face.

29. "In this play the Americans are decidedly the enemy for they are shown as sex happy and almost exclusively sex oriented and sloughing their way through the innocent Vietnamese with arms and genitals alike. Mr. Kupferberg's stateside soldiers are about as likeable as the concentration camp orderlies from the last war." P. W. B., *The Stage and Television Today*, 9 January 1969.

6. AMERICAN I-WITNESSES (RABE, BALK)

1. See, for example, Toby Silverman Zinman, "Search and Destroy: The Drama of the Vietnam War," *Theatre Journal* (March 1990): 5-26, and N. Bradley Christie, "David Rabe's Theater of War and Remembering," in *Search and Clear: Critical Responses to Selected Literature and the Films of the Vietnam War* (Bowling Green, Oh.: Bowling Green State University Popular Press, 1988), 105-15. Hereafter cited as Zinman and as Christie.

2. *Sticks and Bones* was first produced in 1969 at Villanova University (where Rabe was a student) under the direction of James Christie. It was then staged in New York, 7 November 1971, at the New York Shakespeare Festival's Public Theatre. *The Basic Training of Pavlo Hummel*, though written in 1968, premiered at the Newman Theatre on 20 May 1971. *Streamers* premiered at the Long Wharf Theater on 30 January 1976. Rabe also wrote a less well known play, *The Orphan* (1970), which can be viewed as a disguised treatment of Vietnam. Rabe's main Vietnam Protest Plays are published as follows: *The Basic Training of Pavlo Hummel* and *Sticks and Bones* (New York: Viking Press, 1973), and *Streamers* (New York: Knopf, 1985). The first two plays are hereafter cited as Rabe 1973, the third as Rabe 1985. I will also cite from Rabe's introduction to the 1973 Viking edition of the first two plays.

3. For an interesting discussion of veteran and nonveteran playwrights see Zinman.

4. *The Basic Training of Pavlo Hummel* won the 1971 Drama Desk, Drama Guild, and Obie Awards; *Sticks and Bones* won the 1972 Tony Award for best play as well as the Dramatists Guild, Variety Poll, and Outer Circle Awards; *Streamers* was the New York Drama Critics choice for Best American Play of 1976 (Christie 105).

5. Martin Gottfried, *Women's Wear Daily*, 21 May 1971.

6. "He is black or of Spanish descent, and is dressed in the uniform of a sergeant major and wearing many campaign ribbons" (Rabe, *Sticks and Bones*, 127).

7. This is not an unusual characterization: it rather follows a familiar pattern of sexual prejudice wherein, as Said notes in *Orientalism*, "women are usually the creatures of a male power-fantasy. They express unlimited sensuality, they are more or less stupid, and above all they are willing" (Said 1978, 207).

8. "The hands grasping under his chin, stuffing a rag into his mouth. . . . The other Vietcong approaches and crouches over Parham, holding a knife over him. . . . And he places the blade against Parham's chest, and Parham behind his gag begins to howl, begins to flail his pinioned arms and beat his heels furiously upon the ground. . . . Then the knife goes in" (Rabe 1973, 94).

9. "They're sayin' you can go home when you been hit twice and you don't even check. You wanna go back out, you're thinkin', get you one more gook, get you one more slopehead, make him know the reason why. . . . Poor ole Ryan gets dinged round about Tay Ninh, so two weeks later in Phu Loi you blow away this goddamn farmer" (Rabe 1973, 99).

10. ARDELL: You don't know he's got satchel charges.
    PAVLO: I do. . . .
    ARDELL: When you shot into his head, you hit into your own head, fool! (Rabe 1973, 99-101)

11. See Klaus Theweleit, *Male Fantasies*, vol. 1: *Women, Floods, Bodies, History* [1977], trans. Stephen Conway, foreword by Barbara Ehrenreich (Minneapolis: University of Minnesota Press, 1987). Hereafter cited as Theweleit.

12. "War is described as a biological necessity for the human male; without it, he is somehow only half alive. In the same way reproduction is portrayed as requisite for the social well-being of the human female, something for which she will feel a nostalgia for having 'missed.' These questions suggest that biology and the social construction of gender are in fact inseparable, and to deny this is to risk an unfulfilled human character." Susan Jeffords, *The Remasculinization of America: Gender and the Vietnam War* (Bloomington: Indiana University Press, 1989), 89. Hereafter cited as Jeffords.

13. "The Vietnamese woman, as a direct reminder of birth/death, then must be killed, and the prostitute's apparent reassurance that sexuality can proceed without reproduction can occur only as she is disembodied and no longer a woman at all" (Jeffords 93).

14. For a discussion on the function of advertising images in *Sticks and Bones*, see James A. Robinson, "A Soldier's Home: Images of Alienation in *Sticks and Bones*," in *Search and Clear*, 136-46.

15. "Our newer playwrights are plainly obsessed with film. When the curtain goes up these nights, whether it is on a . . . deep carpeted suburban living room or an ice-cool cabaret, the odds are that someone is going to trot out a movie screen sooner or later, snap it down onto its tripod, and turn out the lights while the projector begins to whir." Walter Kerr, *New York Times*, 14 November 1971.

16. OZZIE: Harriet, the TV is broke.
    HARRIET: What?
    OZZIE: There's a picture but no sound. I don't . . .
    HARRIET: I want to talk about David.
    OZZIE: David's all right. I'm gonna call the repairman. (Rabe 1973, 137)

17. OZZIE: I'll get it fixed. I'll fix it. Who needs to hear it? We'll watch it. (Wildly turning TV channels.) I flick my rotten life. Oh, there's a good one. Ohhh, isn't that a good one? That's the best one. That's the best one.
    DAVID: They will call it madness. We will call it seeing. (Rabe 1973, 216)

18. Jean Baudrillard, *Simulations*, trans. Paul Foss, Paul Patton, and Philip Beitchman (New York: Semiotext[e], 1983), 53.

19. The same break with reality occurs when slides are projected at the beginning of each act supposedly to depict David's family. David as a small child is still

recognizable—"The taller one's David, right?" (Rabe 1973, 120)—but he becomes unrecognizable after he comes home from the war.

20. Dick Bruckenfeld, *Village Voice*, 11 November 1971.

21. *The Dramatization of 365 Days* by H. Wesley Balk [based on the book by Ronald J. Glasser, M.D.] (Minneapolis: University of Minnesota Press, 1972). The play premiered at the Shevlin Arena Theater, University of Minnesota, 9 November 1971. Hereafter cited as Balk.

22. The popular film M*A*S*H* and the TV spin-off were both set in Korea, but the references to Vietnam were clear.

23. "It was perhaps similar feeling that led both Jerzy Kosinski and Ronald Glasser to withhold the movie rights for their books on the one hand, while accepting the possibility of a chamber theater exploration on the other" (Balk 6).

24. "And so it goes, and the gooks know it. They will drop the point, trying not to kill him but to wound him, to get him screaming so they can get the medic too" (Balk 54).

25. "The moonlight came in through the door, cutting a path of light across the floor. . . . The gook was waiting, lying on the ground, no more than two meters from the door. He let off a single round that ripped through the trooper's chest. As he fell back the VC put his weapon on automatic and shot the shit out of the hutch" (Balk 40).

26. In one case two GIs sneak out during the night and kill a sniper who has killed their buddies; in the second case, the murder of a Vietnamese is "justified" because he is a thief.

27. "Strange war. Going for something they didn't believe in or for that matter didn't care about, just to make it 365 days and be done with it" (Balk 46).

28. Even in "left-wing" publications today, stress continues to be placed on *American* casualties in war and war-related eco-disasters. See, e.g., the report on the effects of U.S.-spread pesticides on American GIs (but not native populations) during the Gulf War: Laura Flanders, "Mal de guerre," *The Nation*, 7 March 1994, 292-93.

29. "From the beginning of the nineteenth century until the end of World War II France and Britain dominated the Orient and Orientalism; since World War II America has dominated the Orient and approaches it as France and Britain once did" (Said 1978, 4).

CONCLUSION

1. Susan Sontag, *On Photography* (New York: Doubleday, 1973), 18. Hereafter cited as Sontag.

2. On the relationship between aesthetics and anaesthesia, see again Susan Buck-Morss, "Aesthetics and Anaesthetics: Walter Benjamin's Artwork Essay Reconsidered," *October* 62 (fall 1992): 3-41.

3. "Those occasions when the taking of a photograph is relatively undiscriminating, promiscuous, or self-effacing do not lessen the didacticism of the whole enterprise. This very passivity—and ubiquity—of the photographic record is photography's 'message,' its aggression" (Sontag 7).

4. John Guare, *Three Plays: Cop-Out, Muzeeka, Home Fires* (New York: Grove Press, 1970). *Muzeeka* premiered at the Eugene O'Neill Memorial Theatre Foundation in Waterford, Connecticut on 19 July 1967. Hereafter cited as Guare.

5. See Marshall McLuhan and Quentin Fiore, *The Medium Is the Massage* (New York: Bantam Books, 1967).

6. Jean-Claude van Itallie, *TV* (1966), in his *American Hurrah and Other Plays* (New York: Grove Press, 1978), 57-134. Hereafter cited as van Itallie.

7. Grant Duay, *Fruit Salad*, in *The New Underground Theatre*, ed. Robert J. Schroeder (New York: Bantam Books, 1968). Hereafter cited as Duay.

8. "I began writing screenplays three years ago during which time I received invaluable experience in different phases of film making, working on underground films and pilot TV commercials. *Fruit Salad* is my first play" (Duay 120).

9. A newcomer to Vietnam was commonly called a "cherry" by his peers—a connection to the slang expression referring to a virgin. At the beginning of *The 13th Valley*, John M. Del Vecchio describes a young recruit: "From that day on they called him Cherry. It confused him yet it felt right. He was in a new world, a strange world. . . . It made little difference to him that they called every new man Cherry and that with the continual rotation of personnel there would soon be a soldier newer than he and he would call the new man Cherry." Del Vecchio, *The 13th Valley* (New York: Bantam, 1982), 1.

10. Note that "Milt Orshefsky, the *Life* writer . . . stated that color was good 'for the spectacle part—the chopper patterns, the rockets firing etc. and black and white for the human part, the emotions, the fatigue, the tension,'" Susan D. Moeller, *Shooting War: Photography and the American Experience of Combat* (New York: Basic Books, 1989), 291. Hereafter cited as Moeller.

11. Daniel C. Hallin, *The "Uncensored War": The Media and Vietnam* (Berkeley: University of California Press, 1989), 175. Hereafter cited as Hallin.

12. No such concern obtained for the Vietnamese, whose losses were less and less reported: "The total amount of coverage of civilian [Vietnamese] casualties did not increase—it dropped considerably after Tet" (Hallin 176). While the figure of "57,000" U.S. deaths in Vietnam has been well publicized, no definite figure of Vietnamese casualties has been given—perhaps over two million.

13. Amlin Gray, *How I Got That Story*, in *Coming to Terms: American Plays and the Vietnam War*, ed. James Reston Jr. (New York: Theatre Communications Group, 1985). Hereafter cited as Gray.

14. The production I am referring to was put on by Penn's Intuitons at the University of Pennsylvania, fall 1989.

15. True, the play also includes a few other "events," such as "fragging," that are not commonly found in official media images: "He has to win the absolute confidence of the men in his command. If he's not able to, in combat, when he's giving them an order that requires them to risk their lives, it's possible that one of them may shoot him in the back. The soldiers call this 'fragging'" (Gray 91). But these are rare exceptions.

16. In a similar spirit, in Oliver Stone's film *Born on the Fourth of July* (1989), when Donna recalls seeing on television a murdered girl at Kent State lying in a pool of blood, she is reminded of the poster of My Lai with the women and children also lying in pools of blood. Her reference points are television, posters, and photographic images, i.e., simulacra.

17. Michael Herr, *Dispatches* (New York: Avon, 1968), 246. Hereafter cited as Herr.

18. Gray's reporter turns himself into a mechanical recording device—a mere observer of history and not a participant. One notes that in Wim Wender's film *Wings of Desire* (1988), the Angel played by Bruno Ganz reaches a contrary conclusion: he decides to abandon his role as a passive recorder of history and becomes a participant by entering the world of the living. This too is a version of the classical paradox faced by every anthropologist—to change what one has set out merely to record.

19. A similar scene, played out in Herr's *Dispatches* (1968), indicates that Gray's concerns were shared by real reporters. Herr quotes a marine addressing him: "You mean you guys volunteer to come over here? . . . Oh man, you got to be kidding me. You guys asked to come here?" (Herr 217).

20. Walter Benjamin, "The Work of Art in the Age of Mechanical Reproduction," in his *Illuminations*, trans. Harry Zohn, ed. Hannah Arendt (Great Britain: Fontana, 1982), 244. Hereafter cited as Benjamin.

21. Of course, theatre was not the only medium to criticize the media; in Godard and Gorin's film *A Letter to Jane* (1972) one finds a scathing attack on a photograph taken of Jane Fonda while she was touring North Vietnam.

22. Linda Hutcheon, *The Politics of Postmodernism* (London: Routledge, 1989), 135. Hereafter cited as Hutcheon.

23. Raymond Bellour, "Le spectateur pensif," in *L'être—images* (Paris: La Différence, 1990), 77.

24. How exactly, one could also ask, did a documentary army film function already in Piscator's production of *In Spite of Everything*?

25. "What they [documentary images] suggest instead is that there is no directly and naturally accessible past 'real' for us today: we can only know and construct— the past through its traces, its representations. As we have repeatedly seen, whether these be documents, eye-witness accounts, documentary film footage, or other works of art, they are still representations and they are our only means of access to the past" (Hutcheon 113). Of course, to argue that there is no "direct" access to the past is rather different from arguing that there is no access whatsoever.

26. John Tagg, *The Burden of Representation: Essays on Photographies and Histories* (Amherst: University of Massachusetts Press, 1988), 4. Hereafter cited as Tagg.

27. Despite the fact that there were more women reporters and photographers in Vietnam than in any other war, they were still only a minority (Moeller 359). Those who made it over were often referred to as "the girls" and not taken seriously by their colleagues. See Susan Jeffords, *The Remasculinization of America: Gender and the Vietnam War* (Bloomington: Indiana University Press, 1989), 41.

28. Sontag makes that point in perhaps overly dramatic language: "To photograph people is to violate them, by seeing them as they never see themselves, by having knowledge of them they can never have; it turns people into objects that can be symbolically possessed. Just as the camera is a sublimation of the gun, to photograph someone is a sublimated murder—a soft murder, appropriate to a sad frightened time" (Sontag 14-15).

29. Roland Barthes, *Image-Music-Text*, trans. Stephen Heath (New York: Hill and Wang, 1977), 16.

30. It is this image which recurs more than any other in the protest plays, but one could equally focus on the images of the napalmed little girl or the execution of a Vietcong suspect. For an interesting discussion on the latter, see Robert Hamilton, "Image and Context: The Production and Reproduction of 'The Execution of a VC Suspect' by Eddie Adams," *Vietnam Images: War and Representation*, ed. Jeffrey Walsh and James Aulich (New York: St. Martin's Press, 1989), 171-83.

31. Günter Grass, *Max* [1970], trans. Leslie A. Willson and Ralph Manheim (New York: Harcourt Brace Jovanovich, 1972). The play derives from Grass's better-known novel, *Local Anesthetic*. The play's original title was *Davor* [Before] (Neuwied und Berlin: Hermann Luchterhand Verlag, 1970). Hereafter cited as Grass.

32. This same theme is the focus of an Australian play by Rob George: *Sandy Lee Live at Nui Dat* (1981).

33. Such an ambiguity significantly anticipates Michael Verhoeven's 1990 film *The Nasty Girl*.

34. *Staruch* means "old man" in Polish, a term that Grass, born near Gdansk (Danzig), undoubtedly knew.

35. Fredric Jameson, *Postmodernism; or, The Cultural Logic of Late Capitalism* (Durham: Duke University Press, 1991), 19. Hereafter cited as Jameson 1991.

36. "Only when a dog burns will they catch on that the Yanks are burning people over there—doing it every day" (Grass 33).

37. In his novel *Local Anaesthetic*, Grass stresses the numbing effects of television on memory, having a dentist use television in his office to anaesthetize his patients who watch it while he is operating on them.

38. "The lower house meets on Thursday; Flip will be more or less recovered by Friday; he'll announce a press conference in the hospital and make a statement. . . . Dogs will be burned in several big cities. Later foreign countries will join in. That's called the ritualized form of provocation" (Grass 103).

39. See Peter Humphreys, *Media and Media Policy in West Germany: The Press and Broadcasting since 1945* (New York: Berg, 1990).

40. "We began to read all we could lay our hands on about Vietnam. By far the most useful documents we found were the records of the Fulbright Committee Hearings on Vietnam and China" (Brook 14).

41. Thus, Martin Esslin discusses *US* with Brook before its production: "Brook wanted to have a stage in the theatre, and next to this stage, on the left and right huge television screens . . . many of us, I think, have seen the murder of Oswald on television—that is realism but also a dramatic situation. Now, was it also theatre? And if it was theatre, was it especially good theatre? That is to say: drama is man's only communications form that allows an entry into the inner self and not only the outside, the superficial. From this comes an essential aesthetic difference: in theatre one sees a totality . . . what theatre in the age of television can and must offer is what television cannot: a great performance . . . a totality." Esslin, *Theater Heute* (September 1965): 3.

42. "*US* uses documents and recordings and authentic testimonies not as information, not as material for explanation—but as pictures, as living, embodied documents of our times, confusing and contradictory. *US* uses the forms from TV, radio, and popular culture, in order to expose and infiltrate the strategies of media from which we receive secret information and emotionally exciting messages." Ernst Wendt, "Mit den Bomben spielen," *Theater Heute* (February 1967): 16. The title means "playing with bombs. "

43. Charles Marowitz, citing himself, in *Confessions of a Counterfeit Critic* (London: Methuen, 1973).

44. Alan Brien, *Sunday Telegraph* (cited in Brook 188).

45. See Adrienne Kennedy, *An Evening with Dead Essex*, first performed in November 1973 at the American Place Theatre in New York City; first published in *Theatre* 9, no. 2 (1978): 66–78. Hereafter cited as Kennedy.

46. Walter Benjamin, "Theses on the Philosophy of History" [1940], in Benjamin 257.

47. Arendt adds to this notion an artistic dimension: "The intangible identities of the agents in the story, since they escape all generalization and therefore all reification, can be conveyed only through an imitation of their acting. This is also why theater is the political art par excellence; only there is the political sphere of human life transposed into art." Hannah Arendt, *The Human Condition* (Chicago: University of Chicago Press, 1958), 187–88.

48. In Europe, during the sixties, television was not a commercial enterprise but was regulated by the government. Yet, particularly in West Germany, it also provided many opportunities for independent artists to produce their work. It was a viable source of both income and exposure for beginning filmmakers and writers. The relationship between television and artists was therefore not as antagonistic as in the United States. Raymond Williams actually saw television as a potentially positive and powerful cultural force (see Raymond Williams, *On Television* [New York: Routledge, 1989], and *Television: Technology and Form* [Hanover, N.H.: University Press of New England, 1974]). But, at the time of Grass's *Max*, West Germans were debating whether the State television should become partially privatized and include commercials, which helps explain Grass's references to American commercials on television.

49. To avoid the accumulation of examples, I have not mentioned again David Rabe's *Sticks and Bones*, although, as already noted, it is structured as a parody of the popular television series *Ozzie and Harriet*. Nor have I mentioned Christopher

Durang's *The Vietnamization of New Jersey: An American Tragedy*, which in turn parodies Rabe's *Sticks and Bones*. See Toby Silverman Zinman's "The Drama of the Vietnam War," 14.

50. Thus, Jameson writes about photography "whose extraordinary reinvention today (in theory as well as in practice) is a fundamental fact and symptom of the postmodern period" (Jameson 1991, 173). And Hutcheon: "Photography seems even more apt than television to act as the paradigm of the postmodern" (Hutcheon 122).

51. This, at least, is the gist of Jameson's argument: "But postmodern spatialization here plays itself out in the relationship and the rivalry among the various spatial media. . . . Indeed, we may speak of spatialization here as the process whereby the traditional fine arts are mediatized: that is, they now come to consciousness of themselves as various media within a mediatic system in which their own internal production also constitutes a symbolic message and the taking of a position of the status of the medium in question" (Jameson 1991, 162).

52. In Jameson's terms, there results "the effacement . . . of the older (essentially high-modernist) frontier between high culture and so-called mass or commercial culture, and the emergence of new kinds of texts infused with the forms, categories, and contexts of that very culture industry so passionately denounced by all the ideologies of the modern, from Leavis and the American New Criticism all the way to Adorno and the Frankfurt School" (Jameson 1991, 2).

53. See, in particular, Gilles Deleuze and Félix Guattari, *Anti-Oedipus: Capitalism and Schizophrenia,* trans. Robert Hurley, Mark Seem, and Helen R. Lane (Minneapolis: University of Minnesota Press, 1983). See also Deleuze and Guattari, *A Thousand Plateaus: Capitalism and Schizophrenia,* trans. Brian Massumi (Minneapolis: University of Minnesota Press, 1987).

54. "This is, however, precisely why it seems to me essential to grasp postmodernism not as a style but rather as a cultural dominant: a conception which allows for the presence and co-existence of a range of very different, yet subordinate features" (Jameson 1991, 4).

55. "The disappearance of the individual subject, along with its formal consequence, the increasing unavailability of the personal style, engender the well-nigh universal practice today of what may be called pastiche" (Jameson 1991, 16).

EPILOGUE

1. Trinh T. Minh-ha, *When the Moon Waxes Red: Representation, Gender and Cultural Politics* (New York: Routledge, 1991), 17. Hereafter cited as Trinh.

2. See the statement of purpose published by JUSPAO and reprinted in *Drama Review* 13, no. 4 (summer 1969).

3. Thich Nhat Hanh, *The Path of Return Continues the Journey,* trans. Vo-Dinh Mai and Jim Forest, Foreword by Daniel Berrigan (New York: Hoa Binh Press, 1972). Hereafter cited as Nhat Hanh 1972. This text has been republished as "A Play in One Act"—without the woodcuts that accompanied the original and with additional writings on nonviolence spanning the period from the wars in Indochina and the Persian Gulf to current issues in Vietnam—in his anthology *Love in Action: Writings on Nonviolent Social Change* (Berkeley: Parallax Press, 1993).

4. His stories about Vietnam are contained in his *The Moon Bamboo* (1989); his works of practical meditation include *The Miracle of Mindfulness* (1975), *Being Peace* (1987), *The Sun My Heart* (1988), *Old Path White Clouds: Walking in the Footsteps of the Buddha* (1991), *Peace Is Every Step* (1991), *Transformation and Healing* (1992), *Touching Peace* (1992), and *Thunder Silence* (1993).

5. See Thich Nhat Hanh, "A Buddhist Poet in Vietnam" [June 9, 1966], in *The First Anthology: Thirty Years of the New York Review of Books*, ed. Robert B. Silvers et al. (New York: NYRB, 1993), 35. Hereafter cited as Nhat Hanh 1966.

6. I follow closely the very useful unpublished analysis by Bo Wirmark, "The Buddhists in Vietnam: An Alternative View of the War." This paper (currently in the Berrigan Collection, Kroch Library, Cornell University) was presented at a conference in Varanasi, India, in January 1974, and was later sent to Berrigan. Wirmark was in the Department of Peace and Conflict Research, Uppsala University. Hereafter cited as Wirmark.

7. See further Don Luce and John Sommer, *VietNam: The Unheard Voices* (Ithaca: Cornell University Press, 1969), 267-68.

8. Thich Nhat Hanh, *Vietnamese Buddhist Peace Delegation News Bulletin* [Paris], 1 December 1973, 7; also cited in Wirmark 16-17. Hereafter cited as Nhat Hanh 1973.

9. See Thich Nhat Hanh, *Love in Action: The Nonviolent Struggle for Peace in Vietnam* (Paris: Vietnamese Buddhist Peace Delegation Publications, n.d. [c. 1972–73]).

10. There are four major forms of theatre in Vietnam: the two more traditional, Cheo and Tuong, and the more modern, Cai Luong and Kich Noi. See Colin Mackerras, "Theatre in Vietnam," *Asian Theatre Journal* 4, no. 1 (spring 1987): 1-28. Hereafter cited as Mackerras.

11. Augusto Boal, *Theatre of the Oppressed* (New York: Theatre Communications Group, 1985), 122.

12. See Thich Nhat Hanh, *The Diamond That Cuts through Illusion: Commentaries on the Prajnaparamita Diamond Sutra* (Berkeley: Parallax Press, 1992). Particularly relevant retrospectively to *The Path of Return Continues the Journey* is the section on "nonattachment," 61-64.

13. *The Short Prajnaparamita Texts*, trans. Edward Conze (London: Luzac, 1973), 184.

14. *Astasahasrika Prajnaparamita: The Perfection of Wisdom in Eight Thousand Slokas*, trans. Edward Conze (Calcutta: Asiatic Society/Biblioteca Indica, 1958), 139.

15. "Indeed, one of the features of the Cheo characterization was the special place it gave to women. The main characters were female, and . . . the male roles were more or less disgraced" (Mackerras 3).

16. "A great many of the communist culture-drama organizations are totally female. During the performances they costume themselves as men. " JUSPAO report, "'Them'—seen by us," *TDR* 13 (T44) (summer 1969): 34.

17. "From the standpoint of the Third World, a good deal is wrong with the 'old,' and still prevailing, order. In terms of news and news coverage, the overwhelming majority of world news flows from the developed to the developing countries and is generated by four large transnational news agencies—AP, UPI, AFP, and Reuters." Francis N. Wete, "The New World Information Order and the U.S. Press," in *Global Television*, ed. Cynthia Schneider and Brian Wallis (New York: Wedge Press, 1988), 139.

18. Of course, it is not absolutely different from all Western theatre; on the Symbolist, Expressionist, Dadaist, or Lettrist stage, to take just a few examples, representation can be even more rigorously problematized, even eliminated.

19. Antonio Gramsci, *Selections from the Prison Notebooks*, ed. and trans. Quintin Hoare and Geoffrey Nowell Smith (New York: International, 1971), 149.

20. Richard Watts, "The Case of the Berrigans," *New York Post*, 8 February 1971. Not dissimilarly, a much more hostile response in the conservative press had referred to the play as "nine consecutive sermonettes." W. I. Scobie, "The West Coast Scene," *National Review* 22 (3 November 1970): 1173.

INDEX

147. *See also* Vietnam War
War and Cinema: The Logistics of Perception, 71–72
war mentality, 30. *See also* propaganda
Warner, Marina, 5
Wayne, John, 19
weapons, 56, 71, 87. *See also* bombing of civilians
Weiss, Peter, 6, 15, 28, 41, 58, 62, 68–78, 84, 85, 87, 142, 151–52, 172
Wenders, Wim, 184
When the Moon Waxes Red: Representation,

Gender and Cultural Politics, 175
Why Are We in Vietnam?, 5, 32
women: misogynist portrayal of, 135; as other, 142–43; as playwrights, 35, 148, 183; in protest theatre, 4, 31, 34, 119, 123, 125, 127–28, 133–43, 148, 159, 180, 183–85. *See also* femininity; misogyny; other
Women's Street Theatre (San Francisco), 6
Women's Wear Daily, 27
"Workers Theatre," 7–8
World War II, 2, 11

Nora M. Alter is Assistant Professor of German at the University of Florida, where she teaches film, media, cultural studies, drama, and critical theory. She has written on various aspects of film, literature, and drama. She is currently working on the international essay film.